DISHING UP OREGON

DISHING UP
OREGON

145 RECIPES THAT CELEBRATE FARM-TO-TABLE FLAVORS

ASHLEY GARTLAND

Photography by John Valls

The mission of Storey Publishing is to serve our customers by
publishing practical information that encourages
personal independence in harmony with the environment.

Edited by Margaret Sutherland and Lisa H. Hiley
Art direction and book design by Cynthia N. McFarland,
     based on a design by Tom Morgan of Blue Design

Photography by © John Valls
Map, pages 12–13, by © David Cain

Indexed by Nancy D. Wood

© 2011 by Ashley Gartland

Storey Publishing
210 MASS MoCA Way
North Adams, MA 01247
www.storey.com

Printed in China by R.R. Donnelley
10 9 8 7 6 5 4 3

LIBRARY OF CONGRESS CATALOGING-IN-PUBLICATION DATA

Gartland, Ashley.
  Dishing up Oregon / by Ashley Gartland.
      p. cm.
  Includes bibliographical references and index.
  ISBN 978-1-60342-566-7 (pbk.)
  1. Cooking, American—Pacific Northwest style. 2. Cooking—Oregon.
  3. Farm produce—Oregon. 4. Cookbooks. I. Title.
TX715.2.P32G374 2011
641.59795—dc23
                                    2011020051

For my grandmother, Carmen,
and my mother, Shirleen,
who nurtured my love of good food
and the written word.

✺   ✺   ✺

And for Jake,
who makes me believe
that all things are possible.

contents

ACKNOWLEDGMENTS

THIS BOOK WOULD NOT have been possible without the dedication of the many contributors, suppliers, recipe testers, and colleagues who played a part in its creation.

First and foremost, my thanks go to the chefs, farmers, and food and beverage artisans whose support of *Dishing Up Oregon* made this book possible. They graciously shared recipes from their kitchens and willingly opened their doors when I came calling to study the ways they've shaped Oregon's food scene. No matter how busy they were in the field or at the stove, they never turned me away and for that I am forever grateful.

I am also indebted to John and Theresa Valls, whose hard work and stunning photography brought the pages of this book to life. John, your ability to capture the life of an artisan or the beauty of a dish in a single shot left me awestruck every time.

I owe a big thanks to the cast of characters who helped me turn a tiny idea into a tangible cookbook. Thank you to the entire team at Storey Publishing, particularly Margaret Sutherland, who took a chance on this project, and to Lisa Hiley, who saw it through to the finish with great care. Thank you also to Cindy McFarland for the beautiful design and Amy Greeman and Alee Marsh for helping get the word out about the book.

Thank you to my team of recipe testers and tasters whose honest feedback had a hand in shaping these recipes and to friends and colleagues who answered culinary questions when a recipe had me stumped. Special thanks go to Diane Morgan, who offered her mentorship from the very start of this project, and to Amber Lindros, a dedicated proofreader and enthusiastic recipe taster to boot.

My deepest thanks go to my family for offering their endless encouragement from the beginning of this project. Thank you for listening to my ideas, for sampling recipes, and for offering your opinions on each dish whether they were the ones I wanted to hear or not. Finally and most important, I must thank my husband, Jake, whose appetite, discerning palate, and unfailing support played a vital part in every page of this book.

AN OREGON LOVE AFFAIR

Vitaly Paley of Paley's Place Bistro and Bar

IN THE EARLY NINETIES, my wife and I were fortunate to work at a restaurant in a small French village. One day a beautiful basket of morel mushrooms was delivered to our kitchen. They looked so magical and smelled so fragrant I took a closer look. I thought certainly they were gathered nearby, the French being the original locavores and staunch guardians of traditions. To my surprise they came from Oregon. "*Incroyable!* Impossible!" How could it be? In that inspired instant, my love affair with Oregon's wonderful bounty began.

Armed with that French stamp of approval, we left our tiny New York City apartment and set out on a grand adventure down the Oregon Trail where more connections to France awaited us: the cities of The Dalles and La Grande, the Deschutes River, and the Nez Perce people of eastern Oregon. Some believe that the very name of the state comes from the French word *ouragan,* or "hurricane."

Could it be that the early French settlers stayed here because the rolling hills of the Willamette Valley reminded them of Burgundy, where grapes would thrive, or that the lush Cascades, as grandiose as the Alps, were practically carpeted with wild mushrooms? Or was it the cold, stormy Pacific Ocean, brimming with marine life like the North Atlantic? Did they find their Promised Land?

Yet Oregon offers so much more. The mighty Columbia River slices a gorge through the Cascades, gifting us with stunning rainbows and spawning life before tracing its majestic path to the ocean. The Hood River Valley is filled with fruit and hazelnut orchards and serene pastures dotted with sheep. Central Oregon's high dessert offers endless views, pastel mountains, and crystal clear lakes. The eastern part of the state, the true Wild West with its

pristine environment and rich soil, has the open spaces to grow the best potatoes and wheat. In the south, the intoxicating aromas of ripe summer berries make you feel as though you are standing inside the sweetest jar of jam. The grandeur of Oregon is so breathtaking and the scenery so deeply moving that all of us who live here truly believe we have found our Promised Land.

I love cooking in Oregon. There are no food traditions to follow, no rules on how to cook, just great ingredients. Oysters, Dungeness crab, and salmon; morels, chanterelles, and truffles; elk, rabbit, and lamb — these are just a few of my favorites. We are inventing a unique Oregon style and are having a blast doing it.

Ashley Gartland is a prodigious writer who captures our pioneering spirit and helps us rediscover our gastronomic pathways with creative dishes like Chocolate Crab Bisque, Chanterelle Rillettes, and Elk Tartare. Try quenching your thirst with a Nectarine-Basil Lemonade. Or snack on Cherry-Basil Bruschetta while waiting for your Red Wine–braised Beef Short Ribs to finish cooking. For dessert, enjoy a truly Oregonian Apple-Huckleberry Crisp or Rustic Pear Galette.

Dishing Up Oregon is also an insightful read, full of evocative stories about the farmers, artisans, and chefs who make the Oregon food scene so special. John Valls completes the picture by seducing us with gorgeous photographs of Oregon's vistas, delectable dishes, and the people who make it all happen.

I invite you to find your own culinary adventure on the Oregon Trail. Cook your way through our state's bounty. Discover your own French connection to our land and, as I did, fall in love with Oregon's bottomless well of seasonal ingredients.

INTRODUCTION

I FELL IN LOVE WITH OREGON at a farmers' market. Wandering through downtown Portland one summer weekend, I crested a hill and found myself in a sea of booths filled with snowy white cheeses, taut-skinned tomatoes, and flat upon flat of blushing berries. The market energy was instantly palpable as I watched shoppers fawn over farm-fresh produce and farmers speak with obvious enthusiasm about the ingredients they grow and the products they make.

Everyone was joining the conversation about local food, and so I too stepped into the scene. Slowly, I became more involved in this passionate community and more familiar with the producers who bring their fine ingredients to market each week. I discovered new varieties of apples and pears, met an artisan hazelnut grower, and pawed through tables piled high with such flawless vegetables that I wanted to stop and snap photos at every turn.

As a transplant to Oregon, I had once viewed my adopted state primarily as a producer of beer, berries, and pinot noir. But with each market visit, I discovered that the state's foodways have much more to offer. The diverse terrain is covered with lush farmland, acres of orchards, and plentiful pasture; along the lengthy coastline, a vast ocean sustains fresh seafood year-round. And in every community from big city Portland to small folksy towns, artisans are crafting their own definitions of local fare, whether they're perfecting pear brandy or peddling fresh goat cheese at a neighborhood farmers' market.

When I decided to write a cookbook that celebrated Oregon's farm-to-table culture, I set off on a series of trips to meet the people who make the state's diverse food scene possible. In Central Point, I stopped by an award-winning creamery, and in nearby Jacksonville, I toured a biodynamic vineyard and farm. In Eugene, I spoke with a renowned local chef about the growth of the farm-to-table movement, and in Junction City, I wandered through lush pasture with a respected sheep farmer. A charming chef in Sisters won me over with his seasonal, French-inspired menu, while dinner at a wine country restaurant taught me the pleasures of making local mushrooms the star of the plate.

In every community, these passionate individuals have created a food culture that regards farmers, chefs, fishermen, winemakers, distillers, brewers, cheesemakers, and artisans as celebrities. Whether they work as farmers in the field or chefs at the stove, these individuals have dedicated their time and energy to shrinking the distance between farm and table; through their tireless efforts, they've created opportunities for Oregonians to shop locally and eat well in their own backyard.

It's been more than five years since I serendipitously discovered my local farmers' market, and I have not stopped raving about Oregon's food scene since. With its farm-to-table cuisine and abundance of prized ingredients, Oregon has enchanted my appetite and fed me well year after year. My weekly market visit has become an essential part of my lifestyle. I hope this book will help you make a similar routine part of yours.

Ashley Gartland

WASHINGTON

Astoria

Cannon Beach

HAYSTACK ROCK

Hood River

Portland

MOUNT HOOD

OREGON

0   50
Miles

Willamette River

Lincoln City

Salem

Newport

Corvallis

SMITH ROCK

THREE SISTERS

Bend

Eugene

Florence

Bandon

CRATER LAKE NATIONAL PARK

Rogue River

Medford

Ashland

CALIFORNIA

• Pendleton

IDAHO

NEVADA

©2011 David Cain

Dishing It Up

THIS BOOK SHINES a spotlight on Oregon's farm-to-table culture. The recipes highlight much-loved local ingredients like marionberries, hazelnuts, albacore tuna, pears, and grass-fed lamb; the artisan profiles that accompany them will give you snapshots of the producers who make the state's rich food scene possible day after day.

The book is divided into individual chapters that showcase Oregon ingredients and contain recipes that deliver a true sense of place. Though the format is less traditional, I hope that it offers you an entry point to begin an ingredient-driven approach to cooking. It was, however, impossible to showcase every local ingredient in these hundred-plus recipes. Please consider this book an invitation to explore the abundance of ingredients available within the state's borders.

I haven't included the names of specific farmers or local producers in reference to ingredients in most of the recipes; however, I hope you will seek fresh, local ingredients whenever the opportunity presents itself. Make a trip to the market for fresh fruits and vegetables, buy pasture-raised meat and eggs, and support your local farmers and producers whenever you can. You'll learn to shop and eat in season — enjoying roasted asparagus and morels in the spring and pear-filled galettes in the fall — and quickly understand the pleasures of eating food from your own backyard.

A word about the recipes: I have included suggestions for cooking times for each dish, but I also believe personal judgment is your best asset in the kitchen. Watch the timer, but trust your gut and your senses when you're cooking these dishes and your food will turn out as it should.

I began this project with the intention that this book would celebrate Oregon and encourage you to bring a taste of the state to your table. Start exploring the food culture in your own community and soon you'll have a Rolodex of resources ready to help you eat locally and seasonally year-round.

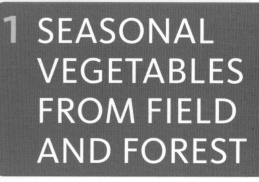

1 SEASONAL VEGETABLES FROM FIELD AND FOREST

Spiced Rhubarb-Cherry Chutney

Most home cooks consider rhubarb a fruit, which is why it has earned the nickname "the pie plant." But rhubarb is actually a vegetable and thus perfectly suited for savory uses as well as desserts. When I spot the first crimson stalks at the farmers' market, I shuttle them home to make this gently spiced rhubarb-cherry chutney. Try it spooned atop slices of roasted pork tenderloin.

¾ cup packed dark brown sugar

⅓ cup red wine vinegar

1½ pounds rhubarb, cut into ½-inch pieces (4 cups)

½ cup dried cherries

   Zest of 1 orange

½ teaspoon ground cinnamon

½ teaspoon ground cloves

½ teaspoon freshly ground black pepper

MAKES ABOUT 2 CUPS

1. Bring the sugar and vinegar to a boil over medium-high heat in a large saucepan. Stir in the rhubarb, cherries, orange zest, cinnamon, cloves, and black pepper with a wooden spoon and bring the mixture back to a boil.

2. Reduce the heat to medium and simmer, stirring occasionally, until the rhubarb is tender and the mixture thickens slightly, about 6 minutes.

3. Let the chutney cool to room temperature before transferring it to an airtight container. Stored in an airtight container in the refrigerator, it will keep for about 1 week. Bring to room temperature before serving.

Morel Mojo

Chef Scott Dolich extends morel season by pickling them into a loose, relishlike condiment he calls mojo. At the restaurant, he dips into his supply to dress up spring vegetables like asparagus or ramps or to garnish grilled meats and fish.

1¼ pounds morel mushrooms
1 cup apple cider vinegar
1 cup beef broth
1 cup vegetable broth
3 garlic cloves, thinly sliced
2¼ teaspoons salt
1 bay leaf
½ teaspoon red pepper flakes
3 tablespoons extra-virgin olive oil

MAKES ABOUT 3 CUPS

1. Submerge the morels in a bowl of cold water and agitate them gently to dislodge any grit. Drain them in a colander and pat dry immediately. Slice off the stems and cut the morels into bite-size pieces.

2. Combine the morels, vinegar, beef broth, vegetable broth, garlic, salt, bay leaf, and red pepper flakes in a large pot. Cover and simmer the mixture over medium heat for 10 minutes.

3. Remove the pan from the heat and let the morel mixture cool slightly. Discard the bay leaf. Drain the morels, reserving the brine. Purée 1 cup of the morels with 1½ cups of the brine in the bowl of a food processor fitted with a steel blade attachment until well combined but not entirely smooth. Add the olive oil in a steady stream with the motor running until well combined.

4. Transfer the purée to a medium bowl and fold in the remaining morels. Discard the remaining brine. Salt to taste. Transfer the relish to an airtight container to cool to room temperature. Stored in an airtight container in the refrigerator, the relish will keep for about 1 month.

NOTE: Morels come into season in early spring and generally stick around through May; find them at grocers like Pastaworks and New Seasons in Portland or through farmers' market vendors like Springwater Farms.

English Pea Pesto

English peas inspired this brilliant green pesto that Chef Matthew Busetto serves with gnocchi at his Portland restaurant. At home, I like to spread it on rounds of toasted bread to serve as a light appetizer. The delicate spread is perfect on its own, but you can also pair it with fresh ricotta (page 103) or shavings of Pecorino Romano cheese.

1 pound English peas, shelled (about 1 cup)

¼ cup extra-virgin olive oil

¼ cup finely grated Pecorino Romano cheese

2 teaspoons finely chopped fresh tarragon

   Sea salt

MAKES ABOUT ¾ CUP

1. Prepare an ice-water bath. Bring a medium pot of salted water to a boil and cook the peas for 1 minute. Drain the peas and immediately transfer them to the ice-water bath to cool. When cool, drain again.

2. Blend the peas and olive oil in the bowl of a food processor fitted with a steel blade attachment until well combined but still slightly coarse.

3. Transfer the pesto to a small bowl. Mix in the cheese and tarragon. Salt to taste and serve immediately.

Fried *Pimientos de Padrón*

Leslie Lukas-Recio and Manuel Recio grow the sweet Spanish peppers known as *pimientos de Padrón* on their Dayton farm. When I asked a market vendor what to do with them, she instructed me to fry the peppers and dust them with sea salt to create this simple appetizer. Be forewarned: Though *pimientos de Padrón* are generally mild, the occasional pepper has a burst of fiery heat. Look for the peppers in late summer and fall at Viridian Farms' Portland Farmers Market booth.

¼ cup extra-virgin olive oil
½ pound Padrón peppers
  Coarse sea salt

4 SERVINGS

1. Warm the olive oil over medium heat in a skillet large enough to hold all of the peppers in a single layer.

2. Add the peppers. Fry over medium heat, turning often, until they are soft and blistered slightly, about 5 minutes.

3. Transfer the peppers to a bowl. Discard the olive oil. Toss the peppers with salt and serve immediately.

VIRIDIAN FARMS

BOOTHS FLUSH WITH FRESH GREENS, flats of berries, and bins of peaches and pears fill the aisles at the Portland Farmers Market each Saturday. But amid stands stocked with familiar regional ingredients, Viridian Farms' Leslie Lukas-Recio and Manuel Recio offer marketgoers a taste of something new: European ingredients like fresh heirloom shell beans, *pimientos de Padrón* peppers, and thick white asparagus grown in Oregon soil on their Dayton farm.

Leslie Lukas-Recio and Manuel Recio

Viridian's market booth provides a snapshot of the niche the couple has pursued since purchasing an established fruit farm in 2004. "We decided if we were going to make it work and really enjoy what we do, we needed to make the farm our own," says Leslie. "One thing we share in common is an understanding and love of good food, produce, and wine. We also met and lived in Spain and love Spanish and European culture. So, we decided to focus on fruits and vegetables from that region of the world."

The couple's decision to grow regional Basque ingredients in Oregon was groundbreaking; Viridian Farms was the first farm to introduce little-known European ingredients to farmers' market clientele and chefs at high-end restaurants like Simpatica, Toro Bravo, and Carafe Bistro. Today the farmers continue to bring coveted heirloom ingredients to market, including the French green known as *ficoide glaciale* and the brick red spice known as *piment d'Espelette* that they make from their Espelette peppers each year.

During the winter, the young farmers take a break from their farm to travel through Italy, France, and Spain and further inspire their work. They spent early trips abroad visiting farms to study growing methods. On more recent trips, however, they met with chefs from Michelin-starred restaurants and mom-and-pop operations to study how to best use the Basque ingredients they grow back home.

The couple returns home each year armed with new ideas and a renewed interest in bringing a taste of the Basque region to Oregon. "We want people to feel the same way that we did when we first started," says Leslie. "I had so many new experiences and tastes and flavors, not only when I lived in Spain but when I go back. We want people to feel that excitement."

Chanterelle Rillettes

Prized for their meaty flavor, chanterelles take the place of pork in this creamy, pâté-like spread. Chef Cathy Whims serves this seasonal starter on her chanterelle tasting menu each fall. Though you can serve it straight from the refrigerator after it chills overnight, she recommends removing the rillettes from the refrigerator approximately one hour before serving to ensure a smooth, spreadable texture.

1 cup (2 sticks) unsalted butter, at room temperature

2 tablespoons extra-virgin olive oil

¾ pound chanterelle mushrooms, coarsely chopped

1 garlic clove, minced

¼ cup dry marsala wine

1 tablespoon tomato paste

Zest and juice of 1 lemon

3 tablespoons finely chopped fresh flat-leaf parsley

Toasted baguette slices

MAKES ABOUT 2 CUPS

1. Warm 6 tablespoons of the butter and the olive oil in a large skillet over high heat until the butter melts. Add the chanterelles and cook, stirring frequently, until they are lightly colored and the liquid they release evaporates completely, about 5 minutes. Add the garlic and stir until fragrant, about 30 seconds. Add the wine, tomato paste, and lemon juice and simmer until the wine evaporates, about 1 minute. Remove the skillet from the heat and let cool.

2. Combine the chanterelle mixture, lemon zest, parsley, and remaining 10 tablespoons butter in the bowl of a food processor fitted with a steel blade attachment. Process the mixture until the chanterelles are finely chopped but not yet a smooth paste.

3. Transfer the spread to a small serving bowl. Cover the bowl with plastic wrap and chill the spread in the refrigerator overnight. Serve with the toasted baguette slices. Stored in an airtight container in the refrigerator, the spread will keep for about 1 week.

Cathy Whims

Shaved Radish "Carpaccio"

Radishes step out of the garnish role to become the main player in this chic salad at Portland's Grüner restaurant. Chef Christopher Israel uses multiple shades of farmers' market radishes to create a colorful canvas to decorate with his favorite herbs. If you can't find pumpkin seed oil, walnut oil is a more widely available substitution.

¼ cup canola oil

2 tablespoons apple cider vinegar

Salt and freshly ground black pepper

16 radishes, trimmed

Pumpkin seed oil

¼ cup finely chopped fresh herbs, such as dill, chives, savory, thyme, or tarragon, or any combination thereof

¼ cup pumpkin seeds, toasted

2 cups microgreens

Fleur de sel, for garnish (optional)

4 SERVINGS

1. Whisk the canola oil and vinegar together in a small bowl. Salt and pepper to taste and set aside.

2. Thinly slice the radishes using a mandoline. Toss the radishes with about half of the dressing in a medium bowl until well dressed. Divide the radishes among four salad plates, arranging them in an overlapping circular pattern starting with the outside edges and circling inward until you reach the center of the plate.

3. Drizzle the radishes with the pumpkin seed oil. Sprinkle the herbs and pumpkin seeds over the radishes.

4. Toss the microgreens in a bowl with the remaining half of the dressing. Mound a handful of the greens in the center of each plate. Garnish with fleur de sel, if desired, and serve immediately.

TRUFFLES

FINDING TRUFFLES, which grow in symbiotic relationship with the roots of trees and mature underground in humid, mild climates, requires not only skill but also luck. These rootless jewels never break the soil's surface and thus, to be harvested properly, must be sniffed out by truffle-hunting dogs. In Oregon, those four-footed foragers search for their treasure underneath Douglas fir trees. It's here that the Oregon black truffle, brown truffle, winter white truffle, and spring white truffle grow.

Though Oregon truffles haven't the reputation of the robust Périgord black truffle or Italy's esteemed white truffle, local truffles are prized, and even preferred, by Northwest chefs. Local gourmands have also grown to appreciate the culinary value of Oregon truffles, which have an earthy, sexy scent that draws comparisons to port, chocolate, and tropical fruit. These truffle fans appreciate Oregon truffles not because they mimic the "real" thing but because they are a unique seasonal ingredient with a flavor and aroma all their own.

During truffle season, which generally begins in late November and can extend into March depending on the weather, local chefs pair truffles with rich cuts of meat and creamy dishes. In particular, the Oregon black truffle's distinctive scent and flavor allow it to shine in simple, straightforward dishes like fresh pasta tossed in a truffle cream sauce or even a simple truffle butter that chefs can use to finish pastas, pan sauces, and vegetable sides.

Experts say truffles are best enjoyed during their peak season, which is when the Oregon Truffle Festival commences. Each January, truffle-loving chefs, truffle hunters, truffle eaters, and truffle growers gather in Eugene for three days of seminars and gourmet experiences to study and celebrate the Oregon truffle industry. Thanks to events like the festival, the fascination with native truffles will continue to grow.

Northwest Black Truffle Butter

When local black truffles are available in the winter, Chef Eric Bechard blends them with butter to use with everything from mashed potatoes to steak and fish. At home, use this aromatic butter to finish risotto, pasta, or pan sauces or to dress a bowl of popcorn as an indulgent snack. Buy truffles at your local farmers' market or through online vendors like Oregon Black Truffles.

½ cup (1 stick) unsalted butter, at room temperature

1¼ ounces fresh Oregon black truffles, finely minced

Coarse sea salt

Eric Bechard

MAKES ABOUT ½ CUP

1. Blend the butter and truffles on medium speed in the bowl of an electric mixer fitted with a paddle attachment until well combined. Salt to taste and transfer the butter to an airtight container.

2. Let the butter sit at room temperature for 2 hours. Cover and refrigerate until ready to use. Stored in an airtight container in the refrigerator, the butter will keep for about 3 days. Bring it to room temperature before serving.

Farmhouse Salad with Lemon-Shallot Vinaigrette

Chef Earl Hook uses butter leaf lettuce and fennel from the restaurant's Skyline Farm in this light update on the retro wedge salad. The versatile lemon vinaigrette keeps the salad tasting clean and bright and belongs in every salad lover's recipe file.

4 SERVINGS

LEMON-SHALLOT VINAIGRETTE

- 3 tablespoons lemon juice
- 1 tablespoon honey
- 1 small shallot, minced (about 1 tablespoon)
- 1 small garlic clove, finely chopped
- ½ cup extra-virgin olive oil
  Salt and freshly ground black pepper

FARMHOUSE SALAD

- 2 small heads butter leaf lettuce
- 1 small fennel bulb, thinly sliced
- ¼ cup pine nuts, toasted
- ¼ cup shaved Parmesan cheese

1. **Make the vinaigrette:** Whisk the lemon juice, honey, shallot, and garlic together in a small bowl. Whisk in the olive oil. Salt and pepper to taste and set aside.

2. **Make the salad:** Quarter the lettuce heads, keeping the root end intact. Rinse well and drain. Arrange two of the wedges, cut side up, on each of four plates.

3. Drizzle 2 tablespoons of the vinaigrette over the wedges on each plate. Toss the fennel and pine nuts together with the remaining vinaigrette in a small bowl. Garnish the salads with the fennel, pine nuts, and Parmesan. Serve immediately.

MERIWETHER'S SKYLINE FARM

IN EARLY FALL, when many chefs are dreaming of braises and stews and roasts, Chef Earl Hook is already thinking about mesclun mix and tomato varieties as he helps plan next year's plots for Meriwether's Restaurant's 5-acre farm. Many Oregon restaurants feature produce from local farms on their menu, but Meriwether's is unique in that every bit of Skyline Farm's more than 8,000-pound harvest is earmarked for Hook. And though the well-connected chef works with a few other vendors, during peak harvest season he fills at least 70 percent of his pantry with produce from the restaurant's farm.

Visit the farm in spring, and Hook and farm manager Danny Percich will point out plots where they're growing cabbage for the chef's farm-fresh slaw, then check in on the newly sprouted fava beans that he'll use to make falafel. They'll walk between

Earl Hook and Danny Percich

rows of tight-lipped spring lettuce to determine whether it's ready to harvest for the restaurant's ever-evolving farmhouse salad. And on a whim, they'll pause to tug sweet spring turnips straight from the soil and enjoy a crisp, midmorning snack.

Every one of the plots they pass is the result of deep discussions between Hook and the farmers who nurture the land. The team studies the previous year's harvest to determine what worked (most recently a three-sisters planting of corn, beans, and squash that thrived) and what didn't (a guava tree experiment that didn't survive the winter). Then they plan next year's plots around past successes and the new experiments they want to pursue. That willingness to experiment is the reason Hook has corn to make fresh masa at Meriwether's and why there are almond trees growing between the farm beds.

Back at Meriwether's, guests make the connection between farm and table by glancing at a list on the menu that highlights in-season produce from the farm. The connection also comes full circle from October to April when the chef hosts monthly family-style Sunday Suppers. He prepares produce from the farm on the restaurant's hearth and rotisserie and invites Skyline Farm's staff and special guests to speak about their work and answer questions from guests while they eat.

"The dinners are about bringing people in, talking about the community, and talking about what Meriwether's vision and story is," Hook says. "It's nice for everyone to meet the farmers and for the farmers to sit down and enjoy the food and see how their produce is being used."

Shaved Zucchini and Basil Salad
with Guajillo Chile Vinaigrette

Chef Brendan Mahaney's raw zucchini salad is a great use for a bumper zucchini crop. The vinaigrette gives the salad a burnished red hue and hint of heat, while basil adds a cooling note. Use zucchini that are about 4 inches long, as they have thinner skins and more tender flesh than mature squash.

½ cup extra-virgin olive oil

2 medium dried guajillo chiles, stemmed and seeded

2 garlic cloves, thinly sliced

¼ cup sherry vinegar

Salt

6 medium green and yellow zucchini (about 2 pounds)

1 cup tightly packed fresh basil leaves, torn

Parmesan cheese shavings, for garnish

4–6 SERVINGS

1. Warm the olive oil in a small skillet over medium-low heat. Add the chiles and garlic and cook, stirring constantly, until the chiles are bright red and the garlic fragrant, about 30 seconds. Remove the skillet from the heat.

2. Transfer the chiles to a blender with a slotted spoon. Set the olive oil and garlic aside to cool slightly.

3. Pulse the chiles in the blender until finely chopped. Blend in the vinegar and a pinch of salt until well combined. Add the olive oil and garlic and blend until the vinaigrette is brick red and well combined. Strain the vinaigrette through a fine-mesh strainer. Discard the pulp. Salt to taste.

4. Trim the ends off the zucchini and cut them in half lengthwise. Shave into long, thin ribbons using a mandoline. Discard any unusable scraps.

5. Toss the zucchini and basil with the vinaigrette until well combined. Divide the salad among four to six plates and garnish with shavings of Parmesan before serving.

Broccoli Rabe Salad
with Lemon Vinaigrette and Prosciutto

Portland-based chef Chris DiMinno accents broccoli rabe, the slightly bitter green also known as rapini, with delicate herbs, crunchy pistachios, and a creamy lemon vinaigrette. The salad is outstanding on its own but even better topped with a poached egg.

NOTE: The lemon oil for the dressing needs to sit for 12 hours before making the vinaigrette.

LEMON VINAIGRETTE

Zest of 5 lemons
1 cup extra-virgin olive oil
2½ tablespoons lemon juice
1 tablespoon late-harvest sauvignon blanc vinegar
1½ teaspoons honey
1½ teaspoons white wine vinegar
¾ teaspoon Dijon mustard
1 egg yolk
Salt and freshly ground black pepper

NOTE: This dish contains raw eggs. Consuming raw eggs may increase your risk of foodborne illness.

BROCCOLI RABE SALAD

2 bunches broccoli rabe (about 10 pieces each), trimmed
½ cup unsalted pistachios, toasted and roughly chopped
2½ tablespoons finely chopped fresh chives
2½ tablespoons finely chopped fresh flat-leaf parsley
2½ tablespoons finely chopped fresh tarragon leaves
Salt and freshly ground black pepper
8 slices prosciutto

4 SERVINGS

1. **Make the vinaigrette:** Mix the lemon zest with the olive oil in a small bowl. Cover the bowl and let sit in a warm, draft-free environment (such as the microwave) for 12 hours.

2. Strain the olive oil through a fine-mesh strainer into a small bowl. Discard the lemon zest. Blend the lemon juice, sauvignon blanc vinegar, honey, white wine vinegar, mustard, and egg yolk in a blender until well combined. Drizzle the oil into the blender with the motor running on medium speed until well combined. Salt and pepper to taste and set aside.

3. **Make the salad:** Bring a large pot of salted water to a boil. Place a cooling rack over a kitchen towel. Cook the broccoli rabe until bright green and tender, about 1½ minutes. Drain and arrange in a single layer on the cooling rack to cool.

4. Toss the broccoli rabe, pistachios, chives, parsley, and tarragon with the vinaigrette to taste in a large bowl. Salt and pepper to taste. Arrange 2 prosciutto slices in the center of each of four dinner plates. Divide the broccoli rabe salad among the plates. Drizzle any remaining dressing over the salads, if desired, and serve immediately.

NOTE: An excellent label for the late-harvest sauvignon blanc vinegar is Katz and Company. The vinegar is available at specialty grocers like Pastaworks and online at www.katzandco.com.

Radicchio Salad with Parsley-Hazelnut Pesto

Though the chefs at Portland's Ned Ludd restaurant are known for the inventive dishes they cook in their wood-fired oven, I fell for this cool radicchio salad. Rather than require a specific amount of olive oil for the pesto, the chefs suggest letting your eyes guide you. When the pesto is bright green and smooth, but not runny, you've added enough oil. Less intuitive cooks can expect to add ½ to ¾ cup olive oil.

PARSLEY-HAZELNUT PESTO

- 1 cup hazelnuts, lightly toasted and skinned
- 1 bunch fresh flat-leaf parsley, stemmed
- ¼ cup finely grated Parmesan cheese

  Zest of 1 lemon
- 1 garlic clove, peeled

  Extra-virgin olive oil

  Salt

RADICCHIO SALAD

- 2 heads radicchio, cored and leaves separated

  Juice of 1 lemon
- 2 tablespoons extra-virgin olive oil

  Salt
- ½ cup fresh flat-leaf parsley
- 2 crisp, slightly tart apples, cored and chopped into ½-inch pieces
- ¼ cup finely grated Parmesan cheese

4–6 SERVINGS

1. **Make the pesto:** Blend the hazelnuts, parsley, Parmesan, lemon zest, and garlic in the bowl of a food processor fitted with a steel blade attachment until well combined. Scrape down the sides of the bowl with a rubber spatula. Add the olive oil with the motor running and blend until the sauce is bright green and smooth. Salt to taste.

2. **Make the salad:** Soak the radicchio leaves in a large bowl of salted ice water for 15 minutes. Rinse and dry, then trim into ½-inch slices and transfer to a large salad bowl.

3. Dress the radicchio with the lemon juice and olive oil. Add 2 to 3 tablespoons of the pesto to the bowl and toss gently to combine. The leaves should be lightly coated but not overly so. Add additional lemon or salt to taste. Add the parsley and apples and toss until well combined.

4. Garnish the salad with the Parmesan and serve immediately. Reserve the remaining pesto for another use. Covered with a thin layer of olive oil and stored in an airtight container in the refrigerator, the pesto will keep for about 3 days.

Recipe from COWHORN VINEYARD & GARDEN

Asparagus Vichyssoise

Cowhorn's winemaker-farmers Bill and Barbara Steele use asparagus from their biodynamic farm to update the classic potato-leek soup known as vichyssoise. A fresh chive garnish adds a delicate onion flavor that partners well with the grassy notes from their farm-fresh asparagus. Serve this soup as a starter at a refined spring meal.

4 SERVINGS

- 1 pound asparagus, trimmed
- 1 tablespoon canola oil
- 1 cup thinly sliced leeks, white and light green parts only
- ¼ cup dry white wine, such as Cowhorn Vineyard's Spiral 36 blend
- 4 cups water
- 1 large (about ¾ pound) russet or Yukon Gold potato, peeled and cut into ½-inch pieces
- 2 fresh parsley sprigs
- 2 fresh thyme sprigs
   Salt and freshly ground black pepper
- ¼ cup heavy cream
- ¼ cup finely chopped fresh chives

1. Cut the asparagus into 1-inch pieces. Separate the tips from the stalk pieces. Set the stalk pieces aside; place the asparagus tips in a small bowl, cover, and refrigerate until ready to use.

2. Heat the canola oil in a large saucepan over medium-low heat. Add the leeks and cook, stirring occasionally, until softened but not browned, about 3 minutes. Add the wine. Continue cooking the leeks until nearly all of the wine evaporates, about 2 minutes.

3. Add the asparagus stalks, water, potato, parsley, and thyme. Bring the mixture to a boil. Cover and simmer over medium-low heat until the potatoes are tender when pierced with a fork, about 20 minutes.

4. Discard the parsley and thyme. Purée the vegetable mixture in the bowl of a food processor fitted with a steel blade attachment until creamy and well combined. Salt and pepper to taste. Transfer the soup to a large bowl, cover with plastic wrap, and refrigerate until chilled, about 2 hours.

5. Bring a small pot of lightly salted water to a boil. Add the reserved asparagus tips and cook until just tender, about 2 minutes. Drain the tips and rinse them under cold water to halt the cooking process.

6. Whisk the cream in a small bowl until soft peaks form. Ladle the soup into four shallow bowls and garnish with a dollop of whipped cream. Divide the asparagus tips among the bowls, gently placing them atop the whipped cream. Garnish the soup with the chives and serve immediately.

Bill Steele

COWHORN VINEYARD & GARDEN

MOST CONSUMERS RECOGNIZE the Cowhorn name from the Rhône-style biodynamic wines they produce, among them a nuanced syrah and a complex white blend known as Spiral 36. But Bill and Barbara Steele's biodynamic vineyard is notable for more than the wines it produces: Shortly after the Steeles planted their first grapevines, they began farming the land as well.

The couple's farming venture began with a 250-pound asparagus harvest in 2007. Demand for their produce grew so quickly that the Steeles and their staff harvested more than 4,000 pounds of asparagus in 2009. Today artichokes, squash, cherries, and hazelnuts thrive alongside the vines and keep the farmers busy with harvests year-round. And the Steeles will keep expanding and diversifying the farm as long as local chefs and market shoppers covet their purple and green asparagus and variety of seasonal crops.

The Steeles raise all of their crops without the use of pesticides, herbicides, or fertilizers, just as they do with their grapes. These efforts earned Cowhorn the first biodynamic and organic certifications among southern Oregon wineries and ensure that their soil is as healthy as possible. The Steeles also recycle everything from corks to wine bottles to act as true stewards of the land.

Apple–Celery Root Salad

Celebrate winter with a crunchy salad that makes use of two of winter's unsung heroes: earthy celery root and palate-cleansing parsley. If you haven't worked with celery root before, don't be alarmed by its gnarly exterior. Once you remove its tough outer skin with a knife, you'll have a crisp, clean root vegetable perfect for partnering with pleasingly tart apples and a mustard vinaigrette.

2 tablespoons coarse-ground Dijon mustard

2 tablespoons lemon juice

1 tablespoon apple cider vinegar

½ teaspoon salt, plus more for seasoning

¼ teaspoon freshly ground black pepper, plus more for seasoning

¼ cup extra-virgin olive oil

1 small (about ½ pound) celery root, peeled and cut into ¼-inch matchsticks

1 large Granny Smith apple, cored and cut into ¼-inch matchsticks

1½ cups fresh flat-leaf parsley

¼ cup walnuts, lightly toasted and roughly chopped

Parmesan cheese shavings, for garnish

4–6 SERVINGS

1. Whisk the mustard, lemon juice, vinegar, salt, and black pepper together in a small bowl. Whisk in the olive oil until well combined.

2. Toss the celery root, apple, parsley, and walnuts with the vinaigrette in a large bowl. Salt and pepper to taste.

3. Divide the salad among four to six plates and garnish with shavings of Parmesan before serving.

Moroccan Tomato Soup

During tomato season on their Gaston farm, Anthony and Carol Boutard often use their summer crop to make this chilled Moroccan soup. The gently spiced dish, which the couple adapted from the *New York Times*, takes tomatoes beyond gazpacho to hit the spot on a hot summer day.

3¼ pounds heirloom tomatoes, cored and cut into 1-inch pieces

3 tablespoons extra-virgin olive oil

3 garlic cloves, crushed

2 tablespoons paprika

2 teaspoons ground coriander

½ teaspoon ground cumin

Juice of ½ lemon

Salt

½ cup finely diced celery (from about 2 stalks)

4 SERVINGS

1. Purée the tomatoes in a blender, working in batches if necessary. Pass the purée through a fine-mesh strainer and into a large bowl, pressing on the solids to extract as much liquid as possible. You should have about 5 cups tomato purée. Discard the solids and set the purée aside.

2. Warm the olive oil in a small saucepan over medium-low heat. Add the garlic, paprika, coriander, and cumin and cook, stirring constantly, until fragrant, about 3 minutes.

3. Stir the spice mixture and lemon juice into the tomato purée. Salt to taste. Cover the bowl with plastic wrap and refrigerate the soup until chilled, about 2 hours.

4. Divide the soup among four shallow bowls. Garnish the soup with the celery and serve immediately.

Ayers Creek Farm

Anthony and Carol Boutard

ANYONE WHO FREQUENTS the Hillsdale Farmers' Market will recognize Anthony and Carol Boutard. The gregarious farmers have peddled their fine produce, sought-after polenta, and small-batch jams from their booth through winter rain and summer heat for more than 150 market days. And they've continued to show up each week because they truly understand the importance of being present for both their customers and their farm.

When the couple bought their Gaston berry farm in 1998, they didn't have a market presence or a farming background. So for a year, they mostly watched the previous owners at work. "I didn't know anything about berry culture at this scale, and I certainly didn't know anything about having a crew of 150 people working for you. And I didn't speak Spanish. We had to learn all of those things," says Anthony. "It was very lucky that we handled it that way. We just watched and then afterward started making our changes and our mistakes, which is what you do."

One such change was pursuing a direct-sales model that allowed the Boutards to sell their produce to local restaurants and grocers. The transition also opened the door for the farmers to anchor the Hillsdale market and start diversifying their crops based on conversations with marketgoers. "We are very interested in what people want to eat," says Carol. "We are not really influenced by market trends but by the personal eating habits of the people we talk to."

Conversations with customers, along with the couple's personal whims, have become strong influences on the crops they grow on their 144-acre farm. The Boutards now cultivate corn, legumes, tomatoes, and orchard fruits alongside their berries. They're also working on producing walnuts, ginger, and table grapes and expect that there will be new projects to pursue in the years to come. "I want people to know us as a moveable feast," says Anthony. "We change throughout the year and we change from year to year."

Parsnip-Almond Soup
with Kumquat-Caperberry Garnish

Years ago, I greatly enjoyed lunching on this modern winter soup at Park Kitchen restaurant in Portland. I have been dying for an excuse to request the recipe ever since. The lively soup is silky and bright and proof that a talented chef can transform a lowly root vegetable into something incredibly refined.

4 SERVINGS

KUMQUAT-CAPERBERRY GARNISH

- ¼ cup sliced almonds, toasted
- ¼ cup thinly sliced caperberries
- ¼ cup thinly sliced kumquats
- 1½ tablespoons minced fresh rosemary
- ⅓ cup extra-virgin olive oil
- 1 tablespoon sherry vinegar

PARSNIP-ALMOND SOUP

- 4 medium parsnips, peeled and cut into 1-inch pieces (about 4 cups)
- 6 large garlic cloves, peeled
- ¼ cup plus 2 tablespoons whole skinless almonds, toasted
- 4 cups low-sodium vegetable broth
- ½ cup sherry
- 1 cup extra-virgin olive oil
- ¼ cup sherry vinegar
  Salt

1. **Make the garnish:** Mix the almonds, caperberries, kumquats, and rosemary together with a rubber spatula in a small stainless steel bowl. Mix in the olive oil and vinegar until just combined. Cover and let the garnish sit for 30 minutes at room temperature before using.

2. **Make the soup:** Combine the parsnips, garlic, almonds, broth, and sherry in a large pot and simmer, covered, over medium-low heat until the parsnips are tender when pierced with a knife, about 30 minutes.

3. Purée the parsnip mixture in a food processor fitted with a steel blade attachment, working in batches if necessary. Mix in the olive oil, then the vinegar, with the motor running.

4. Strain the soup back into the pot through a fine-mesh strainer. Salt to taste. Divide the soup among four shallow soup bowls and garnish with the kumquat-caperberry mixture. Serve immediately.

French Onion Soup

Eugene's venerable Marché restaurant serves this aromatic soup without fail each fall, thus satisfying the appetites of locals who have waited all year for its return. When making this soup at home, caramelize the onions slowly; don't brown them, as browned onions can quickly become crispy, bitter, and undesirable. A homemade or high-quality purchased beef broth delivers the full-bodied flavor desired of this classic French dish.

3 tablespoons unsalted butter

1 tablespoon extra-virgin olive oil

1½ pounds yellow onions (about 5 medium onions), peeled and sliced into thin rings

1 teaspoon salt, plus more for seasoning

¼ teaspoon sugar

3 tablespoons all-purpose flour

2 quarts beef broth, preferably homemade

½ cup dry white wine

2 teaspoons fresh thyme

Freshly ground black pepper

12 thinly sliced baguette rounds, toasted

2 cups coarsely grated Gruyère cheese

¾ cup coarsely grated Parmesan cheese

6 SERVINGS

1. Warm the butter and olive oil in a medium heavy-bottomed saucepan over medium-low heat until the butter melts. Add the onions and cook, covered, for 15 minutes. Uncover the saucepan and raise the heat to medium. Stir in the salt and sugar. Cook the onions, stirring frequently, until they have caramelized and turned golden brown, about 30 minutes longer. Sprinkle the flour over the onions, and cook, stirring constantly, over medium heat for 1 minute longer. Remove the saucepan from the heat.

2. Meanwhile, bring the beef broth to a boil in a large pot. Combine the onions with the boiling broth. Add the wine and thyme. Simmer the soup, partially covered, until rich and deeply flavorful, about 35 minutes. Salt and pepper to taste.

3. Preheat the oven to broil. Ladle the soup into six oven-safe bowls or crocks. Top each bowl with 2 baguette rounds and a generous layer of the Gruyère and Parmesan. Heat the bowls briefly under the broiler until the cheese bubbles and browns, about 5 minutes. Remove the bowls from the oven and serve immediately.

MARCHÉ

STEPHANIE PEARL KIMMEL'S work to promote Oregon's local food movement has been nothing short of trailblazing. After running the Excelsior Café in Eugene for more than two decades and helming King Estate Winery's culinary program, she continued to celebrate her passion for locally grown and gathered food by opening the aptly named Marché in 1998.

At the time, the local food scene was just taking hold, providing the opportunity to run a restaurant focused on regional food and to introduce Eugene to market-driven cooking. "I wanted to buy as locally as possible, and I wanted all the food to be sustainably raised and organic, if possible," Pearl Kimmel says. "I wanted the menu to evolve with the seasons, and I wanted to make sure our presentations were perfectly executed in terms of technique but designed to really bring out the essential flavor of each ingredient."

To support the regional marketplace, Pearl Kimmel shopped at farm stands and nearby farms and pored over seed catalogs with local farmers in the winter. She researched new produce varieties while traveling in France, then encouraged local farmers to experiment with growing European heirloom varieties in Oregon soil. And she developed a network of farmers and artisan producers, such as Laughing Stock Farm, Cattail Creek, Creative Growers, and Groundwork Organics, that helped turn Marché into a leader on Oregon's seasonally driven dining scene.

After more than a decade, Marché's Northwest–French–inspired menus continue to evolve with the seasons and offer intensely flavored, beautifully presented dishes. Only now, the local ingredients that define those menus are easier to come by. "It is so wonderful to see this region mature and develop as a gastronomic destination," says Pearl Kimmel. "We have such great people working here in the farms, restaurants, and stores, and in artisanal food production. Everyone is so dedicated and everything is so pristine and flavorful. It really is a piece of paradise, and we get to celebrate it. We are so lucky, absolutely lucky."

Stephanie Pearl Kimmel

Whole Roasted Fava Beans
with Maitakes and Ricotta

Fava beans have earned a reputation for being a labor-intensive ingredient, since home cooks usually must double-shell the lumpy spring beans before eating them. At Metrovino, Chef Gregory Denton skips the shelling and instead roasts the fava beans whole, rendering the pod and bean edible. If you want to use homemade ricotta here, make Denton's house-made ricotta (page 103).

24 whole fava bean pods, rinsed, dried, and trimmed of fibrous string and tips

½ cup extra-virgin olive oil, plus more for garnish

Kosher salt and freshly ground black pepper

4 maitake mushrooms, each broken into 3 or 4 pieces

1 cup fresh ricotta cheese

¼ cup aged balsamic vinegar

12 fresh mint leaves, torn

1 teaspoon finely chopped fresh flat-leaf parsley

Pecorino cheese shavings

Fleur de sel

4 SERVINGS

1. Position a rack in the center of the oven and preheat the oven to 425°F.

2. Toss the fava bean pods with the olive oil and a pinch of salt and pepper in a large bowl. Roast them on a baking sheet until slightly brown and blistered on the bottom, about 10 minutes.

3. Toss the mushrooms with the olive oil remaining in the bowl and transfer them to the baking sheet with the fava beans. Flip the beans over and roast until they are deep brown and the mushrooms have softened, about 5 minutes longer.

4. Divide the fava beans among four small plates. Garnish each plate with the mushrooms, ricotta cheese, balsamic vinegar, and additional olive oil. Sprinkle the mint, parsley, and shavings of pecorino cheese over the top of each plate. Season with a pinch of the fleur de sel and serve immediately.

Seared Asparagus
with Hard-Boiled Eggs, Crispy Morels, and Mustard Crème Fraîche

Southern Oregon-based chef Matthew Domingo celebrates the harvest season with a series of farm dinners and seasonal dishes like this sharable spring starter, in which he crowns a bed of bright green asparagus spears with crispy morels and hard-boiled eggs. A mustard-laced crème fraîche sauce ties the components of the dish together beautifully.

4 **SERVINGS**

- 4 **eggs**
- ¼ **cup crème fraîche**
- 2 **tablespoons Dijon mustard**
  Salt
- 12 **medium morel mushrooms**
- 3 **tablespoons extra-virgin olive oil**
- 2 **tablespoons unsalted butter**
- 1 **pound asparagus, trimmed**
  Fresh tarragon leaves, for garnish

1. Prepare an ice-water bath. Fill a large saucepan two-thirds full with water and gently lower the eggs into the water. Bring the water to a boil, then turn off the heat and cover for 10 minutes. Transfer the eggs to the ice-water bath. When the eggs are cool, crack and peel them. Cut in half lengthwise and set aside.

2. Whisk the crème fraîche, mustard, and a pinch of salt together in a small bowl. Add water by the teaspoonful, if needed, to achieve a pourable consistency. Set aside.

3. Submerge the morels in a bowl of cold water and agitate them gently to dislodge any grit. Drain in a colander and pat dry immediately. Slice off the stems and cut the mushrooms in half lengthwise.

4. Warm 2 tablespoons of the olive oil and the butter in a small skillet over medium heat until the butter melts. Add the morels and cook until they are golden brown and crispy around the edges, about 5 minutes. Salt to taste. Transfer the morels to a small bowl. Cover to keep warm and set aside.

5. Warm the remaining 1 tablespoon of olive oil in a large cast-iron skillet over medium-high heat. Add the asparagus and cook until slightly browned on one side, about 3 minutes. Turn and cook for 2 minutes longer. The asparagus should be cooked through but still have a bite to it.

6. Drizzle a few spoonfuls of the crème fraîche–mustard sauce in the center of a serving platter. Arrange the asparagus on the platter and drizzle with additional sauce. Arrange the eggs and morels around and on top of the asparagus spears. Garnish with the tarragon leaves and serve immediately.

Matthew Domingo

Honey-Paprika Potatoes

A honey-paprika glaze gives this potato side dish from Chef Adam Sappington a sweet-hot flavor that's welcome at the table morning, noon, or night. If you can't find ricotta salata cheese, you can serve the potatoes with a spoonful of fresh ricotta instead.

4 SERVINGS

1½ pounds red potatoes (about 3 large), cut into ½-inch pieces

3 tablespoons extra-virgin olive oil

2 tablespoons finely chopped fresh rosemary

Salt and freshly ground black pepper

2 tablespoons honey

2 teaspoons garlic powder

2 teaspoons dried oregano

2 teaspoons paprika

4 ounces ricotta salata cheese, crumbled (about 1 cup)

¼ cup fresh flat-leaf parsley, finely chopped

1. Position a rack in the center of the oven and preheat the oven to 400°F.

2. Toss the potatoes with the olive oil, rosemary, and a pinch of salt and pepper in a medium bowl. Transfer the potatoes to a baking sheet and roast until crispy and fork-tender, about 30 minutes.

3. Warm the honey in a large skillet over medium heat until it liquefies. Stir in the garlic powder, oregano, and paprika. Remove the skillet from the heat and toss the potatoes in the honey and spices until well combined. Add the cheese and toss gently.

4. Transfer the potatoes to a serving dish. Garnish with the parsley and serve immediately.

Grilled Corn on the Cob
with Roasted Poblano Aioli and Parmigiano-Reggiano

Chef Ben Bettinger slathers sweet summer corn with a roasted poblano aioli to create an addictive side dish that is juicy, crunchy, and creamy at once. At Portland-based Beaker & Flask, Bettinger uses liberal amounts of aioli on the corn; if you prefer a lighter dressing, add the aioli to your taste and refrigerate any leftovers for another use. When making the aioli, do not rinse the poblano pepper under water after grilling it. Any charred bits clinging to the flesh will intensify the aioli's flavor.

- 6 ears corn in the husk, top and stem ends trimmed but left intact
- 1 large poblano pepper
- 1 tablespoon extra-virgin olive oil
- 1½ teaspoons kosher salt
- 2 egg yolks
- 2 garlic cloves, grated on a Microplane
- 1 tablespoon Dijon mustard
- 1 tablespoon lime juice
- ¼ teaspoon freshly ground black pepper
- 1 cup canola oil
- ½ cup finely grated Parmigiano-Reggiano cheese

NOTE: This dish contains raw eggs. Consuming raw eggs may increase your risk of foodborne illness.

6 SERVINGS

1. Preheat the grill for direct grilling over hot charcoal or high heat. Oil the grill grates. Grill the ears of corn, turning occasionally, until the husks begin to blacken, about 7 minutes. Remove the corn from the grill and set aside to cool.

2. Toss the pepper with the olive oil and 1 teaspoon of the salt in a medium bowl until well coated. Grill the pepper, turning occasionally, until it is charred black on all sides, about 5 minutes. Return the pepper to the bowl and cover tightly with plastic wrap to steam for 15 minutes.

3. Whisk the egg yolks, garlic, mustard, lime juice, remaining ½ teaspoon of salt, and black pepper together in a medium bowl until well combined. Maintaining a steady whisking motion, slowly add the canola oil, a few drops at a time. After the aioli has thickened and you've added about ¼ cup of the oil, continue adding the oil in a slow, thin stream, whisking constantly, until all of the oil is incorporated and the aioli is thick and smooth.

4. Peel the pepper and slice it in half lengthwise. Remove the stem and seeds. Finely chop the pepper and mix it into the aioli with a rubber spatula until well combined. Set the aioli aside.

5. Peel the husks away from the cooled ears of corn and fold them back over the stem. Remove a long strand of husk from each cob and tie it around the remaining husk strands to create a handle. Remove any silk from the kernels.

6. Grill the corn over high heat, turning occasionally, until cooked through, about 5 minutes. Remove the corn from the grill. Heavily coat each cob with aioli and sprinkle generously with the Parmigiano-Reggiano. Serve immediately.

Recipe from CHEF JOHN HELLEBERG

Cremini-stuffed Squash Blossoms

Chef John Helleberg buys squash blossoms from a local farm, then stuffs them with a creamy mushroom-ricotta filling to create a midsummer appetizer. Helleberg serves the squash blossoms with a spoonful of arugula-hazelnut pesto. Serve yours plain or with your favorite pesto as a dinner party appetizer.

CREMINI STUFFING

- 1 pound cremini mushrooms
- 2 tablespoons extra-virgin olive oil
- 1 teaspoon salt, plus more for seasoning
- 2 medium shallots, finely diced (about ½ cup)
- 5 tablespoons ricotta cheese
- ¼ cup plain dried bread crumbs
- 3 tablespoons finely chopped fresh chives
  Freshly ground black pepper

TEMPURA BATTER

- 1 cup all-purpose flour
- ½ teaspoon kosher salt
- 1 cup chilled sparkling water

- 24 large squash blossoms, stems trimmed to 1 inch and stamens removed
  Canola oil, for frying

8 SERVINGS

1. **Make the stuffing:** Chop the mushrooms in the bowl of a food processor fitted with a steel blade attachment until finely chopped. Warm the olive oil in a large skillet over medium heat. Add the mushrooms and salt and cook, stirring occasionally, until the mushrooms start to brown and most of the liquid they release has evaporated, about 3 minutes. Add the shallots and cook until softened, about 2 minutes longer. Remove the skillet from the heat and let cool.

2. Mix the mushroom mixture, cheese, bread crumbs, and chives together in a medium bowl. Salt and pepper to taste. Cover the bowl with plastic wrap and refrigerate until ready to use.

3. **Make the tempura batter:** Whisk the flour, salt, and sparkling water together in a medium bowl. Set aside.

4. Roll tablespoon-sized portions of the mushroom mixture into ovals roughly the length and width of the squash blossom. Gently stuff the mushroom mixture into the blossoms. Twist the petals to seal. The mixture should take up about half the interior cavity of the blossoms.

5. Line a large plate with paper towels. Fill a large pot one-third full with canola oil. Heat the oil over medium heat until a deep-frying thermometer inserted in the oil reads 350°F.

6. Dip the stuffed squash blossoms into the tempura batter and allow any excess batter to drip off. Fry the squash blossoms in small batches until golden brown, turning occasionally, about 2 minutes per batch. Transfer them with a slotted spoon to the paper towel–lined plate to drain. Sprinkle with salt and arrange on a large platter. Serve immediately.

Italian Sandwiches with Kale "Butter"

Gabrielle Rysula and Chad Hahn cook kale from their southern Oregon farm low and slow to create a meltingly soft vegetarian sandwich filling. Upon trying the tender kale, one of the couple's CSA members declared it kale "butter." The name stuck — and so did the rustic sandwich the couple makes whenever kale is in season.

¼ cup extra-virgin olive oil

1 pound lacinato kale, ribs removed and leaves thinly sliced

1 small yellow onion, peeled and finely chopped (about ¾ cup)

4 garlic cloves, minced

2 tablespoons fresh oregano, finely chopped

2 cups mushroom broth

2 tablespoons soy sauce

Salt and freshly ground black pepper

4 ciabatta rolls, halved lengthwise

4 bocconcini-size fresh mozzarella balls, thinly sliced

4 SERVINGS

1. Heat the olive oil in a large skillet over medium heat. Add the kale, onion, garlic, and oregano and cook until wilted, about 2 minutes. Stir in the mushroom broth and soy sauce. Lower the heat to medium-low and simmer, stirring occasionally, until the kale is meltingly tender and most of the liquid has evaporated, about 20 minutes. Salt and pepper to taste.

2. Position a rack in the center of the oven and preheat the oven to 400°F.

3. Divide the kale mixture among the bottom halves of the rolls, allowing the broth to soak the bread a bit. Divide the cheese among the sandwiches. Cover the sandwiches with the top half of the rolls and transfer to a baking sheet.

4. Bake the sandwiches until the cheese melts and the sandwiches are warmed through, about 5 minutes. Serve immediately.

Slow-roasted Tomatoes

A long, slow roast and scattering of herbs turn up the flavor of everyday Roma tomatoes. Use them on pizzas and grilled sandwiches or try them atop Three-Cheese Macaroni and Cheese (page 124).

2 pounds Roma tomatoes

3 tablespoons extra-virgin olive oil

2 garlic cloves, crushed

2 teaspoons finely chopped fresh rosemary

2 teaspoons fresh thyme

¾ teaspoon kosher salt

½ teaspoon sugar

½ teaspoon freshly ground black pepper

MAKES ABOUT 1 CUP

1. Position a rack in the center of the oven and preheat the oven to 225°F.

2. Trim away the stem end of the tomatoes. Halve the tomatoes lengthwise and remove the cores and seeds.

3. Toss the tomatoes in a large bowl with the olive oil, garlic, rosemary, thyme, salt, sugar, and black pepper until well combined. Spread them on a rimmed baking sheet.

4. Bake the tomatoes until they crinkle and shrink to about half their original size, about 3 hours. Use immediately, or cool and transfer to an airtight container. Stored in the refrigerator, the tomatoes will keep for about 1 week.

Hashed Brussels Sprouts

I used to turn my nose up at stinky Brussels sprouts. But that was before I learned that the much-maligned vegetable becomes a welcome winter side dish when you "hash" the sprouts and sauté them in butter and olive oil. Dressing them with coarse-ground Dijon mustard adds another layer of flavor and makes them an ideal accompaniment for winter roasts.

1 pound Brussels sprouts, trimmed
1½ tablespoons apple cider vinegar
1 tablespoon unsalted butter
1 tablespoon extra-virgin olive oil
2 tablespoons dry white wine
1 tablespoon coarse-ground Dijon mustard
Salt and freshly ground black pepper

4 SERVINGS

1. Rinse the Brussels sprouts in cold water in a large bowl. Drain and halve lengthwise. Slice each of the wedges into ⅛-inch strips and toss with the vinegar in a medium bowl.

2. Warm the butter and olive oil in a large skillet over high heat until the butter melts. Lower the heat to medium and add the sprouts. Cook, stirring occasionally, until they have wilted slightly but are still bright green and slightly crisp, about 4 minutes.

3. Add the wine and continue cooking the sprouts over medium heat, stirring occasionally, for 1 minute longer. Remove the skillet from the heat. Stir in the Dijon mustard until well combined. Salt and pepper to taste. Transfer the sprouts to a serving bowl and serve immediately.

Roasted Cauliflower
with Currants and Crème Fraîche

A chef I once knew called cauliflower the redheaded stepchild of the veggie world, mainly because of its less-than-desirable scent. To help promote a positive image of this cruciferous vegetable, serve this side dish, which pairs cauliflower florets with bright ingredients like parsley, lemon juice, and crème fraîche.

4 SERVINGS

- 1 large cauliflower (about 1 pound), trimmed and separated into small florets
- 2 tablespoons extra-virgin olive oil
  Salt and freshly ground black pepper
- ¼ cup fresh flat-leaf parsley, chopped
- 2 tablespoons dried currants
- 2 teaspoons finely grated lemon zest
- 1 teaspoon lemon juice
- 2 tablespoons fresh bread crumbs, toasted
  Crème fraîche, for garnish

1. Position a rack in the center of the oven and preheat the oven to 400°F.

2. Toss the cauliflower florets with the olive oil and a pinch of salt and pepper in a medium bowl until evenly coated. Transfer them to a baking sheet and roast until they are tender when poked with a fork, about 15 minutes.

3. Toss the florets with the parsley, currants, lemon zest, and lemon juice in a medium bowl. Transfer to a serving plate and sprinkle the bread crumbs over the top. Drizzle with the crème fraîche and serve immediately.

Recipe from CHEF ALLEN ROUTT OF THE PAINTED LADY RESTAURANT AND ASHLEY GARTLAND

Heirloom Tomato Tart

Chef Allen Routt tops tiny tarts with beautiful vine-ripened heirloom tomatoes at his charming Newberg restaurant. I've streamlined his recipe using puff pastry to create large tarts to slice and share among friends. To make this tart sing, splurge on heirloom tomatoes, fresh mozzarella, and high-quality puff pastry.

1 sweet onion, peeled and thinly sliced

¼ Gala apple, peeled, cored, and thinly sliced

1 garlic clove, thinly sliced

2 tablespoons champagne vinegar

2 teaspoons sugar

1 teaspoon salt, plus more for seasoning

1 sheet (about 9 ounces) puff pastry, thawed

1 (4-ounce) ball fresh mozzarella cheese, cut into ¼-inch slices

¾ pound heirloom tomatoes, stemmed and thinly sliced

6 medium fresh basil leaves, torn

1 tablespoon extra-virgin olive oil

1 teaspoon balsamic vinegar

Freshly ground black pepper

6 SERVINGS

1. Combine the onion, apple, garlic, champagne vinegar, sugar, and salt in a medium saucepan. Cook the mixture over low heat, stirring occasionally, until the onions are tender but not brown and most of the liquid has evaporated, about 15 minutes. Remove the saucepan from the heat and set aside.

2. Position a rack in the center of the oven and preheat the oven to 400°F. Line two medium baking sheets with parchment paper.

3. Roll the puff pastry out on a lightly floured work surface into a ⅛-inch-thick rectangle measuring about 12 by 16 inches. Cut the rectangle in half to form two 12- by 8-inch pieces. Transfer the pieces to the prepared baking sheets. Pierce the pastry with a fork, leaving about a ½-inch border unpricked around the edges.

4. Scatter the onion mixture over the pastry sheets, leaving a ½-inch border on all sides. Fold over the sides of the pastry to create a nice edge, pressing lightly to secure the corners. Bake the tarts, rotating the baking sheets halfway through, until the pastry is golden brown and the edges are puffed, about 17 minutes.

5. Remove the baking sheets from the oven and layer the cheese over the onion mixture. Top the tarts with the tomatoes and bake until the edges and underside of the pastry are deep brown and the cheese has just started to melt, about 5 minutes. Place the baking sheets on a cooling rack to rest for 10 minutes.

6. Transfer the tarts to a cutting board and scatter the basil over them. Whisk the olive oil and balsamic vinegar together in a small bowl and drizzle it over the tarts. Salt and pepper to taste, slice, and serve immediately.

PORTLAND FARMERS MARKET

THE EARLY BIRDS ARRIVE at Portland Farmers Market's Saturday market promptly at 8:30 AM, just in time to hear the bell that marks the beginning of another busy morning at the market. Toting their woven baskets and ecofriendly shopping bags, in the spring these shoppers will have their pick of conical morels, slim asparagus spears, and the season's first strawberries. Come summer, they'll snatch up flats of marionberries and, in fall, discover tables laden with crisp apples and juicy pears. For them, the early visit is worth the effort: By midday, signboards reading "sold out till next week" start appearing at the bustling vendor stalls.

Such is the popularity of a market that has been growing steadily for nearly two decades. The

FRESH OREGON GROWN BERRIES

market first opened in 1992 in a gravel parking lot with 13 vendors. A few years later, the operation moved to its current site on the tree-lined park blocks at Portland State University. Today it hosts about 120 vendors and attracts 10,000 shoppers each week. Together the PSU market and a handful of neighborhood markets have increased sales for market vendors to nearly $6 million annually.

Market vendors reapply for their stalls each winter, allowing the staff to keep current on what vendors will be bringing to market. It also gives them a chance to manage the balance between farm stands and vendors selling value-added products like baked goods, preserves, and hard cider. Since the market's mission is to support local farms, the staff aims to have 75 percent of the stalls dedicated to farming and 25 percent reserved for value-added foodstuffs.

Farmers from Springwater Farms, Spring Hill Farm, and more have sold their produce at the market since the opening day. Not surprisingly, earning a spot among these veteran vendors can be tough, though not impossible. In fact, the market has given a few notable businesses their start. "Salvador Molly's started with us as a tamale cart and Pine State Biscuits also started with us. Those are businesses whose first day of business was at the market," says senior market manager Jaret Foster. Other artisan businesses like Two Tarts Bakery and Pix Pâtisserie honed their business models at the market before launching successful brick-and-mortar stores in town.

Though the cast of market characters changes slightly each year, the staff's mission to support family farms and small businesses remains the same. The challenge now is attracting locals who don't already support local agriculture or make market trips part of their routine. "There are still a ton of people who don't pay attention to seasonality and shopping locally or who don't recognize that a dollar spent at farmers' markets bounces around in the local economy a whole lot more than spending it at say, Fred Meyer, where the money is immediately exported," says Foster.

In the coming years, the staff hopes to increase the percentage of produce bought at farmers' markets substantially. "There was a study done a number of years ago that found that only 2 percent of fruits and vegetables are purchased at farmers' markets in Portland," says Foster. "We'd like to grow that number to 10 percent. It's a heady goal, but that would be our ideal."

Balsamic-braised Radicchio Risotto

Risotto strewn with glossy braised radicchio gives a popular winter chicory life beyond the salad course. Serve the risotto on its own for supper or with Chef Dustin Clark's fork-tender beef short ribs (page 218) nestled in the rice.

3 strips thick-cut bacon, diced into ¼-inch pieces

1 head radicchio, halved and thinly sliced

2 medium shallots, thinly sliced

¼ cup plus 2 tablespoons balsamic vinegar

2 tablespoons packed dark brown sugar

2 teaspoons dried currants

4 cups vegetable broth

2 tablespoons unsalted butter

¼ cup finely diced fennel bulb

¼ cup finely diced yellow onion

1 cup Arborio rice

1 tablespoon mascarpone cheese

Salt and freshly ground black pepper

4 SERVINGS

1. Cook the bacon in a large skillet over medium-low heat until crisp. Add the radicchio and shallots and cook until the radicchio wilts, about 2 minutes. Add 2 tablespoons of the vinegar, the sugar, and the currants and continue cooking over medium-low heat, stirring occasionally, until the radicchio is tender and slightly jammy, about 20 minutes.

2. Meanwhile, bring the broth to a boil in a medium saucepan. Reduce the heat to low and cover to keep warm.

3. Melt the butter in a medium skillet over medium-low heat. Add the fennel and onion and cook, stirring occasionally, until softened, about 5 minutes. Stir in the rice and continue cooking, stirring occasionally, until the grains of rice are opaque, about 2 minutes longer.

4. Stir in the remaining ¼ cup vinegar and cook over medium-low heat until absorbed. Ladle 1 cup of the broth over the rice and simmer, stirring frequently, over medium-low heat until absorbed. Continue to add the broth ½ cup at a time and reduce it, stirring frequently, until the rice is creamy and tender but still slightly chewy in the center, about 20 minutes. Remove the skillet from the heat. Reserve any remaining broth for another use.

5. Stir in the cheese and radicchio mixture until well combined. Salt and pepper to taste. Divide the risotto among four plates and serve immediately.

Fresh Nettle Pappardelle

After taking a dip in boiling water, nettles shed their stinging properties and make possible this deep green pasta that Chef JC Mersmann partners with his Spring Lamb Ragù (page 188). For a lighter dish, toss the pasta with a splash of olive oil, freshly grated Parmesan cheese, and seasonal market vegetables. You can find nettles in early spring through farmers' market vendors like Gathering Together Farm and Groundwork Organics, or forage for them yourself.

NOTE: This recipe requires a kitchen scale and pasta machine. Fortunately, both tools are cheap and easy to find.

½ pound nettles

1 ounce baby spinach (about 1 cup loosely packed spinach)

1½ cups semolina flour

1–2 tablespoons water

4 SERVINGS

1. Bring a large pot of salted water to a boil. Working in batches, blanch the nettles and spinach in the water until wilted, about 10 seconds. Drain the greens in a colander and rinse with cold water. Remove and discard any stems and squeeze the liquid out of the greens using a clean kitchen towel until they weigh ¼ pound.

2. Purée the greens in the bowl of a food processor. Add the flour and 1 tablespoon of the water and blend until the dough just comes together. Add the remaining 1 tablespoon water if the dough is too dry. Turn the dough out onto a lightly floured work surface and knead until smooth, about 5 minutes. Shape into a ball and cover with plastic wrap. Let the dough rest at room temperature for 1 hour.

3. Divide the dough into four pieces. Working with one piece at a time, flatten it into a rectangle slightly thinner than the pasta machine's widest setting. Dust the dough lightly with flour and feed it through the machine five times at the widest setting. Continue to run the piece through the machine, adjusting to the next thinnest setting every five passes, until the dough is about 2 feet long. Using the pasta machine or a knife, cut the pasta into wide noodles. Repeat the process with the remaining dough.

4. Bring a pot of salted water to a boil. Cook the noodles until they are al dente, about 2 minutes. Serve immediately with desired accompaniments.

Rustic Sausage and Kale Pasta

When kale is in season, I devour it daily in dishes like this rustic pasta. You can use any type of kale here, whether you prefer lacinato kale or a heartier variety. Don't be alarmed by the amount of raw kale called for. The pieces shrink dramatically as they cook, leaving you with the perfect amount of greens to toss with the pasta.

2 tablespoons extra-virgin olive oil

1 small red onion, finely diced

¾ pound ground spicy Italian pork sausage

1 tablespoon unsalted butter

1 bunch kale, ribs removed and leaves cut into ½-inch slices (about 5 cups)

Juice of 1 lemon

Salt

1 pound fresh pasta, such as rigatoni or orecchiette

¼ cup grated Parmesan cheese, plus more for garnish

4–6 SERVINGS

1. Warm 1 tablespoon of the olive oil over medium heat in a large skillet. Add the onion and cook, stirring occasionally, until softened, about 5 minutes. Add the sausage and continue to cook over medium heat until cooked through and browned, stirring and breaking up the sausage into small pieces with a wooden spoon as it cooks.

2. Meanwhile, bring a large pot of salted water to a boil. While the pasta water is heating, warm the butter and remaining 1 tablespoon olive oil in a large skillet over medium heat until the butter melts. Add the kale and cook over medium heat, stirring occasionally, for 2 minutes. Add the lemon juice and continue cooking, stirring occasionally, until slightly wilted, about 2 minutes longer. Remove the skillet from the heat and salt to taste.

3. When the water boils and the sausage is nearly done cooking, cook the pasta until al dente according to the package instructions.

4. Drain the pasta, reserving ¼ cup of the cooking water. Toss the pasta with the reserved cooking water, sausage and onion, three-quarters of the kale, and the Parmesan. Transfer the mixture to a large bowl and garnish with the remaining kale and additional Parmesan before serving.

Recipe from CHEF DAVID ANDERSON OF GENOA

Sunchoke and Fennel Gratin

To the uninitiated, knobby brown sunchokes are a curious market find. They are also, as Chef David Anderson discovered, an excellent candidate for a winter gratin. Genoa's chef layers the root vegetables (which are also called Jerusalem artichokes) with fennel, Parmesan, and a cream-butter sauce to create this rich, earthy rendition. A mandoline is a useful tool for slicing the vegetables into thin pieces, but a sharp knife will work as well.

½ cup (1 stick) unsalted butter
¼ cup minced shallots
2 garlic cloves, minced
1 tablespoon fresh thyme
2 cups heavy cream
½ teaspoon grated nutmeg
   Juice of 1 lemon
2 pounds sunchokes, scrubbed
2 medium fennel bulbs
1 cup grated Parmesan cheese
   Salt and freshly ground black
      pepper

David Anderson

8 SERVINGS

1. Position a rack in the center of the oven and preheat the oven to 325°F.

2. Melt 7 tablespoons of the butter over medium heat in a small saucepan. Stir in the shallots, garlic, and thyme and cook until the shallots have softened, about 3 minutes. Stir in the cream and nutmeg and simmer until warm but not boiling. Set the sauce aside to cool.

3. Fill a large bowl with cold water, and add the lemon juice. Thinly slice the sunchokes and place them in the lemon water.

4. Remove the tough inner cores from the fennel bulbs with a sharp knife and thinly slice the fennel.

5. Coat the bottom and sides of a 9- by 13-inch baking dish with the remaining 1 tablespoon butter. Cover the bottom of the baking dish with a layer of the sliced sunchokes and fennel. Spoon a few tablespoons of the cream mixture over the vegetables and sprinkle with a few tablespoons of Parmesan and a pinch of salt and black pepper. Continue to create layers with the sunchokes, fennel, Parmesan, cream sauce, and salt and pepper until you have used up the sunchokes and fennel. Pour any remaining cream sauce over the top of the gratin and sprinkle with any remaining Parmesan.

6. Cover the baking dish with foil. Bake the gratin until you can pierce the vegetables easily with the tip of a knife, about 1 hour 30 minutes. Remove the foil, turn the oven to broil, and brown the gratin under the broiler for 5 minutes. Let cool for 30 minutes before slicing and serving.

2 SAVORY CELEBRATIONS OF SEASONAL FRUITS

Recipe from CHEF RICHARD WIDMAYER OF SCREEN DOOR

Peach-Herb Salad
with Pickled Red Onions and Balsamic Vinaigrette

Herbs and peaches prove perfectly complementary in this light summer salad. Shavings from a firm cheese like Juniper Grove Farm's fruity Redmondo or a crumbled goat cheese are a nice garnish for this salad as well. Look for fennel pollen in specialty food stores.

NOTE: Be sure to start pickling the onions at least an hour before mealtime.

PICKLED RED ONIONS

- 1 cup red wine vinegar
- ¼ teaspoon red pepper flakes
- 1 black peppercorn
- 1 small bay leaf
- ½ cup thinly sliced red onion

PEACH-HERB SALAD WITH BALSAMIC VINAIGRETTE

- 2 tablespoons balsamic vinegar
- 1 tablespoon minced shallot
- ¼ cup extra-virgin olive oil
  Salt and freshly ground black pepper
- 3 ripe peaches, peeled (optional), pitted, and cut into sixths
- 1½ ounces baby arugula
- 1 medium fennel bulb, thinly sliced
- ½ cup loosely packed fresh basil leaves, torn
- ½ cup loosely packed fennel fronds
- ½ cup loosely packed fresh mint leaves, torn
  Fennel pollen, for garnish

4 SERVINGS

1. **Make the pickled onions:** Bring the vinegar, red pepper flakes, peppercorn, and bay leaf to a boil in a small saucepan over medium heat. Remove the saucepan from the heat. Place the onion slices in a small lidded container and cover them with the hot vinegar mixture. Let the onions cool at room temperature for 1 hour. Cover and refrigerate until ready to use.

2. **Make the peach salad and vinaigrette:** Whisk the vinegar and shallot together in a small bowl. Let the shallot rest in the vinegar for 10 minutes. Whisk in the olive oil. Salt and pepper to taste and set aside.

3. Drain the onions. Discard the peppercorn and bay leaf. Mix the onions, peaches, arugula, fennel, basil, fennel fronds, and mint together in a large bowl. Toss the salad gently with the vinaigrette until well combined.

4. Transfer the salad to a serving bowl. Garnish with a pinch of fennel pollen and serve immediately.

Recipe from CHEF KRISTEN MURRAY

Nectarine-Basil Lemonade

Pastry chef Kristen Murray uses colorful cubes of nectarine and a basil-infused simple syrup to update from-scratch lemonade. The lemonade is on the sweeter side, so if you prefer a more mouth-puckering thirst quencher, use five lemons instead of four.

6 cups water

1½ cups sugar

¼ pound basil stems and leaves (about 2 tightly packed cups), plus more leaves for garnish

4 ripe nectarines

Juice of 4–5 lemons

MAKES ABOUT 9 CUPS

1. Heat 2 cups of the water and the sugar over medium heat in a large saucepan until the sugar dissolves. Remove the saucepan from the heat and stir in the basil. Let the basil syrup cool to room temperature. Strain the syrup and discard the basil. Pour the syrup and the remaining 4 cups water into a large glass pitcher.

2. Remove the pits from the nectarines and cut them into ½-inch pieces. Add the nectarines and juice from 4 lemons to the pitcher. Stir gently with a wooden spoon. Taste the lemonade and add the remaining juice if needed. Refrigerate for at least 1 hour before serving. Serve over ice with a few small basil leaves for garnish.

Blackcurrant Barbecue Sauce

Blackcurrants lend from-scratch barbecue sauce a pleasing tang and deep burgundy hue. Tommie and Peter van de Kamp make the sauce when blackcurrants ripen on their Scio farm from late June through July. Serve the fruity condiment brushed over grilled steak, chicken, or lamb.

1 tablespoon canola oil

1 small red onion, finely chopped (about 1 cup)

½ dried arbol chile, finely chopped (seeds optional)

1 pint (about 2 cups) fresh blackcurrants

½ cup ketchup

¼ cup plus 2 tablespoons apple cider vinegar

¼ cup packed dark brown sugar

1 tablespoon molasses

¼ teaspoon dried thyme

⅛ teaspoon ground allspice

MAKES ABOUT 1½ CUPS

1. Warm the canola oil in a medium saucepan over medium-low heat. Add the onion and cook, stirring occasionally, until softened and just beginning to brown, about 5 minutes.

2. Stir in the arbol chile and cook for 30 seconds longer. Stir in the blackcurrants, ketchup, vinegar, sugar, molasses, thyme, and allspice. Bring the sauce to a boil over medium heat.

3. Reduce the heat to low and simmer, stirring occasionally, until the currants break down and the sauce thickens, about 15 minutes.

4. Remove the saucepan from the heat. Use the sauce immediately, or cool to room temperature and transfer to an airtight container. Stored in the refrigerator, the sauce will keep for about 3 weeks.

Boysenberry Vinaigrette

Portland-based culinary instructor Michele Knaus developed this vinaigrette to serve at a berry-themed cooking class I attended years ago. Not only does it deliver superb flavor, but it boasts a striking hue as well. Use the vinaigrette to dress a simple green salad.

MAKES ABOUT 2 CUPS

1 pint (about 2 cups) fresh or frozen boysenberries

¼ cup honey

¼ cup water

½ cup champagne vinegar

¼ cup finely chopped shallots

1 tablespoon minced garlic

1 teaspoon Dijon mustard

1 teaspoon Tabasco sauce

¼ teaspoon ground coriander

½ cup walnut or hazelnut oil

¼ cup canola oil

Salt and freshly ground black pepper

1. Combine the boysenberries, honey, and water in a small saucepan and simmer over medium heat until the boysenberries soften. Pour the boysenberries and liquid through a fine-mesh strainer into a small bowl, pressing on the solids with a rubber spatula to extract the berry juice but leaving the seeds behind. Discard the seeds.

2. Purée the berry juice, vinegar, shallots, garlic, mustard, Tabasco, and coriander in a blender or the bowl of a food processor fitted with a steel blade attachment. Drizzle in the walnut oil and canola oil with the motor running. Salt and pepper to taste.

3. Adjust the flavor with additional honey or Tabasco as needed. Use the vinaigrette immediately, or transfer to an airtight container. Stored in the refrigerator, it will keep for about 5 days.

Cherry-Basil Bruschetta

Summer cherries need not be limited to clafouti and pie. In this seasonal starter, they mingle with fennel and basil to create an unexpected topping for bruschetta. Skeptics might question the pairing initially, but the combination of juicy cherries and cooling basil and fennel will quickly win guests over. Shaving the fennel bulb thinly on a mandoline before chopping it keeps it from overpowering the dish.

1½ cups sweet dark cherries, pitted and halved

¼ cup finely chopped fennel bulb

2 tablespoons thinly sliced basil leaves, plus more leaves for garnish

½ teaspoon finely grated lemon zest

1 tablespoon lemon juice

1 tablespoon extra-virgin olive oil

¼ teaspoon freshly ground black pepper

20 (¼-inch) slices baguette, toasted

½ cup fromage blanc or similar soft, fresh cheese

MAKES 20 PIECES

1. Mix the cherries, fennel, basil, lemon zest, lemon juice, olive oil, and black pepper together with a rubber spatula in a medium bowl until well combined.

2. Spread each of the toasted baguette slices with a thin layer of the cheese. Top each slice with a small spoonful of the cherry mixture and garnish with a small basil leaf. Arrange the bruschetta on a platter and serve immediately.

Recipe from CHEF MATTHEW BENNETT OF SYBARIS BISTRO

Grilled Oregonzola Figs

When figs come into season in late summer, Chef Matthew Bennett prepares this classic Italian antipasto for diners at his Albany bistro. The figs come off the grill plump and slightly jammy — just make sure to remove the figs from the grill right after the prosciutto crisps or the cheese can melt onto the grill grates and create a sticky, scalding mess.

8 fresh Black Mission figs

2 ounces blue cheese, such as Rogue Creamery's Oregonzola

8 paper-thin slices prosciutto

1 tablespoon honey
   Freshly ground black pepper

4 SERVINGS

1. Make a small incision from the fig's stem toward the middle of the fruit. Gently open the fig and fill the opening with about 1 teaspoon of the cheese. Wrap the fig in the prosciutto. Secure the prosciutto with a toothpick, if necessary. Repeat with the remaining figs.

2. Preheat the grill for direct grilling over hot charcoal or high heat. Oil the grill grates. Place the figs on the grill and cook, turning once, until the prosciutto crisps and the cheese is warm but not melting, about 5 minutes.

3. Remove the toothpicks from the figs, if needed, and arrange the figs on a serving plate. Drizzle with honey and sprinkle with a pinch of black pepper. Serve immediately.

Baby Romaine Salad with Pickled Blueberries
and Creamy Tarragon Dressing

The textural contrast of plump, pickled blueberries, crisp baby romaine lettuce, and creamy tarragon dressing makes this a summer salad worth repeating. When you're pickling the blueberries, keep a close eye on the stovetop. You want to warm the fruit, not make jam, so a brief boil is all they need.

NOTE: Pickle the blueberries a few hours before mealtime so they have adequate time to chill.

PICKLED BLUEBERRIES

- 15 fresh thyme sprigs
- 6 allspice berries
- 6 black peppercorns
- 1½ cups sugar
- ½ cup champagne vinegar
- 1 pint (about 2 cups) fresh blueberries

BABY ROMAINE SALAD WITH TARRAGON DRESSING

- ½ small shallot, finely chopped (about 2 tablespoons)
- 2 tablespoons white wine vinegar
- 2 teaspoons Dijon mustard
- 2 teaspoons tightly packed fresh tarragon leaves
- 1 egg yolk
- ¼ cup plus 2 tablespoons canola oil
  Salt and freshly ground black pepper
- 10 ounces baby romaine lettuce
  Hard sheep's milk cheese shavings, such as Juniper Grove Redmondo cheese, for garnish

NOTE: This dish contains raw eggs. Consuming raw eggs may increase your risk of foodborne illness.

6 SERVINGS

1. **Make the pickled blueberries:** Tie the thyme, allspice berries, and peppercorns together in a small cheesecloth sachet. Bring the sachet, sugar, and champagne vinegar to a boil in a medium saucepan, whisking occasionally, until the sugar dissolves. Remove the saucepan from the heat. Let the syrup cool slightly, then gently stir in the blueberries with a wooden spoon.

2. Put the saucepan back on the stove and cook the blueberries over medium heat until the liquid just comes to a boil. Remove the saucepan from the heat. Discard the cheesecloth sachet and let the mixture cool. Transfer the blueberries and pickling juice to a lidded container and refrigerate for at least 2 hours or overnight.

3. **Make the salad and dressing:** Mix the shallot and vinegar together in a small bowl and let rest for 10 minutes. Blend the shallots, vinegar, mustard, tarragon, and egg yolk in a blender on low speed until well combined. Add the canola oil in a steady stream with the motor running until well combined. Salt and pepper to taste.

4. Toss the lettuce with the dressing in a large salad bowl and divide among six plates. Using a slotted spoon, remove the blueberries from the pickling juice and divide them equally among the plates. Discard the pickling juice. Garnish the salads with a few shavings of the cheese and serve immediately.

SIMPATICA DINING HALL

THERE ARE MOMENTS during every Simpatica Dining Hall dinner when the chatter at the communal tables suddenly ceases and the room becomes reverently quiet. The only sounds are of silverware clinking as diners dip into bowls of shrimp bisque or slice into a *boudin blanc* on a plate of *choucroute garnie*. There may be a shared sigh over a starter of Dungeness crab puffs or the first bite of warm chocolate-whiskey cake, but for the most part diners pause their conversations when the courses arrive at the tables.

Simpatica launched in 2004 as a traveling supper club, born from the need of local butchers Benjamin Dyer and John Gorham to get back behind the stove. In 2005, the traveling chefs found a permanent home in a former music club in Portland's Eastside. In the spare, industrial dining room, devoted locals and tourists from near and far now gather for single-seating Friday and Saturday night dinners and Sunday brunch.

Fans find out about the dinners by registering for the warm, witty e-mails Dyer sends out weekly to announce the upcoming menus. Those menus take shape around local ingredients from a small roster of farms as well as the whims of Chef Scott Ketterman. Every week, the chef studies what's in season and then hatches a theme and multicourse menu from the list of available ingredients.

One night Ketterman might celebrate spring with a menu of fennel and green garlic soup, slow-roasted Chinook salmon, and lemon pound cake garnished with strawberry ice cream and sweet basil syrup. On another evening, he'll take guests on a trip through Spain with a tapas menu featuring *mussels rellenos* and smoked pork ribs with a *piment d'Espelette* glaze. "What it always boils down to is that I want people to come, eat good food, and have a good time," says Ketterman.

Over the years, the Simpatica crew members have continued to diversify their interests and expand their footprint on Portland's food culture, most notably by opening a butcher shop–steakhouse hybrid, Laurelhurst Market, in 2009. But the everyday reinvention truly happens over dinner at the supper club. In more than five years, the chefs have not repeated a dinner menu. Instead, they continually dream up new, inspired meals that give diners plenty of reasons to pause.

Blueberry, Corn, and Basil Salad

My mother often made a version of this colorful corn salad to serve at barbecues and family suppers. I've replaced the bell peppers in the original recipe with sweet blueberries and added cooling basil to update the dish without losing any of its picnic potential.

3 cups fresh corn kernels (from about 6 ears corn)

¼ cup water

1 medium red onion, finely chopped (about 1 cup)

1½ cups fresh blueberries

¼ cup lime juice

¼ cup extra-virgin olive oil

Salt and freshly ground black pepper

½ cup thinly sliced fresh basil leaves

6 SERVINGS

1. Steam the corn with the water in a large saucepan over medium heat, covered, until bright yellow, about 4 minutes. Remove the lid and continue to cook the corn, stirring frequently, until the water evaporates, about 3 minutes longer.

2. Transfer the corn to a large bowl and let it cool slightly. Mix in the red onion, blueberries, lime juice, and olive oil. Salt and pepper to taste. Cover the bowl and refrigerate until chilled, about 2 hours.

3. Remove the salad from the refrigerator and mix in the basil with a rubber spatula. Serve immediately.

Berry, Burrata, and Arugula Salad
with Sherry-Orange Vinaigrette

Chef Earl Hook of Meriwether's and Chef Dolan Lane of Clarklewis served a berry, burrata cheese, and farm greens salad to launch their mid-July Plate & Pitchfork dinner at Smith BerryBarn. I adapted their salad for home cooks and paired it with an easy vinaigrette. The sweet berries, peppery greens, and creamy cheese mingle under the blanket of the sherry-orange vinaigrette to create a farm-fresh summer salad.

3 tablespoons extra-virgin olive oil

1 tablespoon sherry vinegar

⅛ teaspoon orange zest

1 tablespoon orange juice

½ teaspoon honey

Salt and freshly ground black pepper

2 fresh figs, stemmed and quartered

½ cup fresh blackberries

½ cup fresh raspberries

¼ cup fresh blueberries

4 ounces baby arugula

2 (4-ounce) burrata or fresh mozzarella balls, cut into ¼-inch slices

¼ cup hazelnuts, toasted, skinned, and roughly chopped

Salt, such as fleur de sel, for garnish

4 SERVINGS

1. Whisk the olive oil, vinegar, orange zest, orange juice, and honey together in a small bowl. Salt and pepper to taste and set aside.

2. Scatter the figs, blackberries, raspberries, and blueberries across a large platter. Toss the arugula with the vinaigrette in a medium bowl until well combined. Salt and pepper to taste. Pile the arugula over the berries.

3. Garnish the salad with the cheese and hazelnuts. Sprinkle a pinch of the fleur de sel over the salad and serve immediately.

NOTE: Burrata, a soft, fresh Italian cheese made from mozzarella and cream, is available in some supermarkets and specialty grocers. Fresh mozzarella is a good substitute.

PLATE & PITCHFORK

IT'S A HOT SUNDAY AFTERNOON on the outskirts of Portland, and to the unassuming eye everything looks as it should at Smith BerryBarn's U-pick farm. Parents are heading out to the berry fields with buckets and kids in tow, while young couples stand sorting through fresh produce and farm eggs in the farm's red barn. And everyone, it seems, has clued in to the fact that the farm's famous milkshakes are the best way to beat the summer heat.

But the orchard that sits beyond the berry brambles hides a surprise. Here, Erika Polmar and a team of volunteers are transforming a grassy patch of land into an elegant outdoor dining room for Plate & Pitchfork's weekend farm dinner. Soon the tables will be covered with crisp white linens and sparkling glassware and the evening's chefs — Earl Hook of Meriwether's and Dolan Lane of Clarklewis — will enter the outdoor kitchen to prep a true farm-to-table meal.

Polmar works with local chefs each summer to create the Plate & Pitchfork dinner series she founded with Emily Berreth in 2002. The women's initial plan was to host a series of dinners that matched chefs with local farms and reconnected diners with the dedicated people who grow, catch, raise, and prepare local food.

In their first year, they hosted three small, successful dinners; since Berreth stepped down in 2010, Polmar has continued to coordinate a dozen farm dinners each year that honor the series' initial mission. "The core values of Plate & Pitchfork remain the same," says Polmar. "Every dinner focuses on products from the host farm and a farm tour. The difference is that now people ask more questions and are more curious [about the farm]."

Each dinner begins with appetizers and an insightful tour of the host farm. Coupled together, the tour and multicourse meal highlight the benefits of eating local and the farm's sustainable practices. But each evening serves a purpose beyond education as well. Polmar also donates a portion of each season's proceeds to nonprofits that support small farms, environmental literacy, and food security.

Back at Smith BerryBarn, Polmar slips into a floral print dress and countrified cowboy boots before greeting the evening's first guests. Diners arrive to a warm welcome: a table spread with bright fava bean bruschetta, shooters of chilled cucumber soup, and glasses of viognier from Dominio IV Wines. With that first bite of farm-fresh food and first sip of local wine, the educational evening has begun. In mere minutes, the empty tables in the orchard have come to life.

Erika Polmar

Chilled Marionberry-Peach Soup

A recipe for chilled blackberry-lime soup from Janie Hibler's comprehensive *The Berry Bible* cookbook inspired this light, delicate dish. Peaches and a splash of lime juice add complexity to the berries in a chilled soup that works well as a starter or as a less traditional dessert. Serve the soup in white bowls, which contrast with its deep purple hue.

1 cup water

⅓ cup honey

3 pints (about 6 cups) fresh marionberries

2 medium peaches, peeled, pitted, and quartered

¾ cup low-fat plain yogurt

Juice of 1 lime

4 fresh mint leaves

4 SERVINGS

1. Warm the water and honey in a large saucepan over medium heat until the honey liquefies. Stir in the marionberries and peaches and reduce the heat to medium-low. Simmer, stirring occasionally, until the marionberries release their juices and the peaches soften, about 10 minutes.

2. Remove the saucepan from the heat. Let the fruit mixture cool slightly. Purée the fruit mixture in the bowl of a food processor fitted with a steel blade attachment. Strain the purée through a fine-mesh strainer into a large bowl, pushing it through with a spatula to extract the juice. Discard the seeds. Cover the bowl with plastic wrap and refrigerate until well chilled, about 4 hours.

3. Whisk ½ cup of the yogurt and the lime juice into the chilled soup. Divide the soup among four shallow soup bowls. Garnish with a dollop of the remaining ¼ cup yogurt and a mint leaf. Serve immediately.

Oregon Berry Industry

FROM RADIANT RED RASPBERRIES to bright Hood strawberries to the native marionberry, summers in Oregon are awash in berries. From June through September, berries abound at local grocers, farmers' markets, and rural roadside fruit stands; an abundance of U-pick berry farms lets locals experience the delight of plucking sun-kissed berries fresh from the field.

Oregon is the leading producer in the nation of blackberries, marionberries, loganberries, boysenberries, and black raspberries, and the state ranks second in the nation in raspberry production. At last count, growers harvested more than 77 million pounds of caneberries alone for fresh market sales and the individually quick-frozen (IQF) product market.

Professional chefs and home cooks in Oregon prize berries for being versatile, intensely flavored ingredients. Pastry chefs make the most of the berry bounty by serving berry cobblers, crisps, and shortcakes all summer long, while ice cream and gelato shops dish out pint upon pint of berry ice cream and gelato. Local chefs have also discovered that berries can cross over to the savory side of the menu in sauces, salads, mains, and sides. But for many individuals, the greatest pleasure still comes from enjoying juicy local berries fresh and unadorned.

Strawberry Risotto

Chef Robert Reynolds teaches culinary professionals and home cooks to become more intuitive chefs at his intimate Portland cooking school. With this recipe, he showcases a savory use for early spring strawberries, which lack the developed sugars of peak-season berries and thus work well in a main-course risotto. When sweet, peak-season strawberries arrive at the market, it's time to tuck this recipe away for another year.

4 cups low-sodium chicken broth

2 tablespoons unsalted butter

2 tablespoons extra-virgin olive oil

¼ cup finely diced shallots

Salt

1½ cups Arborio rice

1 cup white wine

1 pint (about 2 cups) early spring strawberries, hulled and thinly sliced

¼ cup finely grated Parmesan cheese

Aged balsamic vinegar

Freshly ground black pepper

4 SERVINGS

1. Bring the broth to a simmer in a large saucepan over medium heat. Reduce the heat to low and cover to keep warm.

2. Warm the butter and the olive oil in a medium skillet over medium heat until the butter melts. Add the shallots and a pinch of salt and cook, stirring often, until the shallots are soft but not brown, about 2 minutes. Stir in the rice and continue cooking until the grains of rice are opaque, about 2 minutes longer.

3. Stir in the wine and cook the rice over medium-low heat until it absorbs the wine. Ladle 1 cup of the hot broth over the rice and simmer, stirring frequently, over medium-low heat until absorbed. Continue to add the broth ½ cup at a time and reduce it, stirring frequently until the rice is creamy and tender but still slightly chewy in the center, about 20 minutes. Remove the skillet from the heat and salt to taste. Reserve any remaining broth for another use.

4. Just before serving, gently fold the strawberries into the risotto. Divide the risotto among four bowls. Garnish each serving with 1 tablespoon of the Parmesan, a drizzle of balsamic vinegar, and a pinch of black pepper. Serve immediately.

Robert Reynolds

Roasted Pears with Sage

Finely sliced sage adds a savory note to these caramelized pears. Use them to adorn cheese plates, salads, and grilled meats. Or do as Chef Jenn Louis suggests and purée them into potato-leek soup to give it a subtle sweetness. Use firm, underripe pears for this recipe, as ripe pears will turn soft and mushy in the oven.

3 firm pears, such as Bosc, peeled, cored, and quartered

2 tablespoons extra-virgin olive oil

2 tablespoons sugar

2 fresh sage leaves, finely sliced
   Freshly ground black pepper

4 SERVINGS

1. Position a rack in the center of the oven and preheat the oven to 450°F. Place a rimmed baking sheet on the center rack to warm.

2. Gently toss the pears, olive oil, sugar, sage leaves, and a pinch of black pepper together in a medium bowl. The pears should be well seasoned and slick with olive oil but not drenched.

3. Spread the pears on the hot baking sheet and bake until golden and caramelized on the side touching the pan, about 10 minutes. Turn the pears over and roast until caramelized on the second side, about 8 minutes longer. Check the pears occasionally to make sure they do not get too soft. They should be warmed through but retain a firm texture.

4. Transfer the pears to a serving plate. Let cool slightly before serving.

Mixed Green Salad with Cranberry Vinaigrette

Sustainably grown cranberries from Clearwater Cranberries form the foundation of this pleasantly pink vinaigrette. Farmer Gretchen Farr spoons the dressing over a wintery salad of mixed greens, apples, candied walnuts, and dried cranberries to put the collaborative's harvest to good use at home.

CRANBERRY VINAIGRETTE

- 1 cup fresh or frozen cranberries
- ⅓ cup sugar
- ⅓ cup water
- ½ cup apple cider vinegar
- 1½ teaspoons Dijon mustard
- 3 tablespoons extra-virgin olive oil

MIXED GREEN SALAD

- 5 ounces mixed baby greens
- 1 tart apple, cored and chopped into ½-inch pieces
- ⅓ cup crumbled blue cheese
- ⅓ cup dried cranberries
- ⅓ cup Glazed Walnuts (page 209)

  Salt and freshly ground black pepper

4 SERVINGS

1. **Make the vinaigrette:** Combine the cranberries, sugar, and water in a small saucepan and cook over medium heat, stirring occasionally, until the cranberries pop, about 5 minutes.

2. Pour the cranberry mixture into a blender or the bowl of a food processor fitted with a steel blade attachment. Add the vinegar and mustard and pulse until just combined. Add the olive oil and pulse until smooth.

3. **Make the salad:** Toss the greens with enough dressing to coat the leaves in a medium salad bowl. Add the apple, cheese, dried cranberries, and walnuts and toss gently. Salt and pepper to taste and serve immediately with any remaining dressing on the side.

CLEARWATER CRANBERRIES

GRETCHEN AND RANDY FARR had been farming their 23-acre cranberry farm on the southern coast for 5 years when their efforts drew attention from the South Coast Watershed Council. In addition to growing and harvesting about a half million pounds of cranberries each year, the couple were applying sustainable farming practices such as water conservation and stream restoration to their family farm.

These sustainable practices earned the couple a spot in a growing collaborative of independent, family-owned farms, aptly named Clearwater Cranberries. In 2009, the Farrs worked with the watershed council and the Oregon Environmental Council to create a new, sustainable business model for the industry. The model, which diverted some of the commodity sales to a specialty market for sustainably grown cranberries, offered what the

Farrs call "a win-win-win solution" for farmers, consumers, and the environment.

In the first year, the collaborative successfully implemented the new model and improved the health of local watersheds. The two participating farms became Food Alliance and Salmon Safe certified, and the farmers sold about half their fruit to the specialty market. More important to the Farrs, however, has been the opportunity to leave their property in better shape than they found it.

We do what we can to put the land back the way it was before we arrived so the native fish have a chance to continue on and so we don't damage their habitat and contribute to the decline of any species," says Gretchen. "We do it for our kids and future generations. We don't want a child to someday ask what a salmon was. We want them to know and experience all the wonderful things that we have been able to experience in our lives."

Pear-Pepper Chutney

Marché's chef and founder Stephanie Pearl Kimmel serves this savory chutney atop her curried shrimp salad (page 138) and with cheese plates and roast chicken.

5   Bartlett pears, peeled and cut
    into ½-inch cubes (about 5 cups)

2   red bell peppers, seeded and
    finely chopped (about 1½ cups)

1   lemon, seeded and finely diced

2¼ cups packed dark brown sugar

1½ cups dried currants

1   cup apple cider vinegar

¼   cup finely diced fresh ginger

1   garlic clove, minced

1   heaping teaspoon salt

¼   teaspoon cayenne pepper

MAKES ABOUT 6 CUPS

1. Combine the pears, bell peppers, lemon, sugar, currants, vinegar, ginger, garlic, salt, and cayenne in a large saucepan. Simmer uncovered over low heat, stirring frequently, until the chutney has thickened and the pears have softened but still hold their shape, about 1 hour.

2. Transfer the chutney to an airtight container and let cool to room temperature. Stored in an airtight container in the refrigerator, the chutney will keep for 1 month.

Recipe from PIPER DAVIS OF GRAND CENTRAL BAKERY

Cranberry-Apple Chutney

Grand Central Bakery has served this cranberry chutney — made using Clearwater Cranberries — on its popular turkey sandwich for years. It's bright, tangy, and equally delicious served on a turkey sandwich or alongside roasted chicken or pork.

2 teaspoons extra-virgin olive oil

2 medium red onions, peeled and finely diced (about 1⅔ cups)

2 teaspoons finely minced garlic

1 teaspoon finely grated fresh ginger

3–4 large apples, peeled, cored, and diced into ¼-inch cubes (about 4 cups)

1½ cups fresh or frozen cranberries

1⅓ cups apple cider vinegar

1¼ cups packed dark brown sugar

½ cup dried currants

½ cup golden raisins

2 teaspoons yellow mustard seeds

1½ teaspoons ground allspice

1 teaspoon cayenne pepper

MAKES ABOUT 4½ CUPS

1. Warm the olive oil in a large saucepan over medium heat. Add the onions and cook, stirring occasionally, until softened and translucent, about 5 minutes. Add the garlic and ginger and cook until fragrant, about 1 minute longer.

2. Stir in the apples, cranberries, vinegar, sugar, currants, raisins, mustard seeds, allspice, and cayenne. Increase the heat to medium-high and bring the mixture to a boil. Reduce the heat to low and simmer, stirring frequently, until the apples and cranberries have cooked down and the sauce has thickened, about 40 minutes.

3. Remove the saucepan from the heat and transfer the chutney to an airtight container to cool. Stored in an airtight container in the refrigerator, the chutney will keep for about 1 week.

Raw Beet Salad with Asian Pears and Goat Cheese

My grandmother spent many hot summer mornings pickling beets to fill her pantry. I prefer to skip the fuss and serve them raw in this Jamie Oliver–inspired salad with creamy goat cheese and crisp Asian pears. Using different colored beets creates a striking contrast on the plate.

¼ cup extra-virgin olive oil

2 tablespoons lemon juice

Salt and freshly ground black pepper

2 medium beets, peeled and cut into ⅛-inch matchsticks

1½ Asian pears, peeled, cored, and cut into ⅛-inch matchsticks

4 ounces goat cheese, such as Rivers Edge chèvre, crumbled

¼ cup pine nuts, toasted

4 large fresh basil leaves, torn

Salt, such as fleur de sel, for garnish

4 SERVINGS

1. Whisk the olive oil and lemon juice together in a medium bowl. Salt and pepper to taste. Add the beets and pears and toss gently until glossy.

2. Divide the salad among four small plates. Garnish each plate with 1 ounce of cheese, 1 tablespoon of pine nuts, a scattering of basil, and a pinch of fleur de sel. Serve immediately.

HOOD RIVER COUNTY FRUIT LOOP

JUST A FEW MILES from the windsurfing hub of Hood River, a scenic drive introduces visitors to the agricultural side of the region and the valley's famous fruit. The 35-mile Fruit Loop winds past orchards, farms, and roadside fruit stands below the backdrop of majestic Mount Hood. Orchards bearing cherries, pears, and apples line the scenic route alongside bakeries tucked into rustic red barns and wineries featuring Gorge-grown wines.

By midsummer, day-trippers can escape the fray of their respective cities and roll up to the region's U-pick farms. They'll welcome summer by plucking plump cherries from the trees at places like Draper Girls Country Farm (and likely tote a gallon of the farm's famous nonpasteurized cherry cider home too). As the seasons follow in quick succession, they'll return to pick apples and pears at farms like Kiyokawa Family Orchards, where varieties like shapely Bosc pears and squat Asian pears grow in abundance.

Annual events like Heirloom Apple Days and the Hood River Pear Celebration spotlight prized local fruit and provide even more motivation to visit the region. But many visitors drive the loop to trade their city lifestyle for a rural escape and support local farmers while they take in the sights.

Pear and Prosciutto Pizza

Chef Jennifer Buehler slips this unexpected pizza combination onto her specials menu when pears hit the market. Don't be leery of putting pears on your pie: The combination of the sweet fruit and salty prosciutto is a pleasing one. A preheated pizza stone will help you achieve a crisp, restaurant-quality crust, but a standard pizza pan will also work in a pinch.

- 1 (5½-ounce) ball of pizza dough
  Semolina flour
- ¼ cup coarsely grated mozzarella cheese
- 1 tablespoon coarsely grated Fontina cheese
- ½ Bosc or D'Anjou pear, cored and cut into ⅛-inch slices
- 2 slices prosciutto, roughly chopped
- 1 cup arugula
  White truffle oil (optional)
  Salt, such as Maldon sea salt, for garnish

MAKES 1 (10-INCH) PIZZA

1. Position a rack in the center of the oven and preheat the oven to 425°F. Place the pizza stone in the oven to preheat, if using.

2. Roll the pizza dough out on a lightly floured work surface until you have a circle about 10 inches in diameter. Remove the pizza stone from the oven and sprinkle it lightly with the semolina flour. Transfer the dough to the pizza stone. Sprinkle the mozzarella and Fontina over the dough, leaving a ½-inch border. Layer the pear slices and prosciutto over the cheese.

3. Bake the pizza until the crust is golden and crisp and the cheese has melted, about 15 minutes.

4. Remove the pizza from the oven and garnish with the arugula, a drizzle of white truffle oil, if desired, and pinch of salt. Serve immediately.

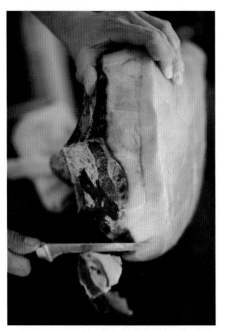

3 OUTSTANDING ARTISAN CHEESE AND DAIRY PRODUCTS

Recipe from GABRIELLE RYSULA AND CHAD HAHN OF MUD PUDDLE FARM

Roasted Beet and Chèvre Spread

Gabrielle Rysula and Chad Hahn blend beets from their Applegate Valley farm with local goat cheese to create this vivid, subtly sweet spread. Try piping the spread onto individual crackers or crostini and topping it with watercress and lemon zest or pickled red onions to give it a bit of zing. For easier entertaining, transfer the spread to a pretty serving bowl and surround it with good crusty bread for dipping.

3   beets, trimmed

1   tablespoon balsamic vinegar
    Salt and freshly ground black pepper

8   ounces goat cheese, such as Mama Terra or Siskiyou Crest chèvre
    Extra-virgin olive oil

MAKES ABOUT 3 CUPS

1. Position a rack in the center of the oven and preheat the oven to 400°F. Place the beets in a roasting pan and toss with the balsamic vinegar and a pinch of salt and pepper.

2. Cover the pan with foil and roast the beets until they are tender when poked with a fork, about 50 minutes. Remove the beets from the oven and uncover the pan. When they are cool enough to handle, peel them and cut into ½-inch pieces.

3. Purée the beets in the bowl of a food processor fitted with a steel blade attachment until partially smooth, about 1 minute. Blend in the cheese, scraping down the sides of the bowl as needed with a rubber spatula, until the beets and cheese are well combined and the spread is smooth. If needed, add about a tablespoon of olive oil to thin the mixture to a spreadable consistency. Salt and pepper to taste.

4. Let the spread cool to room temperature or, if desired, chill it in the refrigerator before serving. Stored in the refrigerator in an airtight container, the spread will keep for about 3 days.

Lemon-Herb Fromage Blanc Spread

I first tried the smooth, creamy fresh cheese known as fromage blanc in a Lyonnaise-style cheese spread at a Paris bistro. When I found a locally made fromage blanc at my grocer, I immediately shuttled it home to re-create the dish I'd first tried — with a few twists. My version gets a lift from lemon zest and a scattering of fresh herbs and added richness from a generous drizzle of extra-virgin olive oil. Toasted slices of baguette or hunks of soft artisan bread are the ideal vehicle for transferring this soft, creamy spread from bowl to mouth.

8 ounces fromage blanc, such as Alsea Acres or Juniper Grove Farm's fromage blanc

¼ cup heavy cream

1½ teaspoons lemon zest

1 teaspoon thinly sliced fresh basil leaves

1 teaspoon finely chopped fresh chives

1 teaspoon finely chopped fresh flat-leaf parsley

Salt and freshly ground black pepper

Extra-virgin olive oil

Salt, such as fleur de sel (optional)

MAKES ABOUT 1 CUP

1. Blend the fromage blanc, cream, lemon zest, basil, chives, and parsley in a medium bowl with a rubber spatula until well combined. The consistency of the cheese will loosen slightly but should not be runny. Salt and pepper to taste.

2. Transfer the mixture to a serving bowl and drizzle a thin stream of olive oil over the top. Sprinkle with fleur de sel, if desired, and serve immediately.

Potted Cheese

Tressa Yellig blends artisan cheese with a bit of butter to create a thrifty appetizer for home entertaining. Though any hard cheese works well in this recipe, Yellig recommends Ancient Heritage Dairy's Hannah Bridge, a hard cheese made from a blend of cow's and sheep's milk. Serve this spread with lightly toasted bread, artisan crackers, or quick pickles for a twist on a traditional cheese plate.

½ cup plus 2 tablespoons (1¼ sticks) unsalted butter, at room temperature and cut into ½-inch cubes

12 ounces hard cheese, such as Hannah Bridge, coarsely grated (about 3 cups)

1 teaspoon kirsch (cherry brandy), such as Clear Creek Distillery's kirschwasser

¼ teaspoon ground allspice

MAKES ABOUT 2 CUPS

1. Cream the butter in an electric mixer fitted with a paddle attachment on medium speed until soft and creamy, about 2 minutes.

2. Wipe down the sides of the bowl with a rubber spatula. Mix in the cheese on medium speed until smooth and well combined, about 3 minutes. Mix in the kirsch and allspice on medium-low speed until just combined.

3. Serve the spread immediately, or pack it into small jars and refrigerate until ready to use. Stored in an airtight container in the refrigerator, it will keep for about 2 weeks.

Tressa Yellig

SALT, FIRE & TIME

ONCE PORTLAND HAD MASTERED the ABCs of the CSA, Tressa Yellig introduced city residents to the next acronym in the local food movement: the community-supported kitchen, or CSK. Like CSAs, sustainable, community-scale CSKs support local farms and offer residents easy access to fresh, local food. But businesses like Yellig's take the process one step further by turning farm-fresh produce and local meats into nutritious pantry staples and meals for their members.

"In food communities like Portland, there is already a huge emphasis on eating locally and on DIY preparations, but that doesn't mean that people have time to make their own food," says Yellig, who launched the Salt, Fire & Time CSK in 2009. "The missing portion is bringing it all together — the food, the nutrition, and the people."

Locals can get involved with Salt, Fire & Time as members and enjoy a weekly supply of regional, seasonal, organic cuisine. The nutrient-dense dishes often emphasize traditional food preparations such as culturing, fermenting, and dehydrating; it's not unusual to see items like potted cheese, sauerkraut, and sour cherry–hazelnut granola on the menu.

But Yellig also encourages locals to get involved on a deeper level. They can volunteer in the kitchen and, in the process, improve their culinary skills under the eyes of a patient instructor. Or they can participate in the family-style feasts and educational classes Yellig hosts to encourage insightful conversations about food. "A CSK is more than a place where food is prepared. It's about building community too," she says. "Food is our one real common denominator."

Recipe from CHEF GREGORY DENTON OF METROVINO

Homemade Ricotta

Chef Gregory Denton makes ricotta in-house to serve with dishes like his whole roasted fava bean appetizer (page 42). His recipe is surprisingly easy to make at home if you arm yourself with the right equipment — namely plenty of cheesecloth and an instant-read thermometer.

2 quarts whole milk

2 cups heavy cream

¼ cup distilled white vinegar

1 tablespoon kosher salt

MAKES ABOUT 4 CUPS

1. Warm the milk and cream in a large saucepan over medium heat. Stir the mixture occasionally with a wooden spoon or rubber spatula until it starts to simmer around the edge of the pan. Continue stirring until an instant-read thermometer inserted in the mixture registers 180°F. Do not let the mixture come to a boil.

2. Remove the saucepan from the heat. Add the vinegar and salt and stir constantly until the mixture curdles and the curds begin to separate, about 1 minute. Cover the saucepan with a clean towel and let sit at room temperature for 2 hours.

3. Line a large colander with three layers of cheesecloth, allowing for several inches of overhang around the top. Set the colander over a large bowl and carefully transfer the ricotta into the colander. Cover the colander and bowl with a clean towel and let the cheese drain for 3 hours.

4. Transfer the cheese to a bowl and use immediately, or transfer it to a lidded container, cover, and refrigerate until ready to use. Discard the liquid in the bowl. Stored in an airtight container in the refrigerator, the ricotta will keep for about 4 days.

Bagna Cauda

Generations of chefs from Portland's legendary Genoa restaurant have served this rich garlic-anchovy dip to diners. Fresh, seasonal vegetables such as blanched cardoons or crunchy carrot sticks and slim breadsticks accompany the sauce-like Italian dip to the table. At home, serve this dip with a mix of raw and blanched vegetables and crisp artisan crackers to create an easy, indulgent first course.

4 cups heavy cream

6 garlic cloves, peeled

8 oil-packed anchovy fillets, rinsed

2 tablespoons unsalted butter, cut into ½-inch cubes

¼ teaspoon cayenne pepper

Salt

8 SERVINGS

1. Combine the cream and garlic in a large saucepan. Reduce the cream by half over low heat, stirring frequently with a wooden spoon or rubber spatula to prevent it from scorching or boiling over.

2. Remove the saucepan from the heat and allow the cream to cool slightly. Transfer the garlic and ¼ cup of the reduced cream to the bowl of a food processor fitted with a steel blade attachment. Add the anchovies and purée until smooth. Add the remaining cream in a thin stream with the motor running and blend until smooth.

3. Return the cream mixture to the saucepan over low heat, and whisk in the butter and cayenne until the butter melts. Taste the dip and whisk in additional cayenne and salt, if needed. Transfer to a serving dish and serve immediately.

Recipe from LOUISA NEUMANN

Eggs Lyonnaise

My good friend Louisa is a brilliant chef, caterer, and cooking instructor, who graciously shared her recipe for these elegant baked eggs. Take care to make good croutons — they're the key to this recipe's success. Fry them until they are crispy and brown but still give a little in the middle. Fresh, local eggs like the pasture-raised eggs from Champoeg Farm are a good choice here. You'll need four 8-ounce ramekins to make this dish.

4 tablespoons (½ stick) unsalted butter, plus more for buttering the ramekins

3 slices artisan bread, diced into ¼-inch pieces (about 1½ cups)

1 small yellow onion, finely diced (about 1 cup)

1½ cups packed spinach, roughly chopped

Salt and freshly ground black pepper

4 eggs

¼ cup heavy cream

2 tablespoons fresh flat-leaf parsley, finely chopped

4 SERVINGS

1. Position a rack in the center of the oven and preheat the oven to 375°F. Lightly butter the insides of four 8-ounce ramekins.

2. Melt 2 tablespoons of the butter over medium heat in a small skillet. Add the bread to the skillet and cook, stirring occasionally, until crispy and brown, about 3 minutes. Transfer the croutons to a small bowl and set aside.

3. Melt the remaining 2 tablespoons butter over medium heat in the skillet. Add the onion and cook, stirring occasionally, until golden brown, about 5 minutes. Divide the onion among the ramekins and layer the chopped spinach over the top. Arrange the croutons on top of the spinach and sprinkle with salt and pepper.

4. Bring a small saucepan of water to a boil. Break an egg into each ramekin and spoon the cream over the eggs, dividing it equally among the ramekins. Set the ramekins in a roasting pan. Pour the boiling water into the roasting pan until it reaches halfway up the sides of the ramekins.

5. Bake the eggs until the whites are set but the yolks are still soft and runny, about 10 minutes. Garnish the eggs with the parsley and additional salt and pepper. Serve immediately.

CHAMPOEG FARM

ON A LUSH GREEN PARCEL OF LAND bordering Champoeg Park, Mark and Catherine Anderson are raising a flock of heritage laying hens and breaking new ground for the poultry industry in Oregon.

A few years ago, the couple began growing marionberries on land that had been in Mark's family since 1856. But poultry was their true passion, so they started raising laying hens on the side. "Then we had a really bad berry year and decided to take some eggs to the farmers' market," says Mark. "We sold out of 50 dozen eggs in three hours." Clearly locals desired pasture-raised eggs.

Unlike commercial egg producers, the Andersons raise their hens outdoors on green grass and move them twice a week to keep plenty of fresh grass underfoot. The grass helps the hens produce rich eggs with vibrant yolks and a health profile unmatched by mass-market eggs. "The hens get so many nutrients and vitamins from the green grass — the omega-3s, the beta-carotene, and vitamin D from the sunshine," says Mark. "The yolks are bright orange, and if the hens catch a grasshopper or grub that day, the yolk is even brighter."

In just a few years, the couple has ramped up production to 650 dozen eggs a week to meet increasing demand from local grocers, farmers' market customers, and restaurants like Paley's Place, Higgins Restaurant and Bar, Nostrana, and Grand Central Bakery. "I really want to be able to provide this product to the masses," says Mark of the farm's future. "I don't want to be an elitist because there are too many elitist products out there already." Instead, he and Catherine want to give everyone a chance to experience the pleasure and benefits of eating pasture-raised eggs.

Recipe from CONSTANCE JESSER OF JACKSONVILLE MERCANTILE

Blue Cheese Cheesecakes

When I first made these savory cheesecakes, I was disappointed when they deflated slightly as they cooled — until my dinner guest announced that she was charmed by their rustic appearance. Their robust flavor, though, won me over in the end. Serve these cheesecakes slightly warm or at room temperature with crispy crackers, grapes, and slices of apple or pear as a pre- or postdinner cheese course.

Unsalted butter

Flour

2 eggs

1 (8-ounce) package cream cheese

4 ounces blue cheese, such as Rogue Creamery's Crater Lake blue cheese

½ teaspoon freshly grated nutmeg

½ teaspoon freshly ground white pepper

MAKES 2 (8-OUNCE) CHEESECAKES

1. Position a rack in the center of the oven and preheat the oven to 350°F. Butter and flour two 8-ounce ramekins.

2. Separate the egg yolks from the whites. Mix the yolks, cream cheese, and blue cheese together in a small bowl with an electric mixer on medium speed until well combined. Mix in the nutmeg and white pepper. Whip the egg whites in a separate bowl using a clean set of beaters until they just hold stiff peaks. Gently fold the egg whites into the cheese mixture with a spatula.

3. Divide the batter between the ramekins and place the ramekins on a baking sheet. Bake the cheesecakes until they are puffed and golden brown on top, about 40 minutes. (Don't open the oven door until the cheesecakes look done or they will collapse and bake unevenly.) The cheesecakes are done when they are firm in the center and a toothpick inserted 1 inch from the side of the ramekin comes out clean.

4. Transfer the ramekins to a cooling rack to rest for 30 minutes. The cheesecakes will deflate slightly as they cool. Carefully run a knife around the edges of the ramekins and gently turn the cheesecakes out onto a serving plate. Serve immediately.

Recipe from CHEF JASON BARWIKOWSKI OF OLYMPIC PROVISIONS

Spring Strata

Chef Jason Barwikowski shifts the ingredients in his satisfying strata with the seasons. In winter, he turns to a foolproof flavor combination of bacon, mushrooms, and potatoes; come spring, he'll swap in asparagus or English peas for a lighter touch. Though he often uses Taleggio cheese in his strata, I've substituted local goat cheese here.

6–8 SERVINGS

- 4 fingerling potatoes
- 6 strips thick-cut bacon, coarsely chopped (about 1 cup)
- ½ pound asparagus stalks, trimmed and cut into ½-inch pieces
- 1 tablespoon minced garlic
- 5 eggs
- 2 cups heavy cream
- 2 tablespoons finely grated Parmesan cheese
- 1 tablespoon Dijon mustard
- 2 teaspoons extra-virgin olive oil
- 1 teaspoon finely chopped fresh thyme
- ¼ teaspoon red pepper flakes
- 3 cups cubed French bread, crust removed
- 4 scallions, white and light green parts only, thinly sliced
- 2 ounces goat cheese, crumbled
  Cooking spray

1. Position a rack in the center of the oven and preheat the oven to 325°F. Place the potatoes in a small saucepan, cover them with water, and bring to a boil. Cook until just tender, about 4 minutes. Drain and cut them into ¼-inch slices.

2. Cook the bacon over medium-low heat in a large cast-iron skillet, stirring occasionally, until the bacon begins to crisp, about 5 minutes. If necessary, drain the fat from the skillet, leaving about 1 teaspoon to coat the pan. Add the asparagus and garlic to the skillet and cook with the bacon over medium heat, stirring occasionally, until the garlic is fragrant and the asparagus is warmed through, about 2 minutes. Remove the mixture from the heat to cool.

3. Whisk the eggs, cream, Parmesan, mustard, olive oil, thyme, and red pepper flakes together in a large bowl. Fold in the potatoes, cooled bacon-asparagus mixture, bread, scallions, and goat cheese with a rubber spatula until well combined.

4. Coat a 9-inch round baking pan with cooking spray. Pour the strata mixture into the pan and bake until the eggs are set and the crust is golden brown, about 35 minutes. Turn on the broiler and broil the strata until browned on top, about 5 minutes. Let cool slightly, then slice into wedges and serve immediately.

Blue Cheese–Chicken Salad Sandwiches

Rogue Creamery cheese makers craft their legendary blue cheeses in a funky country creamery in Central Point. This picnic-worthy chicken salad sandwich gets an update with a hit of tarragon and a layer of a Rogue blue cheese of your choice. Though they make eight different styles, I prefer their signature Rogue River Blue.

2 cups diced cooked chicken breast

⅔ cup diced celery

⅓ cup mayonnaise

4 scallions, white and light green parts only, thinly sliced

2 teaspoons lemon juice

1 tablespoon finely chopped fresh tarragon leaves

Salt and freshly ground black pepper

4 whole-grain sandwich rolls, halved

4 ounces blue cheese

4 SERVINGS

1. Mix the chicken, celery, mayonnaise, scallions, lemon juice, and tarragon together in a large bowl with a rubber spatula until well combined. Salt and pepper to taste.

2. Divide the chicken salad evenly among the bottom halves of the rolls. Sprinkle the cheese over the top of the chicken salad, dividing it evenly. Place the top halves of the rolls on the sandwiches and serve immediately.

ROGUE CREAMERY

THE PAST DECADE has been very good to the unassuming cinderblock cheese-making facility known as Rogue Creamery. The Central Point–based creamery has racked up the awards, winning top honors for its innovative Smokey Blue cheese in competitions from Austin to Paris and earning the distinction of being the World's Best Blue Cheese in 2003 at the World Cheese Awards in London.

The creamery, however, was producing outstanding artisan cheeses long before it received such acclaim. Rogue's roots reach back to the 1930s, when Tom Vella arrived from Sonoma, California, and set his sights on making cheese in the Rogue River Valley. Cheddar was his first love, though an interest in making blue cheese soon followed. Vella began making blue cheese after he'd traveled to Roquefort, France, and armed himself with the knowledge and skills he needed to make fine blue cheese in Oregon. That was in 1957, and the company has made top-tier blue cheeses ever since.

In 2002, David Gremmels and Cary Bryant purchased the company from Vella's son, Ig, with a handshake and a promise that they'd keep the heritage of the company alive. Gremmels and Bryant sustain the creamery by holding steadfast to Rogue's founding principles and by focusing on making a few styles of cheese extremely well. Today, Rogue's lineup of fine cheese includes cheddars, cheese curds, and eight varieties of those famous blues that appear on restaurant menus throughout Oregon and beyond.

Grilled Cheese Sandwiches
with Prosciutto, Arugula, and Honey-soaked Figs

Figs and honey are a natural cheese plate pairing that I like to combine on a sandwich for dinner. To make this grown-up grilled cheese, I soak dried figs in honey simple syrup and slip them between two slices of bread with prosciutto, peppery arugula, and sharp white cheddar cheese. Serve these sandwiches with a mixed green salad and bottle of wine for a meal that feels nostalgic and modern at once.

16 dried Black Mission figs, halved

½ cup honey simple syrup (see Note)

8 ½-inch-thick slices artisan bread

4 thin slices prosciutto

1 cup arugula

4 ounces sharp white cheddar cheese, coarsely grated (about 1 cup)

2 tablespoons unsalted butter

NOTE: To make the honey simple syrup, pour ¼ cup of hot water over ¾ of cup mild honey in a small bowl and stir until the honey has dissolved. Store any remaining syrup in a clean jar at room temperature and use to add an earthy sweetness to iced tea or cocktails.

4 SERVINGS

1. Soak the figs in the warm honey simple syrup in a small bowl until plump, about 10 minutes. Drain the figs and discard the syrup.

2. Arrange 4 slices of the bread on a cutting board. Layer the prosciutto, figs, and arugula over the bread slices, dividing the filling equally between the slices. Sprinkle ¼ cup of cheese over the top of each slice and gently press the second slices of bread over the filling.

3. Melt the butter on a griddle or in a large skillet over medium heat. Place the sandwiches on the griddle and flatten by placing a heavy skillet on top. Cook the sandwiches until golden brown on the bottom, about 5 minutes. Flip the sandwiches, cover with the skillet, and cook until the bread is golden brown and the cheese is melted, about 4 minutes longer. (Alternatively, cook the sandwiches in a panini press for about 5 minutes.)

4. Remove the sandwiches from the griddle. Slice the sandwiches in half and serve immediately.

Rimrocker Cheese–Potato Croquettes
with Chive Crème Fraîche

Chef Damon Jones dreamed up this play on a loaded baked potato after tasting a sample of Rimrocker cheese from Tumalo Farms. At the chef's Ashland restaurant, he serves the croquettes on a bed of microgreens. If you can't find Rimrocker cheese, you can substitute a semihard cheese such as cheddar from a local dairy instead. Make this recipe the day after a holiday dinner when leftover mashed potatoes are in plentiful supply.

CHIVE CRÈME FRAÎCHE

- ½ cup crème fraîche
- 2 tablespoons finely chopped chives

POTATO CROQUETTES

- 2 teaspoons unsalted butter
- ½ cup finely chopped leeks
- 1½ cups mashed potatoes, cooled
- 4 ounces semihard cheese, such as Tumalo Farms's Rimrocker cheese, coarsely grated (about 1 cup)
- ½ cup plus 2 tablespoons plain dried bread crumbs

  Salt and freshly ground black pepper
- 1 egg

  Extra-virgin olive oil

Damon Jones

MAKES 8 CROQUETTES

1. **Make the chive crème fraîche:** Whisk the crème fraîche and chives together in a small bowl until well combined. Cover and refrigerate until ready to use.

2. **Make the croquettes:** Melt the butter in a medium skillet over medium-low heat and cook the leeks, stirring occasionally, until soft, about 5 minutes. Remove the pan from the heat and let cool slightly. Mix the leeks, mashed potatoes, cheese, and 2 tablespoons of the bread crumbs together in a medium bowl with a rubber spatula until well combined. Salt and pepper to taste.

3. Portion the potato mixture into 8 small croquettes using your hands. Lightly beat the egg in a shallow dish. Spread the remaining ½ cup bread crumbs in a separate shallow dish. Place the dishes next to each other and dip the potato cakes in the egg, turning once to coat both sides, and then the bread crumbs, turning once to coat both sides.

4. Line a plate with paper towels. Coat the bottom of a large skillet with olive oil and warm over medium heat. Add the croquettes to the skillet and, working with 4 cakes at a time, cook them over medium-high heat until golden brown, about 3 minutes per side. Transfer the cakes to the paper towel–lined plate to drain; cover the plate with foil to keep warm while you cook the remaining cakes.

5. Divide the croquettes among four plates. Serve piping hot with a dollop of chive crème fraîche.

Rustic Cheese Galette

Fresh goat cheese from Fraga Farm inspired the chefs at EVOO to make this homespun tart. If you can't find chervil to accent the creamy filling, you can substitute an equal amount of parsley with similar results.

GALETTE DOUGH

- 2 cups all-purpose flour
- ½ cup (1 stick) unsalted butter, chilled and cut into ½-inch cubes
- ½ cup shortening, chilled
- ¼ cup ice water
- 1½ tablespoons beaten egg (see Note)
- ¾ teaspoon salt
- ½ teaspoon sugar
- ½ teaspoon distilled white vinegar

CHEESE FILLING

- 5 ounces goat cheese, such as Fraga Farm chèvre
- 4 ounces ricotta cheese
- 3 ounces mozzarella cheese, coarsely grated
- ¾ ounce Parmesan cheese, finely grated
- ¼ cup crème fraîche
- 4 chervil sprigs, leaves removed and minced
- ⅛ teaspoon allspice
- ⅛ teaspoon ground coriander

  Salt and freshly ground black pepper

MAKES 1 (10-INCH) GALETTE

1. **Make the crust:** Combine the flour, butter, and shortening in a large bowl. Set the bowl in the freezer to chill for 5 minutes. Remove the bowl from the freezer and cut the butter and shortening into the flour using a pastry cutter or your hands until the mixture is coarse and crumbly and the butter and shortening are reduced to the size of peas.

2. Whisk the ice water, egg, salt, sugar, and vinegar together in a small bowl. Drizzle the mixture over the flour mixture, using a fork to distribute it evenly through the dough. The dough will be slightly shaggy but should come together when pressed with your hands. If necessary, add another teaspoon of ice water.

3. Turn the dough out onto a lightly floured work surface. Press and fold it gently with your hands until it just comes together. Shape the dough into a disk about 3 inches in diameter. Wrap in plastic wrap and refrigerate for 1 hour or up to 1 day.

4. **Make the filling:** Mix the goat cheese, ricotta, mozzarella, Parmesan, crème fraîche, chervil, allspice, and coriander together in a medium bowl with a rubber spatula until well combined. Salt and pepper to taste.

5. Position a rack in the center of the oven and preheat the oven to 350°F. Line a large baking sheet with parchment paper.

6. Place the chilled dough on a lightly floured work surface and roll it out into a large circle about 12 inches in diameter. Transfer the dough to the prepared baking sheet. Spread the cheese filling over the middle of the dough with a rubber spatula, leaving about a 2-inch border. Fold the edges of the dough over the outer edge of the filling, pleating the dough as needed and leaving the cheese-filled center open.

7. Bake the galette until the crust is golden brown and the filling has set, about 40 minutes. Let cool for 10 minutes on the baking sheet, then transfer to a cooling rack to finish cooling. Serve slightly warm or at room temperature.

NOTE: To make their galette crust, EVOO's chefs halve their traditional pastry crust recipe such that it requires half an egg. To halve an egg, beat a large egg and measure approximately 1½ tablespoons of the beaten egg to use for this recipe. Reserve the remaining egg for another use or discard.

Malfatti with Pumpkin and Sage Brown-Butter Sauce

Malfatti means "poorly made" in Italian, and yet these little ricotta dumplings have loads of appeal. Though they are a bit misshapen, they are also wonderfully delicate and light, making them an ideal starter to pair with everything from a fresh tomato sauce to the sautéed pumpkin Chef Jenn Louis serves them with at her upscale-casual Portland restaurant.

NOTE: The malfatti must be refrigerated overnight.

MALFATTI

4 SERVINGS

- 1 pound Swiss chard, stems and ribs removed
- 9 ounces ricotta cheese
- 2 eggs
- 1½ ounces finely grated pecorino cheese (about ⅓ cup), plus more for garnish
- 1½ tablespoons all-purpose flour
- ¼ teaspoon freshly grated nutmeg
- ½ teaspoon salt
- ⅛ teaspoon freshly ground black pepper
- ½ cup semolina flour

PUMPKIN AND SAGE BROWN-BUTTER SAUCE

- ¾ cup (1½ sticks) unsalted butter, cut into ¼-inch cubes
- 4 fresh sage leaves, torn
- 1 (¾ pound) pumpkin or butternut squash, peeled, seeded, and chopped into ¼-inch dice (about 1½ cups)
- Juice of ½ lemon
- Salt and freshly ground black pepper

1. **Make the malfatti (one day ahead):** Blanch the chard in a large saucepan until it softens slightly. Drain in a colander until cool enough to touch. Gather the chard in handfuls and squeeze over the sink to remove as much water as possible. Use a clean kitchen towel to pat and dry it further, if necessary. Finely chop the chard.

2. Mix the ricotta, eggs, pecorino, all-purpose flour, nutmeg, salt, and black pepper together in a medium bowl until well combined. Fold in the chard until well combined.

3. Pour the semolina flour into a wine glass or other deep, wide glass. Shape a heaping teaspoon of the ricotta mixture into a small ball using your hands. Place the ball in the glass and swirl the glass until the flour coats the ball and a dumpling forms. Place the dumpling in a large, shallow baking dish. Repeat the process with the remaining ricotta mixture. Cover the baking dish with plastic wrap and refrigerate overnight.

4. **Cook the malfatti:** Bring a medium pot of salted water to a boil. Position a rack in the center of the oven and preheat the oven to 250°F.

5. **Make the pumpkin and sage brown-butter sauce:** Brown the butter with the sage over medium heat in a large skillet until golden and nutty, about 5 minutes. Add the pumpkin and lemon juice to the skillet. Cook the pumpkin over medium heat, stirring occasionally, until tender but still holding its shape, about 5 minutes. Salt and pepper to taste. Set aside, covering to keep warm.

6. Reduce the boiling water to a slow simmer. Remove the dumplings from the refrigerator and gently drop a handful into the water. Cook the dumplings until they are set but still creamy and tender, about 4 minutes. Using a slotted spoon, gently transfer the dumplings to a shallow baking pan. Place the pan in the oven to keep warm while you cook the remaining dumplings.

7. Divide the dumplings among four plates. Spoon the pumpkin and sage brown-butter sauce over them. Garnish with additional pecorino and serve immediately.

NOTE: When making the malfatti, the key to success is to dry the blanched greens extremely well before mixing them with the ricotta. This step ensures that the dumplings stay pretty and intact when you boil them — despite a name that suggests otherwise.

JUNIPER GROVE FARM

YOU CAN HEAR THE HEART of Juniper Grove Farm bleating the moment you approach Pierre Kolisch's hand-built creamery. Just beyond the creamery's bright blue front door, his herd of goats stand greeting visitors and munching on alfalfa between milkings. Kolisch and his small staff rise early to milk the goats at 7 AM; they milk them again at 4 PM to keep up with the demand for Juniper Grove's high-quality artisan cheese.

Kolisch chased his dream of becoming an artisan cheese maker in France, appropriately.

After apprenticing with a farmstead cheese maker abroad, he returned home to Oregon in 1987 and bought a farm in the Central Oregon desert. What began as a one-man, hobby-scale cheese-making operation has since grown into a nationally recognized business with a herd of about 85 goats and a selection of 10 different cheeses.

For a small artisan cheese maker, Kolisch makes an impressive range of cheeses, from the mold-ripened Pyramid to the nutty, pecorino-like Redmondo to a full-flavored feta. Such variety is unusual for a small-scale producer and all the

Pierre Kolisch

more impressive because Kolisch has expanded his lineup without decreasing the quality of a single cheese. "That is a very difficult task because getting good at one cheese — well, if you can get good at one cheese, that's adequate for a cheese maker to aspire to," he says.

Local market shoppers and chefs praise many of the farm's cheeses but often gravitate toward the fruity aged Tumalo Tomme and the surface-ripened Bûche that have become Juniper Grove signatures. Kolisch enjoys eating the Bûche during the summer with a glass of chilled white wine,

and he recommends consumers serve his cheeses similarly, free from fancy adornments.

"Think of these cheeses as something that can stand on their own. There is a little too much fussiness among American consumers that cheese has to go with something," he says. "Just eat it by itself. You don't have to pair it with a fig or some quince paste or some honey that came from some exotic place. Just have some good bread and good cheese and wine and appreciate the flavors that are in the cheese."

Three-Cheese Macaroni and Cheese
with Slow-roasted Tomatoes

Making homemade macaroni and cheese dirties more pots and pans than instant boxed brand macaroni-and-cheese varieties, but the intensely rich results make the cleanup worth it. My version is a sturdy, reliable classic with a slight twist — I layer a double batch of Slow-roasted Tomatoes (page 52) over the pasta before blanketing it with crunchy, buttery bread crumbs. Rogue Creamery and Tillamook Country Creamery make sharp cheddars locally, while Juniper Grove Farm produces a seasonal Gruyère. For the Gouda, look to Willamette Valley Cheese Company.

1 pound elbow macaroni

4 cups whole milk

6 tablespoons (¾ stick) unsalted butter

¼ cup all-purpose flour

8 ounces extra-sharp cheddar cheese, coarsely grated (about 2 cups)

4 ounces Gouda cheese, coarsely grated (about 1 cup)

4 ounces Gruyère cheese, coarsely grated (about 1 cup)

1 tablespoon Dijon mustard

⅛ teaspoon cayenne pepper

Salt and freshly ground black pepper

2 batches Slow-roasted Tomatoes (page 52)

1 cup fresh bread crumbs

1½ teaspoons fresh thyme

8–10 SERVINGS

1. Position a rack in the middle of the oven and preheat the oven to 375°F. Bring a large pot of salted water to a boil. Add the macaroni and cook according to the package instructions, until it is al dente. Drain the macaroni.

2. Heat the milk over low heat in a medium saucepan. Do not let it boil. Melt 4 tablespoons of the butter over low heat in a large pot. Whisk in the flour and cook, whisking constantly, for 2 minutes. Add the milk and continue cooking, whisking constantly, until smooth and slightly thickened, about 2 minutes longer.

3. Remove the pot from the heat and stir in the cheddar, Gouda, Gruyère, mustard, and cayenne with a heatproof spatula. Stir in the macaroni until well combined. Salt and pepper to taste.

4. Transfer the macaroni and sauce to a 9- by 13-inch baking dish. Layer the roasted tomatoes over the pasta. Melt the remaining 2 tablespoons butter. Mix the butter, bread crumbs, and thyme together in a small bowl with a wooden spoon or rubber spatula until well combined. Sprinkle the mixture over the tomatoes.

5. Bake the macaroni until the sauce is bubbling around the edges and the bread crumbs and top layer of noodles are golden brown, about 30 minutes. Let rest for 10 minutes before serving.

Fettuccine with Caramelized Onions, Zucchini Ribbons, and Walnuts in Yogurt Sauce

Though simple, this pasta — inspired by a yogurt-sauced fettuccine from Nostrana's Chef Cathy Whims — takes forethought because you need to drain the yogurt at least 8 hours before making the pasta. Getting the caramelized onions and zucchini ribbons ready also takes time, but once you have prepped the mix-ins, the assembly takes mere minutes. Serve this light pasta with the Seared Asparagus with Hard-Boiled Eggs, Crispy Morels, and Mustard Crème Fraîche (page 44) as a spring supper.

6–8 SERVINGS

- 2 cups whole-milk plain yogurt
- ¼ cup extra-virgin olive oil, plus more for garnish (optional)
- 2 medium white onions, peeled and thinly sliced (about 2 cups)
- 1 pound small zucchini
  Salt
- 1 pound fresh fettuccine
- 1 cup finely grated Parmesan cheese
- ¾ cup walnuts, toasted and coarsely chopped
  Freshly ground black pepper
- ¼ cup finely chopped fresh chives

1. Line a colander with cheesecloth and place over a large bowl. Spoon the yogurt into the colander, cover, and refrigerate for at least 8 hours or overnight, allowing the yogurt to drain and become thick.

2. Transfer the yogurt to a clean bowl and let it come to room temperature. Discard the cheesecloth and the liquid.

3. Warm the olive oil over medium-low heat in a large skillet. Add the onions and cook, stirring frequently, until the onions are golden brown and caramelized, about 35 minutes.

4. Meanwhile, slice the ends off the zucchini and cut them in half lengthwise. Shave the zucchini into long, thin ribbons using a vegetable peeler or mandoline. Slice the ribbons in half lengthwise. Discard the ends and any unusable scraps.

5. Place the ribbons in a large colander set over a large bowl. Toss the zucchini with a pinch of salt and let stand for 30 minutes at room temperature to draw out the moisture. Rinse the zucchini under cold running water and drain well. Spread the ribbons on a large, clean kitchen towel. Roll up the towel to absorb excess water.

6. Bring a large pot of salted water to a boil. Add the pasta and cook until al dente, about 3 minutes. Drain the pasta, reserving about ½ cup of the cooking water.

7. Whisk the yogurt and reserved cooking water together in a large bowl until smooth. Toss the pasta with the yogurt sauce until coated. Toss the onions, zucchini, ½ cup of the Parmesan, and ½ cup of the walnuts with the pasta until well combined. Salt and pepper to taste.

8. Transfer the pasta to a large serving bowl. Garnish with the remaining ½ cup Parmesan, ¼ cup walnuts, chives, and a drizzle of olive oil, if desired. Serve immediately.

Recipe from MICHELLE VERNIER OF WILDWOOD RESTAURANT

Yogurt-Peach Coffee Cake

Yogurt stands in for sour cream in this light, spongy coffee cake. The original recipe called for fresh cranberries, but I prefer peaches in this gently spiced cake. If you prefer the flavor of cranberries, simply substitute 1 cup frozen cranberries for the peaches.

STREUSEL TOPPING

- 4 tablespoons (½ stick) unsalted butter, chilled and cut into ½-inch cubes
- ⅔ cup all-purpose flour
- ¼ cup granulated sugar
- ¼ cup packed light brown sugar

COFFEE CAKE

- Cooking spray
- 1⅓ cups all-purpose flour
- ½ teaspoon baking soda
- ¼ teaspoon ground cinnamon
- ¼ teaspoon salt
- ⅛ teaspoon ground ginger
- ⅛ teaspoon ground nutmeg
- 5 tablespoons unsalted butter, at room temperature
- 1 cup packed light brown sugar
- 2 eggs
- 2 teaspoons vanilla extract
- ¾ cup (6 ounces) low-fat plain yogurt
- 1 cup frozen peaches, cut into ½-inch pieces

MAKES 1 (9-INCH) CAKE

1. **Make the streusel topping:** Blend the butter, flour, granulated sugar, and brown sugar with your fingers or a pastry blender in a small mixing bowl until loose and crumbly. Cover the bowl with plastic wrap and place in the freezer until ready to use.

2. **Make the cake:** Position a rack in the center of the oven. Preheat the oven to 350°F and coat a 9-inch round baking pan with cooking spray.

3. Whisk the flour, baking soda, cinnamon, salt, ginger, and nutmeg together in a small mixing bowl. Set aside.

4. Cream the butter and brown sugar on medium speed in the bowl of an electric mixer fitted with a paddle attachment until well combined. Add the eggs and vanilla and continue mixing until well combined, scraping the sides of the bowl with a rubber spatula as needed. Add the yogurt and mix until smooth. Add the flour mixture and mix until well combined.

5. Mix in the peaches with a rubber spatula until evenly distributed throughout the batter. Pour the batter into the prepared baking pan. Remove the streusel topping from the freezer and sprinkle it evenly over the batter.

6. Bake the cake until golden brown on top and a tester stick inserted into the center comes out clean, about 45 minutes. Let cool slightly before serving. Stored covered at room temperature, the cake will keep for about 3 days.

Yogurt Panna Cotta with Strawberry-Rhubarb Sauce

At her Portland restaurant, Chef Cathy Whims turns Nancy's Yogurt into a silky panna cotta that makes diners swoon. She tops it with a strawberry-rhubarb sauce, though any seasonal fruit sauce would be a fine substitution when rhubarb and strawberry season ends.

NOTE: The panna cotta requires an overnight chill.

YOGURT PANNA COTTA

¼ cup water

1 tablespoon unflavored powdered
   gelatin

2 cups heavy cream

1 cup sugar

Salt

2 cups whole-milk plain yogurt

Canola oil

STRAWBERRY-RHUBARB SAUCE

1 rhubarb stalk, trimmed and cut
   into ½-inch slices

½ cup sugar

1 tablespoon lemon juice

1 pint fresh strawberries (about
   2 cups), hulled and quartered

6 SERVINGS

1. **Make the panna cotta:** Pour the water into a small bowl and sprinkle the gelatin over it. Let the gelatin soften for 5 minutes.

2. Warm the cream, sugar, and a pinch of salt in a medium saucepan over low heat, stirring occasionally until the sugar dissolves, about 10 minutes. Add the gelatin-water mixture (it should now be solid like Jell-O) to the saucepan. Stir to dissolve, then remove from the heat. Whisk the yogurt in a medium bowl to smooth out any lumps. Gradually whisk the warm cream mixture into the yogurt to bring the yogurt up to the temperature of the cream.

3. Lightly coat six 6-ounce ramekins with the canola oil. Arrange the ramekins on a baking sheet. Divide the cream mixture among the ramekins and cover them with plastic wrap. Refrigerate overnight.

4. **Make the strawberry-rhubarb sauce:** Cook the rhubarb, sugar, and lemon juice in a small saucepan over medium heat, stirring occasionally, until the rhubarb has softened and the sugar has disolved, about 10 minutes. Add the strawberries and cook over medium heat, stirring occasionally, until the strawberries are warm, about 5 minutes longer. Remove the saucepan from the heat and let cool to room temperature.

5. Remove the ramekins from the refrigerator. Run a knife around the edge of each ramekin and turn it upside down on a small plate. Shake the plate and ramekin downward gently once or twice to release the panna cotta. Serve the panna cotta immediately with a few spoonfuls of strawberry-rhubarb sauce on top.

SPRINGFIELD CREAMERY

SPRINGFIELD CREAMERY'S product line spans from kefir to sour cream, but the company still revolves around the product cofounders Chuck and Sue Kesey hedged their bets on back in 1970: Nancy's Yogurt.

The couple had been bottling milk for nearly a decade when Chuck and bookkeeper Nancy Hamren began tinkering with formulas that blended her grandmother's yogurt recipes with the beneficial bacteria now known as probiotics. They spooned their tangy cultured yogurt into glass canning jars and sold it to natural food stores in Eugene well before words like "live cultures" and "probiotics" were familiar to the mainstream dairy industry.

Today, the same yogurt recipe contains billions of live cultures, as do all of Springfield Creamery's products. But probiotics aren't the only thing that sets the creamery's products apart. The Keseys source their milk from family farms located within a 100-mile radius of the creamery and sweeten many products with local honey from Eugene-based GloryBee Foods. To flavor their fruit yogurts and kefirs, Sue purchases fruit in season from local farms to freeze and use throughout the year. And beyond the creamery walls, the Keseys stay deeply involved in their hometown by hosting cultural events that give back to the arts community in Eugene.

Through it all — including a move to a modern facility, a devastating fire, and a Grateful Dead benefit concert that kept the creamery in business

Sheryl Kesey Thompson and Sue Kesey

in the 1970s — the Keseys have continued to make cultured dairy and soy products the old-fashioned way. And even though they pioneered using probiotics in the dairy industry and now ship to every state, the Springfield Creamery remains a small, family-run company at heart.

"We've held on to all the things we started with," says Sue. "We started out with the idea that we were going to make the best food we could and get it to as many people as we could for the best price we could. That basic mission hasn't changed at all."

4 A WORLD BEYOND CLAM CHOWDER

Dungeness Crab Cakes

Cannon Beach residents and tourists seeking an elegant meal often make dinner reservations at the little mustard yellow house known as Newmans at 988. The chef's refined crab cakes make frequent appearances in the intimate dining room. Don't be put off by the task of making the trio of sauces that accompany them; each one is simple to make and adds bright flavors and colors to the finished plate.

CRAB CAKES

- 2 ounces shelled and deveined shrimp
- 2 ounces fresh scallops
- ¼ cup heavy cream
- Juice of ½ lemon
- ½ pound cooked, shelled Dungeness crabmeat
- ½ cup fresh flat-leaf parsley, finely chopped, plus more leaves for garnish
- 2 tablespoons extra-virgin olive oil

LEMON AIOLI

- 2 egg yolks
- Juice of ½ lemon
- 1 garlic clove, minced
- 1 teaspoon Dijon mustard
- ½ cup extra-virgin olive oil
- Salt and freshly ground black pepper

GREEN OIL

- ½ cup spinach
- ½ cup extra-virgin olive oil

BALSAMIC SYRUP

- 1 cup balsamic vinegar

NOTE: This dish contains raw eggs. Consuming raw eggs may increase your risk of foodborne illness.

MAKES 4 CRAB CAKES

1. **Make the crab cakes:** Blend the shrimp, scallops, cream, and lemon juice in the bowl of a food processor until smooth. Transfer the mixture to a medium bowl and gently fold in the crabmeat and parsley with a rubber spatula. Cover the bowl with plastic wrap and refrigerate until ready to use.

2. **Make the aioli:** Whisk the egg yolks in a small bowl until thick. Whisk in the lemon juice, garlic, and mustard until well combined. Add the olive oil in a slow stream, whisking steadily, until well combined. If the mixture is too thick, substitute a few teaspoons of water for the remaining oil as the aioli comes together. Salt and pepper to taste. Cover the bowl with plastic wrap and refrigerate until ready to use.

3. **Make the green oil:** Blend the spinach and olive oil in the bowl of a food processor until bright green and well combined. Set aside.

4. **Make the balsamic syrup:** Bring the vinegar to a boil in a small saucepan over medium-high heat. Simmer the vinegar until it has reduced to the consistency of maple syrup, about 15 minutes. Remove the saucepan from the heat.

5. While the vinegar reduces, remove the crab mixture from the refrigerator and form it into four ½-inch-thick patties. Heat the olive oil in a large skillet over medium-high heat. Cook the crab cakes until golden brown, about 4 minutes per side.

6. Decorate a plate with drops of the green oil and balsamic syrup. Place a crab cake in the center of the plate and garnish with a spoonful of aioli and chopped parsley. Repeat with the remaining crab cakes and serve immediately.

Recipe from CHEF GILBERT HENRY OF CUVÉE RESTAURANT

Cuvée's Coveted Crab Juniper

Diners flock to Chef Gilbert Henry's intimate wine country bistro for a taste of the French transplant's signature crab juniper. The comforting dish unexpectedly pairs two local winter ingredients, fresh Dungeness crab and sweet Comice pear. Henry cooks this entrée in rarebit dishes, but you can use a large square baking dish in their place if needed. The presentation won't be as elegant, but you can easily transfer the rice and fish to a plate before spooning the warm cream sauce over the top.

- 1 **cup cooked basmati rice**
- 2 **(4- to 6-ounce) petrale sole fillets**
- 2 **cups heavy cream**
- 1 **cup diced Comice pear**
- ¾ **pound cooked, shelled Dungeness crabmeat**
- 1 **tablespoon ruby port**

2 SERVINGS

1. Position a rack in the center of the oven and preheat the oven to 375°F.

2. Divide the rice between two rarebit dishes. Place a fillet on top of the rice in each dish. Bake until the sole is cooked through but still moist, about 10 minutes.

3. While the sole cooks, reduce the cream in a medium nonstick skillet over high heat until the cream starts to brown around the edges of the pan. Do not stir the cream until it begins to brown. If the cream starts to foam, skim the foam off the top and reserve to stir in later rather than reduce the heat.

4. When the cream begins to brown, scrape the edges of the pan with a heatproof spatula and stir in the pear, crabmeat, and any reserved cream. Reduce the heat to medium and continue to cook until the sauce is thick enough to coat the back of a spatula.

5. Remove the sole from the oven. Spoon the cream sauce over the sole and rice and drizzle the port over the top. Serve immediately.

Dungeness Crab

WITH ITS SWEET, DELICATE FLAVOR and moist, flaky meat, Dungeness crab is a prized catch along the Oregon coast. On December 1, fishing fleets leave port to drop their circular pots and, over the course of the next 8 weeks, pull up nearly 75 percent of their annual production. The crab fishery stays open until August, but winter is the prime season to catch Dungeness crab in Oregon.

Fishermen harvest an abundance of crab along the West Coast, with Oregon leading production. "We've been fortunate that the crab gods have smiled favorably on Oregon over the last few years," says Oregon Dungeness Crab Commission Executive Director Nick Furman. In the 2009–2010 season alone, fisherman tallied a 23-million pound catch.

Continuing healthy harvests highlight the fact that the crab fishery is more concerned with sustaining its industry than turning a quick profit. The fishermen look to the future by limiting the harvest to mature male crabs and by returning females and juvenile males to the ocean unharmed. They also ensure healthy stocks by using fishing methods that result in minimal bycatch and by employing gear designed for species conservation. In 2010, the fishermen's efforts earned the fishery a Marine Stewardship Council seal of approval.

"We've harvested Dungeness crab commercially for more than 100 years. It's been part of our coastal culture for decades and we still have a very sustainable, well-managed fishery," says Furman. "Other fisheries are concerned with short-term gains, but we're proud of fact that we are a sustainable fishery."

Recipe from **FOUNDING CHEF AND OWNER STEPHANIE PEARL KIMMEL OF MARCHÉ RESTAURANT**

Curried Bay-Shrimp Salad

Marché's founding chef has made this light salad since the start of her cooking career in Eugene. At her much-loved restaurant, the salad is topped with a spoonful of house-made pear chutney (page 90) before it goes out to diners. Serve this salad with a hunk of crusty French bread and a glass of local riesling as a light evening meal.

1 **pound cooked bay shrimp**
⅓ **cup finely diced celery**
¼ **cup finely diced red onion**
1 **teaspoon curry powder**
½ **teaspoon lemon juice**
⅓ **cup mayonnaise**
   Salt and freshly ground black pepper
1 **medium head butter leaf lettuce**
   Pear-Pepper Chutney (optional)
   Finely chopped fresh cilantro leaves, for garnish

4 SERVINGS

1. Mix the shrimp, celery, and onion together in a medium bowl with a rubber spatula. Whisk the curry powder and lemon juice together in a separate bowl until it forms a smooth paste. Whisk in the mayonnaise and blend until the paste and mayonnaise come together. Gently fold the curry mayonnaise into the shrimp mixture. Salt and pepper to taste.

2. Make a bed of butter lettuce leaves on each of four salad plates. Spoon the curried shrimp salad in the center of the leaves on each plate. Garnish each salad with a spoonful of pear chutney, if desired, and cilantro leaves. Serve immediately.

Steamed Mussels for a Crowd

A splash of the classic Scandinavian spirit aquavit, made stateside by Portland-based House Spirits Distillery, plays up the fennel notes in this rustic dish. If you prefer a richer broth, add ¼ to ½ cup of heavy cream to the pot and bring it to a boil before you spoon it over the mussels. Serve the mussels in wide shallow bowls with crusty bread to mop up the flavorful broth.

2 pounds mussels, scrubbed and debearded

2 tablespoons unsalted butter

2 tablespoons extra-virgin olive oil, plus more for garnish (optional)

2 large leeks, white and pale green parts only, finely chopped (about 2 cups)

2 small fennel bulbs, cored and chopped (about 2 cups), fronds reserved

Salt

2 garlic cloves, crushed

2 teaspoons fennel seeds

1 teaspoon red pepper flakes

1 (2-inch-wide) strip of orange peel

1¼ cups dry white wine

2 tablespoons aquavit

½ pound ground pork sausage

3–4 SERVINGS

1. Look the mussels over and discard any that have cracked or broken shells. Gently squeeze any open shells shut. Discard any mussels that don't close.

2. Warm the butter and olive oil in a large lidded pot over medium heat. When the butter has melted, add the leeks, chopped fennel, and a pinch of salt. Cook the vegetables, stirring occasionally, until they have softened slightly, about 3 minutes.

3. Add the garlic, fennel seeds, red pepper flakes, and orange peel to the pot and cook over medium heat, stirring occasionally, until fragrant, about 1 minute. Add the wine and aquavit to the pot and cook for 2 minutes longer. Reduce the heat to low, cover the pot, and simmer for 20 minutes to let the flavors meld.

4. Stir in the mussels. Cover the pot and cook the mussels over medium heat for 4 minutes. Meanwhile, cook the sausage in a small skillet over medium heat, breaking it up into small bits with a wooden spoon or spatula.

5. Peek at the mussels to see if they have opened. If necessary, cover the pot and cook the mussels until the majority of the shells have opened, up to 2 minutes longer. When the majority of the mussels are open, give them a stir and discard any mussels that remain closed.

6. Divide the mussels between three or four wide shallow bowls. Remove the orange peel and garlic from the pot and discard. Spoon the vegetables and broth over the mussels. Divide the sausage among the bowls. Garnish each bowl with a few fennel fronds and a drizzle of olive oil, if desired. Serve immediately.

Recipe from **DAVID BRIGGS OF XOCOLATL DE DAVID**

Chocolate Crab Bisque

Portland-based chocolatier David Briggs updates classic confections by pairing chocolate with savory infusions such as bacon and pimentón in his lineup of artisan sweets. This chic crab bisque shares the savory-meets-sweet flavor profiles found in his confections thanks to additions of a chocolate roux and bits of dark chocolate bar. The combination of crab and chocolate is unexpected but, like all of Briggs' creations, the results are quite pleasing.

NOTE: This soup is easy to make, but it does need five hours to simmer on the stove.

CHOCOLATE CRAB BISQUE

- 7 tablespoons unsalted butter
- 1 yellow onion, peeled and diced
- ½ cup peeled and finely diced carrots
- ½ cup finely diced celery
- 1 garlic clove, minced
- 1 bay leaf
- 2 fresh oregano sprigs, leaves removed
- 1½ teaspoons salt
- 1 teaspoon red pepper flakes
- ⅔ cup dry white wine
- 2 quarts low-sodium vegetable broth or water, or any combination thereof
- 1 whole, cooked Dungeness crab, cleaned, shells and meat reserved

- ¼ cup all-purpose flour
- 1 tablespoon unsweetened natural cocoa powder, such as Dagoba
- ¼ cup heavy cream
- 1½ tablespoons roughly chopped 70 percent or higher chocolate
  Lemon juice (from about ½ lemon)
  Salt and freshly ground black pepper

CRABMEAT GARNISH

- Reserved crabmeat
- 2 tablespoons extra-virgin olive oil
- 1 teaspoon lemon zest
  Juice of ½ lemon
- 1 tablespoon fresh flat-leaf parsley
  Salt and freshly ground black pepper

4 SERVINGS

1. **Make the bisque:** Melt 1 tablespoon of the butter in a large lidded pot over medium-high heat. Add the onion, carrots, celery, garlic, bay leaf, oregano, salt, and red pepper flakes. Cook over medium heat, stirring occasionally, until soft, about 5 minutes. Add the wine and bring to a simmer over medium heat. Simmer for 5 minutes, then add the broth and bring the soup back to a simmer. Add the crab shells to the pot and reduce the heat to low. Cover the pot and cook the soup over low heat for 5 hours.

2. **Make the garnish:** Combine the reserved crabmeat, olive oil, lemon zest, lemon juice, and parsley in a small bowl. Salt and pepper to taste. Cover the bowl with plastic wrap and refrigerate until ready to use.

3. Remove the shells and bay leaf from the pot and discard. Purée the soup in small batches in a blender or the bowl of a food processor fitted with a steel blade attachment until

smooth, about 2 minutes per batch. Strain the soup back into the pot through a fine-mesh strainer.

4. Melt the remaining 6 tablespoons of butter over medium-high heat in a small saucepan. Mix in the flour with a wooden spoon or whisk, stirring constantly until the flour turns golden brown. Mix in the cocoa powder until well combined. Turn off the heat and gradually whisk 2 cups of the soup into the flour-cocoa mixture until well combined.

5. Whisk the flour-cocoa mixture into the remaining soup and bring to a simmer. Simmer uncovered until the soup thickens to the consistency of a cream soup, about 10 minutes longer. Whisk in the cream and chocolate over low heat. Turn off the heat and season to taste with lemon juice, salt, and pepper.

6. Divide the soup among four shallow bowls. Top each bowl with a spoonful of the crab garnish and serve immediately.

Recipe from **CHEF ALLEN ROUTT OF THE PAINTED LADY RESTAURANT**

Oregon Shrimp Napoleons

Chef Allen Routt layers a light bay-shrimp salad with cooling cucumbers and buttery avocado in these striking napoleons. I've streamlined his recipe by replacing from-scratch aioli with a doctored citrus mayonnaise. If you don't own the 4-ounce ring molds needed to make the napoleons, you can also serve the shrimp salad with fresh greens or tucked into a baguette with the cucumber slices and crisp lettuce leaves. The ring molds, however, are worth the small price if you desire an eye-catching, no-cook starter to serve to company on hot summer days.

CITRUS MAYONNAISE

- ¼ cup mayonnaise
- Juice of ½ lemon
- Zest of ½ orange

SHRIMP SALAD

- 1 English cucumber
- ½ pound cooked bay shrimp
- ¼ cup pine nuts, toasted
- ¼ cup golden raisins, finely chopped
- 1½ teaspoons finely chopped fresh chives
- 1½ teaspoons finely chopped fresh flat-leaf parsley
- Salt and freshly ground black pepper
- 1 avocado
- 2 cups microgreens
- 1 tablespoon extra-virgin olive oil
- 1½ teaspoons lemon juice

4 SERVINGS

1. **Make the citrus mayonnaise:** Mix the mayonnaise, lemon juice, and orange zest with a rubber spatula in a small bowl. Set aside.

2. **Make the shrimp salad:** Place a 4-ounce ring mold in the center of each of four plates. Thinly slice three-quarters of the cucumber on a mandoline. Layer the slices inside the ring molds, distributing them evenly among the plates.

3. Peel the remaining cucumber and chop it into ¼-inch pieces. Mix the cucumber, shrimp, pine nuts, raisins, chives, parsley, and citrus mayonnaise in a medium bowl with a rubber spatula until well combined. Salt and pepper to taste.

4. Fill each ring mold about three-quarters full with the shrimp salad. Peel the avocado and cut it into ¼-inch pieces. Arrange the avocado on top of the shrimp, dividing it equally among the molds. Carefully unmold each napoleon.

5. Dress the microgreens with the olive oil, the lemon juice, and a pinch of salt. Top each napoleon with a small handful of microgreens and serve immediately.

Oysters on the Half Shell
with Strawberry Mignonette

The first strawberries of the season inspired Portland-based chef Michael Hanaghan to create a berry-stained mignonette for local oysters. The delicate, floral strawberries nicely complement the slightly sweet Kumamoto oysters.

NOTE: Be sure to make the strawberry mignonette at least 8 hours before serving the oysters.

1 small shallot
¼ cup red wine vinegar
1 tablespoon honey
2 medium strawberries, hulled and quartered
   Freshly ground black pepper
1 dozen small oysters, such as Kumamoto oysters, scrubbed

4 SERVINGS

1. Cut the shallot in half. Thinly slice half of the shallot; wrap the remaining half in plastic wrap and refrigerate until ready to use.

2. Combine the sliced shallot, vinegar, honey, and strawberries in a small saucepan and bring the mixture to a boil. Reduce the heat to medium-low and simmer for 3 minutes. Transfer the mignonette to a lidded container to cool. Refrigerate for at least 8 hours and up to 1 day.

3. Strain the mignonette through a fine-mesh strainer into a small bowl, pressing on the strawberries and shallots to extract as much juice as possible. Discard the strawberry-shallot pulp.

4. Finely chop the remaining half shallot. Whisk the chopped shallot and a pinch of black pepper into the mignonette.

5. Open the oysters and discard the upper shell. Arrange the oysters on a serving plate over a bed of crushed ice. Spoon the mignonette over the oysters or serve it on the side in a small ramekin. Serve immediately.

Steamed Clams in Tomato-Fennel Broth
with Dill-Hazelnut Pesto

Dill pesto and a fennel-scented broth dress up simple steamed clams in this party-worthy dish from Portland supper club chef Courtney Sproule. Round out the meal with a crisp green salad, thick slices of grilled bread, and a bottle of chilled white wine.

3 pounds manila clams, scrubbed

2 tablespoons extra-virgin olive oil

¼ pound pancetta, roughly chopped

½ medium sweet onion, peeled and diced into ¼-inch pieces (about ½ cup)

Salt

2 garlic cloves, minced

1 pound tomatoes, peeled, cored, and diced into ¼-inch pieces

1½ tablespoons fresh thyme

1 tablespoon fennel seeds, lightly toasted and crushed

1 bay leaf

2 cups dry white wine

1½ cups low-sodium chicken broth

½ medium fennel bulb, chopped into ¼-inch dice (about ½ cup)

Freshly ground black pepper

¼ cup Dill-Hazelnut Pesto (page 147)

NOTE: To peel the tomatoes, bring a large saucepan of water to a boil. Prepare an ice-water bath. Cut a small, shallow X into the bottom of each tomato. Dip the tomatoes in the boiling water until the skin just starts to pucker and loosen, about 30 seconds. Drain the tomatoes and immerse them in the ice-water bath. Peel the loosened skin off the tomatoes with a small knife.

4 SERVINGS

1. Look the clams over and discard any that have cracked or broken shells. Gently squeeze any open clams together. Discard any clams that don't close.

2. Line a small plate with paper towels. Heat 1 tablespoon of the olive oil over medium-low heat in a large skillet. Add the pancetta, and cook, stirring occasionally, until crisp. Transfer the pancetta to the plate to drain.

3. Heat the remaining 1 tablespoon olive oil in a large pot over medium heat. Add the onion and a pinch of salt and cook, stirring occasionally, until the onion is soft but not brown, about 5 minutes. Add the garlic and cook until fragrant, about 1 minute longer.

4. Add the tomatoes, thyme, fennel seeds, and bay leaf to the pot and cook at a gentle simmer over medium heat until the liquid in the tomatoes has evaporated. Add the wine and chicken broth and simmer over medium heat until reduced by half. Stir in the fennel. Salt and pepper to taste.

5. Bring the broth to a boil and add the clams. Cover and simmer over medium-high heat until the clams pop open, about 6 minutes. Discard the bay leaf and any clams that have not opened.

6. Divide the remaining clams among four shallow bowls. Divide the broth among the bowls. Garnish each serving with the pancetta and 1 tablespoon of the pesto. Serve immediately.

Dill-Hazelnut Pesto

din din's Courtney Sproule uses her Dill-Hazelnut Pesto to garnish steamed clams. The pesto is also great to use as a garnish for omelets and fish or as a light summer pasta sauce. If you can't find hazelnut oil, walnut oil is an excellent substitute.

1⅓ cups fennel fronds
1 cup fresh dill fronds
¼ cup roasted hazelnuts, skinned
1 garlic clove, minced
Zest of ½ lemon
1 teaspoon lemon juice
¼ cup hazelnut oil
2 tablespoons extra-virgin olive oil
Salt and freshly ground black pepper

MAKES ⅔ CUP

1. Blend the fennel, dill, hazelnuts, garlic, lemon zest, and lemon juice in the bowl of a food processor fitted with a steel blade attachment until well combined.

2. Add the hazelnut oil, then the olive oil in a slow, steady stream with the motor running. Salt and pepper to taste. Use the pesto immediately or transfer to an airtight container, cover with a thin layer of olive oil, and refrigerate until ready to use. Stored in the refrigerator, the pesto will keep for about 1 week.

Razor Clam Po' Boys

Chef John Stewart updates the po' boy with local razor clams at his Portland-based sandwich shop. Though the po' boy special only occasionally joins shop favorites like the Park Kitchen sandwich on the blackboard menu, it's an easy recipe to replicate at home after a day of clamming at the coast. You can find razor clams at local seafood markets and grocers if you aren't the clamming type.

JICAMA SLAW

¼ head napa cabbage, thinly sliced (about 1 cup)

½ jicama, peeled and coarsely grated (about 1 cup)

1 red bell pepper, seeded and thinly sliced

1 large carrot, peeled and coarsely grated

½ jalapeño chile, seeded and thinly sliced

2 tablespoons fresh cilantro leaves

½ cup mayonnaise

½ cup orange juice

2 tablespoons sugar

1 teaspoon lemon juice

Salt and freshly ground black pepper

RAZOR CLAM PO' BOYS

6 razor clams, cleaned and butterflied

1 cup all-purpose flour

Salt and freshly ground black pepper

1 cup milk

1 egg

2 cups panko (Japanese bread crumbs)

Canola oil

2 tablespoons unsalted butter

4 (5-inch) hoagie rolls or baguettes, split and toasted

4 SERVINGS

1. **Make the jicama slaw:** Mix the cabbage, jicama, bell pepper, carrot, jalapeño, and cilantro together in a large bowl.

2. Whisk the mayonnaise, orange juice, sugar, lemon juice, and a pinch of salt and black pepper together in a small bowl. Pour the dressing over the slaw and toss until well combined. Cover the bowl with plastic wrap and refrigerate until ready to use.

3. **Make the po' boys:** Slice the clams into 2 pieces in the center at their thinnest part. Tenderize the clams thoroughly with a meat tenderizer.

4. Line a large plate with paper towels. Add the flour to a shallow dish and lightly season with salt and pepper. Whisk the milk and egg together in another shallow dish. Add the panko to a third shallow dish. Working with one piece of clam at a time, place the clam in the flour, turning once to coat. Dip the clam in the egg-milk mixture, turning once to coat. Dip the clam in the panko, turning once to coat. Set aside. Bread the remaining clams.

5. Heat about 1 inch of canola oil in a large skillet over medium-high heat until the oil is shimmering. Add the butter to the skillet and, working in batches, gently ease a few breaded clams into the oil with a large spoon. Fry the clams, turning once, until they are golden brown. Transfer the clams to the prepared plate using a slotted spoon or kitchen tongs. Fry the remaining clams.

6. Divide the fried clams among the bottom halves of the rolls. Spread the jicama slaw on top of the clams, dividing it equally among the sandwiches, and top with the second half of the roll. Slice the sandwiches in half and serve immediately.

John Stewart

Heirloom Carrot Bisque
with Manila Clams and Chorizo

Chef Gregory Denton makes creamy carrot bisque from heirloom carrots, then gives the soup a spicy finish with diced jalapeño and a pinch of cayenne pepper. The first time I served this soup, those spicy elements left my eyes watering — and my husband devouring his bowlful. If, like me, you have a low tolerance for spicy foods, simply omit the jalapeño and cut back on the red pepper flakes and cayenne as needed. Served spicy or just shy of spicy, you'll love the combination of carrots, chorizo, and manila clams in this winter soup.

HEIRLOOM CARROT BISQUE

- ½ cup (1 stick) unsalted butter
- 2 tablespoons extra-virgin olive oil
- 6 garlic cloves, minced
- 1 teaspoon red pepper flakes
- 2 cups finely diced heirloom carrots
- ½ cup finely diced celery
- ½ cup finely diced yellow onion
- ¼ cup finely diced red bell pepper
- ¼ jalapeño chile, seeded and finely diced (optional)
- ½ cup all-purpose flour
- 1 cup white wine
- ¼ cup plus 1 tablespoon brandy
- 2 cups water
- 4 cups heavy cream
- 1 tablespoon plus 1 teaspoon paprika
- ¼ teaspoon cayenne pepper
- Salt and freshly ground white pepper

CLAM-CHORIZO GARNISH

- 2 pounds manila clams, scrubbed
- ½ pound cured Spanish chorizo sausage, diced into ¼-inch pieces
- 1 medium carrot, peeled and shaved into long, thin ribbons, blanched and cooled
- ¼ cup plus 2 tablespoons heavy cream
- ¼ cup finely chopped fresh chives

6 SERVINGS

1. **Make the soup:** Warm the butter, olive oil, garlic, and red pepper flakes in a large pot over medium heat. Cook until the garlic starts to brown, about 2 minutes. Add the carrots and cook over medium heat, stirring occasionally, until the carrots start to soften, about 5 minutes. Stir in the celery, onion, bell pepper, and jalapeño pepper, if desired. Cook, stirring occasionally, over medium heat until the vegetables start to soften and brown, about 5 minutes.

2. Mix in the flour with a wooden spoon and cook over medium heat for 1 minute. Stir in the wine and ¼ cup of the brandy. As the soup starts to thicken, scrape the sides and edges of the pot to fully incorporate the flour into the soup. Add the water and stir as the bisque comes to a boil. Add the cream and continue stirring as the bisque comes back to a boil.

3. Reduce the heat to low and stir in the paprika, cayenne, and remaining 1 tablespoon brandy. Salt and pepper to taste.

Cover the soup and simmer over low heat, stirring occasionally, for 20 minutes.

4. Blend the soup in the bowl of a food processor fitted with a steel blade attachment until smooth. Strain the soup back into the pot through a fine-mesh strainer and adjust any seasoning if necessary. Cover to keep warm.

5. **Make the garnish:** Look the clams over and discard any that have cracked or broken shells. Gently squeeze any open clams together. Discard any that don't close.

6. Fill a large pot with about 1 cup of water and add the clams to the pot. Cover and bring the water to a boil. Reduce the heat to medium-low, then cook the clams undisturbed for 5 minutes. Lift the lid and check to see if the majority of the shells have opened. If they are open, remove the pot from the heat; if they are still closed, cook for up to 2 minutes longer. Remove the clams from the water and transfer the meat to a small bowl; discard the shells.

7. Cook the chorizo in a large skillet over medium-high heat until it starts to release its oil. Stir in the clams and blanched carrot peels and cook until just warmed through, about 2 minutes. Set aside.

8. Whisk the cream with a hand mixer on medium speed in a small mixing bowl until soft peaks form. Set aside.

9. Bring the bisque back to a boil, then remove from the heat. Divide the bisque among six shallow soup bowls. Garnish each bowl with a spoonful of the whipped cream. Drape the carrot peels over the whipped cream and gently spoon the chorizo and clams on top of the carrots. Drizzle the soup with any remaining chorizo oil in the skillet and sprinkle the chopped chives over the top. Serve immediately.

Recipe from EARL AND HILDA JONES OF ABACELA VINEYARD & WINERY

Abacela Paella

Earl and Hilda Jones have perfected paella to serve for weeknight suppers at home and at special winery events like their fiestas. This surf-and-turf paella brings a taste of Spain to the table with Oregon shellfish, chicken, sausage, and chorizo. Enjoy it with a bottle of one of Abacela's fine tempranillos. If you do not own a paella pan, a large skillet will work for this recipe as well.

¼ cup extra-virgin olive oil

4 boneless, skinless chicken thighs

½ pound sausage, such as kielbasa or linguica, cut into ½-inch slices

¼ pound cured Spanish chorizo sausage, cut into ¼-inch slices

6 small bay scallops

6 medium shrimp, shelled and deveined

1 medium yellow onion, peeled and finely chopped

1 garlic clove, minced

½ teaspoon fresh cilantro leaves, finely chopped

½ teaspoon fresh oregano leaves

½ teaspoon fresh tarragon leaves, finely chopped

½ teaspoon red pepper flakes

¼ teaspoon ground cumin

¼ teaspoon fresh thyme

¼ teaspoon freshly ground black pepper

1 (28-ounce) can Roma tomatoes, drained, seeded, and roughly chopped

3 cups low-sodium chicken broth

¼ teaspoon crumbled saffron threads

1½ cups medium-grain paella rice, such as Bomba variety

¼ pound green beans, blanched

6 manila clams, scrubbed

6 mussels, scrubbed

Salt

1 red or yellow bell pepper, roasted, peeled, seeded, and thinly sliced

1 lemon, quartered

4–6 SERVINGS

1. Warm 3 tablespoons of the olive oil in a 16-inch paella pan or large skillet. Add the chicken and cook over medium heat, turning occasionally, until browned all over, about 10 minutes. Transfer the chicken to a large plate.

2. Cook the sausage and chorizo over medium heat in the skillet until light brown, about 2 minutes. Transfer the sausage and chorizo to the plate. Heat the remaining 1 tablespoon olive oil in the skillet over medium heat. Add the scallops and shrimp and cook until the scallops are light brown and the shrimp are barely pink, about 1 minute. Transfer the scallops and shrimp to the plate.

3. Position a rack in the lower half of the oven and preheat the oven to 375°F.

4. Add the onion and garlic to the skillet and cook over medium-low heat, stirring occasionally, until soft and light brown, about 5 minutes. Stir in the cilantro, oregano, tarragon, red pepper flakes, cumin, thyme, and black pepper, and cook over medium-low heat until fragrant. Add the tomatoes and cook, stirring frequently, over medium-low heat until the liquid evaporates and the sauce thickens, about 10 minutes longer.

5. Add the chicken broth and saffron. Bring the broth to a boil. Sprinkle the rice evenly over the broth. Turn off the heat and add the chicken, sausage, chorizo, and green beans to the skillet. Loosely cover the skillet with foil and bake until the rice starts to soften, about 15 minutes.

6. While the paella cooks, look the clams and mussels over and discard any that have cracked or broken shells. Gently squeeze any open clams or mussels together. Discard any that don't close.

7. Remove the skillet from the oven and stir the rice lightly with a wooden spoon. Do not break the grip the rice has on the bottom of the pan. Push the scallops, shrimp, clams, and mussels deep into the rice. Loosely cover the skillet with the foil and bake until the liquid is absorbed and the rice is tender but not soft, about 10 minutes longer.

8. Remove the skillet from the oven and discard any clams or mussels with unopened shells. Let the paella stand uncovered for 5 minutes. Salt to taste. Garnish the paella with the bell pepper and lemon wedges and serve immediately.

Earl and Hilda Jones

Oregon Albacore Tuna Melts

Luan Schooler updates the pedestrian tuna melt with high-quality Oregon albacore tuna and upscale mix-ins of preserved lemons, capers, and a specialty tarragon mustard she carries at her gourmet mercantile. Though one can of tuna seems a small amount for four sandwiches, you'll be surprised how far this thrifty recipe stretches the fish. If you can't find Edmond Fallot Tarragon Dijon mustard, you can mix 2 teaspoons of Dijon mustard with 1 teaspoon of finely chopped fresh tarragon leaves to serve as a substitute.

- 1 (6-ounce) can Oregon albacore tuna
- 2 tablespoons chopped oil-cured black olives
- 1 tablespoon chopped preserved lemons
- 1 tablespoon chopped salt-cured capers
- 3 tablespoons extra-virgin olive oil
- 2 teaspoons Edmond Fallot Tarragon Dijon mustard, plus more for the rolls
- 4 small ciabatta rolls, halved
  Freshly ground black pepper
- 6 ounces extra-sharp white cheddar cheese, coarsely grated (about 1½ cups)
- 2 tablespoons unsalted butter

4 SERVINGS

1. Drain the liquid off the tuna and break it into large chunks with a fork in a medium bowl.

2. Rinse the olives, lemons, and capers with water and squeeze the moisture out of them with a paper towel. Mix the olives, lemons, and capers with the tuna using a rubber spatula. Whisk the olive oil and mustard together in a small bowl. Stir the mustard dressing into the tuna mixture with a rubber spatula.

3. Spread a thin layer of mustard on the top half of each of the rolls and sprinkle liberally with black pepper. Spread the tuna on the bottom half of each of the rolls, dividing it equally among the rolls. Sprinkle the cheese over the top of the tuna, dividing it equally among the rolls. Gently press the two sides of the sandwich together.

4. Melt the butter on a griddle or in a large skillet over medium heat. Place the sandwiches on the griddle and flatten by placing a heavy skillet on top. Cook the sandwiches until golden brown on the bottom, about 5 minutes. Flip the sandwiches, cover with the skillet, and cook until the bread is golden brown and the cheese is melted, about 4 minutes longer. (Alternatively, cook the sandwiches in a panini press until cheese is melted and the bread is crisp, about 5 minutes.)

5. Remove the sandwiches from the griddle. Slice in half and serve immediately.

Luan Schooler and Tim Wilson

OREGON ALBACORE TUNA

SALMON MIGHT BE OREGON'S STATE FISH, but local albacore is poised to become the star of the coastal waters. From late June through October, Oregon fishermen troll the water 50 to 200 miles off the coast in search of the mild, meaty Pacific albacore that has in-the-know consumers hooked.

To preserve the environment that fuels their livelihood, tuna fishermen use a sustainable hook and line method to catch the fish; the method — also called troll or pole fishing — brings the tuna in one at a time to reduce bycatch and keep the ocean habitat healthy. The fishermen's environmentally conscious efforts have kept local albacore stocks strong and abundant. And they've earned the fishery a "best choice" label from the Monterey Bay Aquarium and certification from the Marine Stewardship Council as a sustainable, well-managed fishery.

Consumers appreciate the fact that local albacore is an environmentally responsible seafood choice. But for many individuals, the preference for local albacore is a matter of taste as well. Pacific albacore are mild, distinctive, and incredibly fresh. And in the case of custom-canned tuna, the quality and flavor of the fish trumps that of mass-market brands many times over.

Many midsize fishermen have their catch custom canned at local canneries to preserve the essential flavors and texture of the fish. Whereas big-brand tuna producers double-cook their tuna and use juices, water, or oil to enhance its flavor, coastal canneries natural-pack local tuna using the same methods savvy do-it-yourselfers use to can tuna at

home: They fillet and process the tuna by hand and cook it only once in the can. The resulting tuna is meaty and incredibly moist — just one more way you can eat local and well along the Oregon coast.

Spaghetti with Albacore Tuna Ragù

At Bandon's upscale wine bar and restaurant, Chef Jeremy Buck marries summer tomatoes, peppers, and eggplants from local farms with fresh Oregon albacore tuna to create a light, flavorful ragù. Buck uses fresh albacore loin in his pasta, but I've streamlined his recipe by substituting canned albacore tuna. Because local canned albacore tuna is caught by hook and line and processed by small coastal canneries, the fish retains the flavor and quality needed to serve as a substitute in recipes like this.

1 small eggplant, peeled and cut into ½-inch cubes (about 2 cups)

Kosher salt

3 tablespoons extra-virgin olive oil

3 garlic cloves, thinly sliced

4 medium tomatoes, peeled (see Note, page 146), seeded, and roughly chopped

2 red bell peppers, seeded and cut into ¼-inch strips

⅓ cup thinly sliced fresh basil leaves, plus more for garnish

1 pound spaghetti

2 (6-ounce) cans Oregon albacore tuna

¼ cup finely chopped fresh flat-leaf parsley, plus more for garnish

3 tablespoons brine-packed capers, rinsed

Freshly ground black pepper

4–6 SERVINGS

1. Place the eggplant in a colander and sprinkle generously with salt. Toss well and let sit for 30 minutes over the sink or a large plate to draw out the water. Rinse the eggplant and wrap in a clean kitchen towel to squeeze out any remaining water.

2. Warm the olive oil over medium heat in a large skillet. Add the garlic and cook over medium-low heat until fragrant, about 2 minutes. Remove the garlic from the skillet and discard.

3. Increase the heat to high and add the eggplant to the skillet, shaking the skillet gently so the eggplant doesn't stick. Cook until lightly browned, stirring occasionally, about 5 minutes. Reduce the heat to medium-low and add the tomatoes, bell peppers, and basil to the skillet. Simmer, stirring occasionally, until the tomatoes break down and the sauce thickens, about 20 minutes.

4. Bring a large pot of salted water to a boil. Add the spaghetti to the pot and cook according to the package instructions until al dente.

5. While the spaghetti cooks, drain the tuna and break it into small pieces with a fork in a small bowl. Add the tuna, parsley, and capers to the skillet and simmer over medium-low heat for 5 minutes longer. Salt and pepper to taste.

6. Drain the spaghetti and divide it among four to six plates. Top the spaghetti with the ragù, dividing it equally among the plates. Garnish with additional chopped basil and parsley. Serve immediately.

Halibut Ceviche

Chef Kenny Hill changes the menu at his locally influenced Oaxacan-style restaurant every two weeks to keep it hyperseasonal; when halibut season begins in early spring, he brings back this citrus-spiked ceviche. Marinating the fish in freshly squeezed citrus juices "cooks" it while it rests in the refrigerator. Serve the ceviche family-style in a large bowl with tortilla chips on the side or divide it among small bowls to serve as a refreshing starter at a Mexican-themed dinner party.

1 cup lime juice

½ cup orange juice

¼ cup apple cider vinegar

2¼ teaspoons ground coriander

2¼ teaspoons ground cumin

Zest of 1 lemon, finely chopped

½ teaspoon minced garlic

Salt and freshly ground white pepper

1 (1-pound) halibut fillet, cut into ½-inch cubes

1 large cucumber, peeled, seeded, and diced into ¼-inch cubes (about 1½ cups)

1 small red onion, peeled and finely chopped (about 1 cup)

1 serrano chile, minced

1 medium bunch spinach, stems removed

Fresh cilantro leaves

4 SERVINGS

1. Whisk the lime juice, orange juice, vinegar, coriander, cumin, lemon zest, garlic, and a pinch of salt and pepper together in a large bowl. Mix in the halibut, cucumber, onion, and serrano chile with a rubber spatula. Cover and refrigerate until the halibut is opaque, about 2 hours.

2. Line a large, shallow bowl (or four small bowls) with a layer of the spinach leaves. Using a slotted spoon, transfer the ceviche to the serving dish(es). Drizzle a few spoonfuls of the marinade over the top of the ceviche. Discard the remaining marinade.

3. Garnish the ceviche with a small handful of cilantro leaves and serve immediately.

Kenny Hill

Crispy-Skinned Black Cod with Salsa Mojo Verde

Chef Anthony Cafiero marries a Northwest fish with a classic Canary Islands sauce to brighten the flavor and color of this seafood entrée at Tabla. At the Portland-based restaurant, he often serves the cod with a red quinoa salad and lemon confit. Home cooks can serve this simplified recipe with a side of couscous, quinoa, or brown rice.

SALSA MOJO VERDE

- 1 bunch fresh cilantro (about ⅓ pound)
- 3 tablespoons sherry vinegar
- 2 garlic cloves, crushed
- 1 tablespoon ground cumin
- ½–¾ cup extra-virgin olive oil
  Salt

BLACK COD

- 6 (5-ounce) skin-on black cod fillets
  Salt
- 2 tablespoons extra-virgin olive oil
- 1 tablespoon unsalted butter

6 SERVINGS

1. **Make the salsa:** Blend the cilantro stems and leaves, vinegar, garlic, and cumin in the bowl of a food processor fitted with a steel blade attachment. Slowly pour ½ cup of the olive oil into the machine with the motor running, stopping the motor and scraping down the sides of the bowl with a rubber spatula as needed. Add up to ¼ cup more olive oil if needed; the sauce should be slightly loose but not runny. Salt to taste and set aside.

2. **Make the cod:** Position a rack in the center of the oven and preheat the oven to 450°F. Season the top of the fillets with salt. Heat a large cast-iron skillet over medium-high heat and warm the olive oil and butter until the butter melts. Place the fillets in the pan, skin side down. Firmly press down on each fillet with a spatula to make sure all of the skin touches the skillet.

3. When the skin is crispy, after about 2 minutes, flip each fillet over and place the skillet in the oven. Bake the cod until cooked through, about 5 minutes depending on the thickness of the fillets.

4. Place a fillet, skin side down, on each of six plates. Garnish each serving with a generous spoonful of the salsa and serve immediately.

NEWMAN'S FISH COMPANY

JOHN HENRY NEWMAN opened Newman's Fish Company in 1890 in Eugene, when he was just 13 years old. He delivered fish to locals from a horse-drawn cart and, later, a 1912 Model T Ford truck and provided the small community with high-quality seafood and service for more than 70 years. Today, Newman's values live on under the direction of Dwight Collins and John Cleary. The partners have upheld the original owner's high standards while also expanding the company's reach. Newman's Fish now encompasses a respected wholesale operation, two retail locations in Eugene, and a high-end fish market in Portland.

At Newman's Fish Market in northwest Portland, customers have their pick of fresh fish fillets, delicate smoked trout, and live crab cooked to order; in Eugene, offerings of salmon, crab, rockfish, petrale sole, and lingcod abound. The fish is extremely fresh, the quality is superior, and, whenever possible, the fish locally caught as well. Though the company purchases seafood from a variety of locations, they also bring in albacore, salmon, shellfish, and more from Astoria and Newport a few times a week.

Additionally, the owners have developed relationships with local fishermen and buy about 20 percent of the company's volume directly from Oregon watermen. The fishermen benefit from this direct-sales structure, as do consumers who get access to a fresher, higher-quality product than they would through conventional sourcing methods. "If you look at the fish industry's structure, you have the fishermen, the processor, the wholesaler, the retailer, and the consumer. In most cases the consumer is the fifth person in the chain, and in most cases that process has to happen in a very short time," says Cleary. "We cut one link out of that chain, and occasionally we cut two links out of that chain when we deal directly with the fisherman."

Over the past decade, Newman's Fish has also developed a niche selling seafood to small, chef-owned restaurants that seek higher-quality, more carefully handled fish than larger businesses can deliver. "The larger company's scope is less handling and higher volume and ours is just the opposite — more handling and less volume," says Cleary. "We are very hands-on. Our commitment is to quality."

John Cleary

Coastal Stew

At their Cannon Beach cooking school, Chef Bob Neroni and Chef Lenore Emery give a coastal staple their own twist by combining razor clams, halibut, and rockfish in a coriander-and-oregano-scented broth.

6–8 SERVINGS

- 3 tablespoons extra-virgin olive oil, plus more for garnish
- 1 medium carrot, peeled and finely diced (about 1 cup)
- 1 medium fennel bulb, finely diced (about 1 cup)
- 1 medium onion, finely diced (about 1 cup)
- 2 shallots, finely diced (about ½ cup)
- 6 garlic cloves, minced
- 2 (14.5-ounce) cans diced tomatoes, with juice
- 1½ cups dry red wine
- 2 teaspoons dried oregano
- 1 teaspoon ground coriander
  Salt
- 1 pound razor clams, cleaned and roughly chopped
- 2 medium Yukon Gold potatoes, peeled and cut into ½-inch pieces
- 1 pound halibut, cut into 1-inch pieces
- 1 pound rockfish, cut into 1-inch pieces
  Freshly ground black pepper
- ½ cup fresh basil leaves, torn

1. Warm the olive oil over medium heat in a large lidded pot. Add the carrot, fennel, onion, shallots, and garlic, and cook, stirring occasionally, until the vegetables are aromatic but still firm, about 5 minutes. Add the tomatoes, wine, oregano, coriander, and a pinch of salt. Bring the liquid to a simmer and stir in the razor clams. Reduce the heat to low, cover, and simmer until the clams are tender, about 45 minutes.

2. Add the potatoes to the pot. Cover and cook over low heat until the potatoes are fork-tender, about 15 minutes longer. Gently stir in the halibut and rockfish. Increase the heat to medium-low, cover the pot, and cook until the fish is cooked through, about 5 minutes longer. Salt and pepper to taste.

3. Ladle the stew into six to eight soup bowls. Garnish each serving with about 1 tablespoon of the basil and a drizzle of olive oil. Serve immediately.

EVOO Cannon Beach Cooking School

WHEN CHEFS BOB NERONI AND LENORE EMERY made a permanent move to their favorite coastal vacation spot, they sought a way to introduce their passion for cooking to their new community. So they purchased a little beach bungalow in downtown cannon Beach and turned it into a cooking school that doubles as a charming gourmet shop when classes aren't in session.

Students visiting from as far as the East Coast and as nearby as down the beach have been filling the cozy classroom since the duo opened the school in 2004. The ever-changing lineup of lively classes helps students learn to make everything from chewy artisan breads to peppercorn-crusted strip steak and coastal stew.

EVOO has made the artsy coastal town even more appealing to tourists and residents, but the school isn't the only way Neroni and Emery have shaped Cannon Beach's culinary scene. The couple were also instrumental in launching a farmers' market in town. Thanks to these passionate chefs, locals can now follow the school's sustainable mantra by shopping for fresh market fare in their own community.

Lenore Emery and Bob Neroni

Gin and Citrus Salt–cured Salmon Gravlax

Curing your own salmon is a crowd-pleasing way to show off a beautiful piece of fish. Chef Anthony Cafiero cures fresh Chinook salmon with locally made Aviation gin and a citrus-salt blend to make gravlax for the fish plate at his Portland restaurant. Serve the gravlax as part of an appetizer plate or, for breakfast, in a dish like Polenta Cakes with Goat Cheese, Cured Salmon, and Poached Eggs (page 168).

1 cup kosher salt

½ cup sugar

Zest of 1½ lemons

Zest of 1 orange

2 tablespoons gin

1 pound center-cut Chinook salmon fillet, skin and pin bones removed

4–6 SERVINGS

1. Blend the salt, sugar, lemon zest, and orange zest in the bowl of a food processor fitted with a steel blade attachment until well combined, about 10 seconds.

2. Spread a piece of plastic wrap slightly larger than the salmon fillet on a clean work surface. Spread a thick layer of the citrus-salt cure on the plastic wrap and drizzle 1 tablespoon of the gin over it. Set the salmon on top of the cure. Pack the remaining cure evenly on top of the fillet. Drizzle the remaining 1 tablespoon gin over the salmon.

3. Place a second piece of plastic wrap on top of the salmon. Seal the edges of the plastic wrap together and expel any air from the packet while tightly wrapping the fillet. Wrap the fillet in a final layer of plastic wrap. Transfer the fish to a nonreactive pan large enough to hold the salmon lying flat. Place a flat-bottomed dish on top of the fillet and weight it down with a few heavy cans.

4. Refrigerate the salmon for 24 hours, turning the fish every 8 hours or so to distribute the cure evenly. At the 24-hour mark, remove the plastic wrap and check the salmon for firmness. If the salmon still feels raw and fleshy to the touch, rewrap the fish and continue to cure until firm and translucent, up to 12 hours longer.

5. When the salmon is firm, unwrap it and rinse thoroughly under cold running water. Pat the fillet dry with a paper towel and slice it thinly on the bias to serve. Stored in an airtight container in the refrigerator, the gravlax will keep for about 2 weeks.

Smoked Salmon and Sea Bean Salad
with White Wine–Chive Vinaigrette

When briny sea beans come into season in late spring, Chef Brendan Mahaney pickles pounds of them to use in dishes like this brightly flavored salad. The pickled sea beans partner with sweet raisins, smoked salmon, and fresh sea beans to give a delicate lettuce and bitter endive salad contrasting flavors and textures in every bite.

Spindly sea beans, which are also called glasswort, grow in the shallow waters along the coast and are available at farmers' markets from late spring through early fall from vendors like Misty Mountain Mushrooms. Note that the pickled sea beans require an overnight soak.

4 SERVINGS

PICKLED SEA BEANS

- 1 cup water
- 1 cup white wine vinegar
- ½ teaspoon black peppercorns
- 1 ounce (about ¼ cup) sea beans

WHITE WINE–CHIVE VINAIGRETTE

- ¼ cup plus 2 tablespoons extra-virgin olive oil
- 2 tablespoons white wine vinegar
- 1 tablespoon finely chopped fresh chives

  Salt and freshly ground black pepper

SALAD

- ¼ cup golden raisins
- 1 (1-pound) head red oak leaf lettuce, leaves separated
- 2 heads Belgian endive, leaves separated
- ½ pound smoked salmon, broken into bite-size pieces
- 1 ounce (about ¼ cup) sea beans

1. **Make the pickled sea beans:** Bring the water, vinegar, and peppercorns to a boil in a small saucepan. Turn off the heat. Place the sea beans in a small jar or lidded container and pour the liquid over the top, covering the sea beans completely with the liquid. Let the liquid cool, then cover, and refrigerate overnight.

2. **Make the vinaigrette:** Whisk the olive oil and vinegar together in a small bowl. Whisk in the chives. Salt and pepper to taste. Set aside.

3. **Make the salad:** Place the raisins in a small bowl and cover with boiling water. Cover the bowl and allow the raisins to sit for 5 minutes to plump. Drain the raisins.

4. Toss the lettuce and endive leaves with the vinaigrette in a large bowl. Divide the lettuce and endive leaves among four salad plates. Garnish the salads with the drained pickled sea beans, raisins, salmon, and fresh sea beans. Serve immediately.

Hazelnut-crusted Salmon
with Brown Butter and Balsamic Vinegar

When local salmon is in season, Chef Aaron Bedard serves this hazelnut-crusted fish to guests at the inn's nightly four-course dinners. Contrasting garnishes of rich brown butter and sweet, tangy aged balsamic vinegar dress up the salmon and make this entrée a favorite with Cannon Beach tourists.

¼ cup roasted hazelnuts, skinned

1 (1-pound) wild salmon fillet

Salt and freshly ground black pepper

2 tablespoons unsalted butter

1 tablespoon aged balsamic vinegar

NOTE: Cooper Mountain Vineyards makes a local aged balsamic vinegar, called Apicio, that I like to use for this dish. Find the vinegar on their website or at purveyors like Cork, Foster & Dobbs, and Pastaworks.

4 SERVINGS

1. Position a rack in the center of the oven. Preheat the oven to 350°F and line a baking sheet with foil.

2. Pulse the hazelnuts in the bowl of a food processor fitted with a steel blade attachment until finely ground. Spread the ground hazelnuts on a large plate.

3. Lightly season the salmon fillet with salt and pepper. Roll the top of the fillet in the ground hazelnuts to form a crust. Transfer the fillet to the prepared baking sheet and patch up any holes in the crust. Bake the salmon until the fish is pale pink and just cooked through and the hazelnut crust is golden brown, about 10 minutes.

4. While the salmon cooks, melt the butter in a small saucepan over medium heat. Continue cooking the butter, swirling the pan occasionally, until it becomes golden brown and has a nutty aroma, about 5 minutes. Remove the saucepan from the heat.

5. Remove the salmon from the oven and transfer it to a serving plate. Drizzle the brown butter and balsamic vinegar over the top of the fillet and serve immediately.

Polenta Cakes with Goat Cheese, Cured Salmon, and Poached Eggs

Though the owners of the Brookside Inn, Bruce and Susan Bandstra, serve these corn-and-scallion-studded polenta cakes to their wine country guests at breakfast, I also enjoy them for dinner with a simple green salad on the side. The Bandstras make the cakes in individual tart pans, but I find it easier to chill the polenta in an 8-inch square baking pan and cut it into wedges or cakes with a large cookie cutter after it chills.

2 tablespoons unsalted butter

¼ cup plus 2 tablespoons fresh sweet corn (from about ½ ear of corn)

¼ cup thinly sliced scallions, white and light green parts only

1½ tablespoons *herbes de Provence*

Salt and freshly ground black pepper

1½ cups whole or reduced-fat milk

½ cup coarse-ground cornmeal

2 ounces goat cheese

4 eggs

1 tablespoon distilled white vinegar

4 slices cured salmon

Sour cream

4 SERVINGS

1. Melt 1 tablespoon of the butter in a medium skillet over medium heat. Add the corn and cook, stirring occasionally, until lightly browned, about 2 minutes. Add the scallions and 1 tablespoon of the *herbes de Provence* and cook for 2 minutes longer. Remove the skillet from the heat. Salt and pepper to taste and set aside.

2. Warm the milk in a medium saucepan over low heat. Slowly whisk in the cornmeal. Simmer, whisking frequently, until the mixture thickens and starts to pull away from the edges of the saucepan, about 15 minutes. Remove the saucepan from the heat.

3. Stir the corn-scallion mixture and cheese into the cornmeal-milk mixture until well combined. Spread the mixture in an 8-inch square baking pan. Cover the pan with plastic wrap and refrigerate for at least 2 hours or overnight.

4. Remove the chilled polenta from the refrigerator. Cut the polenta into four cakes using a 4-inch round cookie cutter. Alternatively, cut it into eight triangular wedges. Discard any scraps and set the cakes aside.

5. Crack each of the eggs into an individual ramekin and line a plate with paper towels. Bring about 2 inches of water to a boil in a large skillet. Add the vinegar and a pinch of salt to the skillet and reduce the heat to low. Slip each egg into the skillet, spacing them evenly apart in the water. Cook until the egg whites are set and the yolks are filmed over but still runny, about 3 minutes. Transfer the eggs from the skillet to the prepared plate using a slotted spoon.

6. While the eggs are poaching, melt the remaining 1 tablespoon butter in a large skillet over medium heat. Add the polenta cakes to the skillet and cook until golden brown, about 3 minutes per side. Divide the cakes among four plates.

7. Top the cakes with a slice of the cured salmon, a poached egg, and a dollop of sour cream. Garnish with the remaining ½ tablespoon *herbes de Provence* and serve immediately.

Local Ocean Seafoods

AT LOCAL OCEAN SEAFOODS' FISH MARKET in Newport, the case labels for fish and shellfish reveal not just the species but also how each fish was caught and what boat hauled it in. "When people visit our restaurant and market and look across the bay, they see all the fishing boats and can make a connection with the harvester," says co-owner Laura Anderson.

Anderson and local fisherman Al Pazar founded Local Ocean Seafoods in 2002 to introduce

accountability and transparency to Oregon's seafood industry. Initially they operated as a coast-based wholesaler and sold exclusively local seafood to upscale grocers and high-end restaurants in Portland. Three years later, they shifted their focus to feeding the local community when they opened a restaurant and seafood market on the Newport Bayfront.

Local Ocean Seafoods has since become a popular fish market and locally focused seafood restaurant. Tourists, fishermen, and neighborhood regulars sit elbow to elbow in the dining room each day, enjoying fresh local seafood in fish tacos, crab po' boys, and fishwives stew. The restaurant's industrious chef, Charlie Branford, obtains more than 95 percent of the seafood on his menu from local waters and visits the docks regularly to purchase seafood directly from the boats. Such dedication to building a business around a local industry supports Oregon fishing families and educates consumers about the wild, sustainable seafood available along the coast.

"We really want to be that showcase for local seafood. Often people come to the coast and have expectations that they'll eat local seafood when in fact most restaurants buy seafood from a distributor, and it could come from anywhere in the world or the Pacific Coast," says Anderson. "We set up a business plan to buy directly from the boats and do our own processing, and that's what sets us apart from other restaurants in town. People actually see the fish come in our back door from the

5 HEARTY FARE FROM GRASS-FED LAMB TO WILD GAME

Thyme-roasted Chicken
with Warm Potato, Kale, and Pancetta Salad

Chef Matthew Busetto nestles golden, crispy-skinned chicken in a warm potato, kale, and pancetta salad in this rustic, Sunday supper–worthy dish. He turns out a superior bird using the Zuni Café technique of seasoning the chicken with salt and thyme two days before roasting it.

NOTE: The chicken requires a 48-hour rest in the refrigerator. To successfully time this dish, start prepping the salad components after the chicken has been roasting for 25 minutes.

1 (3½-pound) whole chicken

3 teaspoons salt, plus more for the vinaigrette

2 teaspoons fresh thyme

4 Yukon Gold potatoes, cut into 1-inch cubes

¾ cup roughly diced pancetta

1 small shallot, finely chopped (about 2 tablespoons)

⅓ cup red wine vinegar

⅔ cup extra-virgin olive oil

Freshly ground black pepper

1 bunch lacinato kale, stems removed and leaves cut into 2-inch slices (about 5 cups)

4–6 SERVINGS

1. Rinse and dry the chicken. Mix 2 teaspoons of the salt and the thyme together in a small bowl. Gently loosen the skin of the chicken around the breast and thighs and push about ½ teaspoon of the salt-thyme mixture under the skin of each breast and thigh. Sprinkle the remaining 1 teaspoon salt over the chicken, making sure that the thicker pieces are coated slightly more than the thinner pieces and that a pinch of salt goes into the cavity on the backbone. Place the chicken in a roasting pan and cover with plastic wrap. Refrigerate for 2 days.

2. Position a rack in the center of the oven and preheat the oven to 400°F. Roast the chicken until the skin is golden brown and the thickest part of the thigh registers 160°F on an instant-read thermometer, about 50 minutes.* If needed, move the pan to the top rack during the last 5 minutes of cooking to brown the chicken skin.

3. While the chicken roasts, bring a large pot of salted water to a boil. Simmer the potatoes over medium heat until soft when poked with a paring knife, but not falling apart, about 25 minutes. Remove the pot from the heat and hold the potatoes in the cooking water to keep warm until ready to use.

4. Cook the pancetta in a small skillet over medium heat until crispy. Transfer the pancetta to a paper towel–lined plate and cover with foil to keep warm. Discard the fat or reserve for another use.

5. Whisk the shallot and vinegar together in a small bowl. Let the shallot rest in the vinegar for 10 minutes to soften its bite. Whisk in the olive oil. Salt and pepper to taste and set aside.

6. Remove the chicken from the oven and let rest for 10 minutes on a cutting board.

7. Bring a large pot of salted water to a boil and blanch the kale until just wilted, about 30 seconds. Drain and pat dry with paper towels. Drain the potatoes. Re-whisk the vinaigrette. Gently toss the kale, potatoes, and pancetta with the vinaigrette in a large bowl until well combined.

8. Transfer the potato salad to a large platter. Cut the chicken into eight pieces (two wings, two breasts, two thighs, and two drumsticks) and arrange the pieces on top of the salad. Serve immediately.

*NOTE: The USDA recommends cooking chicken to an internal temperature of 180°F, but many professional cooks prefer the lower temperature. Use whichever you are more comfortable with.

Recipe from LESLIE LUKAS-RECIO AND MANUEL RECIO OF VIRIDIAN FARMS

Basque-style Chicken with Espelette Piperade

Piperade, the colorful Basque pepper sauce, gets its mild heat from the brick red spice known as *piment d'Espelette* (Espelette pepper powder). At Viridian Farms, Leslie Lukas-Recio and Manuel Recio make their *piment d'Espelette* by drying peppers in the sun for at least six weeks before grinding the dried peppers into a coarse powder. The couple sells the spice at their Portland Farmers Market booth from mid-March through October and through the farm's online store year-round.

½ cup extra-virgin olive oil

3 medium yellow onions, thinly sliced

3 garlic cloves, minced

4 yellow bell peppers, seeds and stems removed and cut into ¼-inch slices

2 red bell peppers, seeds and stems removed and cut into ¼-inch slices

4 large tomatoes, peeled (see Note page 146), seeded, and roughly chopped

3 tablespoons *piment d'Espelette*

¼ teaspoon fresh thyme

Salt and freshly ground black pepper

1 (3½- to 4-pound) chicken, cut into 8 pieces

4–6 SERVINGS

1. Warm ¼ cup of the olive oil over medium heat in a large lidded pot. Reduce the heat to medium-low and cook the onions and garlic, stirring occasionally, until soft but not brown, about 5 minutes. Increase the heat to medium and stir in the yellow bell peppers and red bell peppers. Cover and cook for 10 minutes.

2. Stir in the tomatoes and *piment d'Espelette*. Cover and cook, stirring occasionally, until thickened, about 20 minutes longer. Stir in the thyme and a pinch of salt and pepper and transfer to a large bowl.

3. Wipe out the pot with a paper towel and warm the remaining ¼ cup olive oil over medium heat. Add the chicken and cook, turning occasionally, until browned on all sides, about 10 minutes.

4. Pour the pepper-tomato sauce over the chicken. Cover and simmer over low heat, stirring occasionally, until the chicken is fork-tender and cooked through, about 35 minutes. Salt and pepper to taste. Divide among four to six plates and serve immediately.

NOTE: When Viridian's Basque frying peppers are available in the fall, substitute them for the bell peppers called for here. Serve the meltingly soft peppers and tender chicken with boiled potatoes and green beans as a hearty autumn meal.

Spring Pork Braise

The savvy meat men at Tails & Trotters encourage customers to braise tough cuts of their hazelnut-fed pork to create meltingly tender meat. Though they use pork jowl in this recipe, I prefer the more widely available pork shoulder. Serve the pork in large hunks over fresh fava beans, peas, and new potatoes in the spring, or shred it into smaller pieces, dress it with a light tomato sauce, and serve it with pasta or polenta in any season.

2 tablespoons extra-virgin olive oil

1 (2½-pound) pork shoulder blade roast

1 white onion, thinly sliced

8 fresh sage leaves

3 garlic cloves, minced

1 cup sliced fennel bulb

1 cup white wine

1 cup low-sodium chicken broth

2 tablespoons lemon peel
  Fennel fronds

6 SERVINGS

1. Position a rack in the center of the oven and preheat the oven to 425°F.

2. Warm the olive oil over medium heat in a large lidded oven-proof pot. Brown the pork on all sides. Remove the pork from the pot. Add the onion and sage leaves to the pot and cook, stirring occasionally until the onion softens, about 4 minutes. Add the garlic and cook until fragrant, about 1 minute longer.

3. Add the sliced fennel and wine. Cook, stirring occasionally, until the fennel has softened slightly, about 5 minutes. Stir in the chicken broth, lemon peel, and a small handful of fennel fronds. Return the pork to the pot and roast uncovered for 30 minutes.

4. Lower the oven temperature to 325°F and cover the pot. Roast the pork until fork-tender, about 1 hour 30 minutes longer. Check the pork occasionally and add additional broth or water as needed to keep the meat moist.

5. Transfer the pork to a cutting board and discard the onion, fennel, herbs, and braising liquid. Cover with foil and let it rest for 20 minutes. Trim off any fat and serve immediately.

TAILS & TROTTERS

AARON SILVERMAN'S PASSION for prosciutto started with a snack. Back in 2004, the Eugene-based farmer sat sampling a plate of regional prosciutto in Turin when he began wondering why no one was making prosciutto back home.

On that same trip, he learned that Italian producers use different breeds of pigs and finish them on local acorns to make regionally distinct prosciutto. When he returned to Eugene, Silverman put his new knowledge to good use and started raising pigs to make prosciutto on his farm. But in place of the traditional acorns, he finished his pigs on Oregon hazelnuts instead.

Morgan Brownlow

Once Silverman had a few trial runs under his belt, he moved his family to Portland to pursue his prosciutto-making project in earnest. It was there that he partnered with Morgan Brownlow, a well-known chef who was working on a similar project of his own. With Silverman's farming background and Brownlow's butchery and charcuterie expertise, it has proved a perfect partnership.

The challenge in making high-quality, USDA-certified prosciutto is that it takes many months to cure the pork. While their first batch cured, the pair sold hazelnut-finished pork to chefs and farmers' market shoppers and educated locals on how to use their distinct cuts.

"Morgan's style of butchery is a northern Italian style as far as how he looks at the cuts. There are many very distinctive cuts that we offer to the restaurants and the retail market," says Silverman. "So we definitely do a lot of education at the market about those cuts. We have to be able to tell you what to do with a brisket or a coppa or the inside round of the leg."

When fans of the fresh pork at Tails and Trotters try the prosciutto, it won't taste exactly like old-world prosciutto. The men's goal is to make high-quality prosciutto but also a product that reflects the region. "Instead of doing a European-style prosciutto here, we want to do what the pinot industry did for wine by making a Northwest-style prosciutto from pigs that were finished on hazelnuts," says Silverman.

Grilled Pork Chops with Grilled Nectarine Salsa

Portland's Laurelhurst Market is an artisanal butcher shop by day and a seasonally driven steakhouse by night. Not surprisingly, the staff is well versed in teaching customers how to prepare cuts from their case at home. When it comes to pork, co-owner Benjamin Dyer suggests grilling pork chops and elevating the smoky meat with a citrus-spiked grilled nectarine salsa.

4 **SERVINGS**

- 4 bone-in pork loin chops
  Salt and freshly ground black pepper
- 3 medium nectarines, halved and pitted
- 1½ tablespoons extra-virgin olive oil
- 2 tablespoons finely chopped red onion
- 1 tablespoon lemon juice
- 1 tablespoon lime juice
- 1 tablespoon fresh cilantro leaves, roughly chopped
- 1½ teaspoons fresh mint leaves, finely chopped
- 1 teaspoon seeded, finely chopped jalapeño chile

1. Preheat the grill for direct grilling over hot charcoal or high heat. Sprinkle the pork chops liberally with salt and pepper. Set aside.

2. Oil the grill grates. Brush the nectarines on the cut side with ½ tablespoon of the olive oil. Grill them oiled side down until lightly colored but not black, about 3 minutes. Flip them over and grill 2 minutes longer, skin side down. Remove the nectarines from the grill and set aside.

3. Grill the pork chops, turning once, until their internal temperature reads 150°F on a meat thermometer, about 5 minutes per side. Transfer the chops to a plate and lightly cover with foil to keep warm.

4. Dice the nectarines into ½-inch pieces and place in a medium bowl. Add the remaining 1 tablespoon of olive oil, onion, lemon juice, lime juice, cilantro, mint, and jalapeño to the bowl. Mix the salsa with a rubber spatula until well combined. Salt and pepper to taste.

5. Garnish the pork chops with the nectarine salsa and serve immediately.

Marionberry Pork Mole

The marionberries in this cheater's mole lend the earthy chocolate sauce a subtle sweetness and hit of bright acidity. Braising the pork shoulder in the sauce renders a tender, flavorful meat that I serve shredded and stuffed into homemade tortillas with accompaniments of crumbled cotija cheese and cilantro.

6 SERVINGS

- 2 tablespoons neutral-flavored oil, such as canola or grapeseed oil
- 1 (3-pound) bone-in pork shoulder blade roast, trimmed of visible fat
- 1 medium yellow onion, roughly chopped
- 2 Roma tomatoes, roughly chopped
- 3 garlic cloves, peeled
- 2 cups low-sodium chicken broth
- 1 (14.5-ounce) can tomato sauce
- 3 tablespoons dark brown sugar
- 3 tablespoons distilled white vinegar
- 3 tablespoons sliced almonds, toasted
- 2 tablespoons dried currants
- 2 chipotle chiles in adobo sauce
- 1 dried ancho or pasilla chile, stemmed, seeded, deveined, and roughly chopped
- 1 teaspoon ground cinnamon
- ¼ teaspoon ground cloves
- 1 cup frozen marionberries
- 1 ounce dark chocolate
- Crumbled cotija cheese, for garnish
- Fresh cilantro leaves, for garnish

1. Warm the oil over medium heat in a large lidded pot. Pat the pork dry with a paper towel and brown on all sides. Remove the pork from the pot. Cook the onion, stirring occasionally, over medium heat until translucent, about 5 minutes. Stir in the tomatoes and garlic and cook for 1 minute longer. Stir in the chicken broth, tomato sauce, sugar, vinegar, almonds, currants, chipotles, dried chile, cinnamon, and cloves. Bring to a simmer. Stir in the marionberries and chocolate.

2. Return the pork to the pot. Reduce the heat to low, cover, and simmer gently until the pork is tender and falls easily away from the bone, about 3 hours.

3. When the pork is nearly done, position a rack in the center of the oven and preheat the oven to 350°F.

4. Transfer the pork to a roasting pan, leaving the sauce in the pot. Bake until the pork starts to brown, about 20 minutes.

5. Let the sauce cool slightly, then purée it in a blender or the bowl of a food processor fitted with a steel blade attachment until smooth. Pour the sauce back into the pot and cover to keep warm. The sauce should be thick. If it is too thin, reduce it over medium heat until it thickens.

6. Remove the pork from the oven. Discard the bone and, using two forks, shred the meat. Toss the pork with the mole sauce until well coated. (You may not need all of the sauce.) Garnish with cotija cheese and cilantro leaves and serve immediately.

SWEET BRIAR FARMS

SINCE SHE JOINED SWEET BRIAR FARMS in 2004, Petrene Moreland has come up with a slogan to sell farmer, founder, and partner Keith Cooper's heritage pigs: "Try the rest, then come to us for the best."

And increasingly, local chefs and shoppers at the 12 farmers' markets Sweet Briar Farms serves do just that. Chefs like Simpatica Dining Hall's Scott Ketterman like Sweet Briar Farms' fresh, all-natural pork because their breeds and feed yield intensely flavorful meat. Cooper feeds the pigs ground whole-kernel corn, not recycled grain, and occasionally finishes pigs on ground hazelnut meal to supply chefs with the well-marbled pork they desire.

Now, some 30 years after Cooper's pork-raising project began, Sweet Briar has become a pig farm in transition. On the 40-acre plot on the outskirts of Eugene, the farm is undergoing construction that includes a new barn and pig "condos" that will serve as birthing spaces for the hundreds of baby pigs Cooper raises each year. In these new spaces, Cooper will continue to raise the prized heritage breeds Sweet Briar is known for — Durocs, Berkshires, Hampshires, and Yorkshires — and keep the chefs and market shoppers well supplied.

Petrene Moreland

Steak Salad with Grilled Onions, Fingerlings, Blue Cheese, and Bacon Vinaigrette

Steakhouse salad gets a new look in this modern American dish from Bend-based chef Cliff Eslinger. Though this main-course salad has a lot going on — tender fingerling potatoes, sweet grilled onions, robust blue cheese, and slivers of grilled steak — everything comes together handsomely with the help of a salty-sweet bacon vinaigrette.

1 pound fingerling potatoes, halved lengthwise

2 tablespoons extra-virgin olive oil

Salt and freshly ground black pepper

1 large Hermiston onion or other sweet onion, sliced into ¼-inch-thick rings

1 (1½-pound) flat-iron steak

7 ounces baby arugula

6 ounces smoked blue cheese, such as Rogue Creamery's Oregon Blue, crumbled

Warm Bacon Vinaigrette (page 182)

4 SERVINGS

1. Position a rack in the center of the oven and preheat the oven to 400°F. Toss the potatoes with 1 tablespoon of the olive oil and sprinkle with salt and pepper. Transfer them to a baking sheet and roast until fork-tender and golden brown, about 20 minutes. Remove from the oven and cover with foil to keep warm.

2. While the potatoes roast, prepare the grill for both indirect and direct grilling over hot charcoal or high heat. Oil the grill grates. Toss the onions with the remaining 1 tablespoon olive oil and sprinkle with salt and pepper. Grill the onions over indirect heat, turning once, until they are cooked through and slightly soft, about 10 minutes. Place the onions on the baking sheet with the potatoes to keep warm.

3. Sprinkle the steak with salt and pepper. Grill the steak over direct heat until medium-rare or an instant-read thermometer inserted into the middle reads 135°F, about 5 minutes per side. Let the steak rest on a cutting board for 5 minutes.

4. Toss the potatoes, onions, arugula, and cheese with the vinaigrette in a large bowl. Salt and pepper to taste. Divide the salad among four plates. Thinly slice the steak across the grain and divide equally among the salads. Serve immediately.

Warm Bacon Vinaigrette

Chef Cliff Eslinger uses this indulgent vinaigrette to dress his steak salad (page 180) at 900 Wall. Depending on how well dressed you like your salad, you may have vinaigrette left over. Refrigerate any excess in an airtight container and use within one week. Rewarm the vinaigrette before serving.

4 strips thick-cut bacon, roughly chopped

3 tablespoons diced yellow onion

½ cup warm water

6 tablespoons champagne vinegar

3 tablespoons sugar

1½ teaspoons cornstarch

   Freshly ground black pepper

MAKES ABOUT ⅔ CUP

1. Cook the bacon in a medium skillet over medium heat, stirring occasionally, until crispy, about 5 minutes. Transfer the bacon to a small bowl with a slotted spoon and set aside. Add the onion to the skillet and cook in the bacon fat over medium-low heat, stirring occasionally, until soft, about 5 minutes.

2. Meanwhile, bring ¼ cup plus 2 tablespoons of the water, the vinegar, and the sugar to a boil in a small saucepan. Whisk the cornstarch with the remaining 2 tablespoons water in a small bowl to make a slurry.

3. Add the hot vinegar mixture and the slurry to the skillet and cook over medium heat, stirring constantly, for 2 minutes longer to thicken the vinaigrette. Stir in the bacon. Add a pinch of black pepper. Transfer the dressing to a small bowl, cover, and set aside until ready to use.

Sunday Flank Steak with Sorrel Salsa Verde

My childhood neighbor Janet grilled her famous flank steak for family and friends nearly every Sunday night. I tweaked her recipe slightly and found it a perfect match for bright, lemony Sorrel Salsa Verde. The salsa comes from Courtney Sproule, a talented chef who runs a Portland-based supper club and catering company called din din.

NOTE: Marinate the steak for at least three and up to eight hours before grilling.

1 (1½-pound) flank steak
½ cup low-sodium soy sauce
¼ cup rice vinegar
2 garlic cloves, minced
1 tablespoon honey
2 teaspoons peeled and minced fresh ginger
½ cup Sorrel Salsa Verde (page 184)

4 SERVINGS

1. Place the steak in a shallow lidded container. Whisk the soy sauce, vinegar, garlic, honey, and ginger together in a small bowl. Pour the marinade over the steak. Cover and refrigerate for at least 3 hours and up to 8 hours, turning the steak occasionally to ensure even marinating.

2. Preheat the grill for direct grilling over hot charcoal or high heat. Oil the grill grates. Grill the steak to the desired doneness, about 6 minutes per side for medium-rare. Transfer the steak to a cutting board and let rest for 5 minutes.

3. Thinly slice the steak across the grain. Transfer the slices to a serving platter or four dinner plates and garnish with the Sorrel Salsa Verde before serving.

Sorrel Salsa Verde

Piquant Sorrel Salsa Verde creates a colorful garnish for grilled flank steak but can dress up grilled lamb or omelets as well. Courtney Sproule buys her sorrel from Gales Meadow Farm, but you can get it from numerous farmers' market vendors nearly year-round as well. (If you can't find hazelnut oil, walnut oil is an excellent substitute.)

MAKES 1¼ CUPS

- 3 oil-packed anchovy fillets
- ¼ cup milk
- 1½ cups fresh flat-leaf parsley, roughly chopped
- ¼ pound sorrel, ribs and stems removed and leaves roughly chopped (about 1½ cups)
- 3 tablespoons capers, rinsed, dried, and minced
- 2 tablespoons finely chopped fresh chives
- 1 tablespoon finely minced shallot
  Zest of ½ lemon
- ⅔ cup hazelnut oil
- 3 tablespoons extra-virgin olive oil
  Salt and freshly ground black pepper

1. Soak the anchovies in the milk in a small bowl for 10 minutes to neutralize the packing oil. Rinse, dry, and mince the anchovies; discard the milk.

2. Mix the anchovies, parsley, sorrel, capers, chives, shallot, and lemon zest together in a medium bowl with a rubber spatula. Mix in the hazelnut oil and olive oil until well combined. Salt and pepper to taste. The salsa can be made up to an hour ahead and allowed to sit, covered, at room temperature until ready to use. Stored in an airtight container in the refrigerator, the salsa will keep for about 2 days.

Grilled Quail
with Apple, Sunchoke, and Fennel Salad

When apples, fennel, and sunchokes are in season in late fall, Chef John Eisenhart matches their clean flavor and crisp texture with tender grilled quail. Though he serves the quail in large pieces meant to be eaten with your fingers, you can also pull the quail meat off the bone and toss it into the salad before serving it. Look for fennel pollen in specialty food stores.

½ cup extra-virgin olive oil

2 teaspoons balsamic vinegar

4 semi-boneless quail

2 small Pink Lady apples, cored and cut into ⅛-inch matchsticks

1 small fennel bulb, thinly sliced

6 sunchokes, scrubbed and thinly sliced

Juice of 1 orange

Salt and freshly ground black pepper

Fennel pollen, for garnish

4 SERVINGS

1. Whisk ¼ cup of the olive oil and the balsamic vinegar together in a small bowl. Arrange the quail in a single layer in a small dish and pour the marinade over the top. Turn the quail once to coat. Cover and refrigerate for 4 hours.

2. Preheat the grill for direct grilling over medium-hot charcoal or medium heat. Remove the quail from the refrigerator and let come to room temperature.

3. Remove the quail from the marinade and discard any excess liquid. Oil the grill grates. Grill the quail until just cooked through, about 4 minutes per side. The meat will still be slightly pink. Transfer the quail to a plate and cover it with foil to rest for 5 minutes.

4. Toss the apples, fennel, and sunchokes with the orange juice and the remaining ¼ cup olive oil in a medium bowl. Salt and pepper to taste. Divide the salad among four plates.

5. Cut the quail into quarters, lengthwise and crosswise, and divide among the plates. Garnish with the fennel pollen and serve immediately.

Lamb Meatballs Stuffed with Swiss Chard and Goat Cheese

Chef Adam Sappington serves his spin on the nostalgic meatball at his retro-style restaurant in Portland's Montavilla neighborhood. I am particularly fond of this dish because each meatball has a surprise hidden inside: a winning combination of wilted chard and creamy goat cheese. Serve these large meatballs family-style on a bed of orzo tossed with chopped tomatoes and olives.

¼ cup finely ground bread crumbs (made from hamburger buns)

¼ cup whole milk

1½ pounds ground lamb (80 percent lean)

1 tablespoon dried basil

1 tablespoon dried oregano

1 tablespoon garlic powder

2 teaspoons kosher salt, plus more for seasoning the chard

2 tablespoons extra-virgin olive oil

1 bunch Swiss chard, stems removed and leaves roughly chopped (about 3 cups)

Freshly ground black pepper

2 ounces fresh goat cheese, such as Rivers Edge chèvre

4–6 SERVINGS

1. Position a rack in the center of the oven and preheat the oven to 350°F. Line a large baking sheet with parchment paper.

2. Mix the bread crumbs and milk together in a small bowl and let soak for 5 minutes.

3. Mix the bread crumb–milk mixture with the lamb, basil, oregano, garlic powder, and salt in a large bowl with a rubber spatula until well combined. Cover the bowl with plastic wrap and refrigerate until ready to use.

4. Warm the olive oil in a large skillet over medium heat. Add the chard and sauté, stirring occasionally, until wilted and tender, about 10 minutes. Remove the skillet from the heat. Salt and pepper the chard to taste.

5. Form approximately ½-cup portions of the meat mixture into balls to create 6 meatballs. Split each meatball in half and flatten each half to form a patty. You will have 12 patties.

6. Place 6 of the patties on a clean work surface. Spoon about 2 teaspoons of the chard and 1 teaspoon of the goat cheese in the middle of each patty, leaving a ½-inch border around the filling. Cover each of the chard-topped patties with a plain patty. Seal the edges and gently shape the patties back into meatballs.

7. Arrange the meatballs on the prepared baking sheet and bake until browned and cooked through, about 40 minutes. Transfer to a serving dish and serve immediately.

THE COUNTRY CAT DINNER HOUSE & BAR

THERE ARE MANY HIGH-PROFILE, farm-to-table restaurants in the locavore-filled town of Portland. But only one restaurant has embraced the challenge of reimagining classic American dishes with local ingredients to give its countrified menu a decidedly Oregon twist.

At The Country Cat Dinner House & Bar, Chef Adam Sappington straps on his trademark overalls and serves down-home cuisine that hints at his Midwest roots and his deep understanding of Northwest ingredients and producers. Each dish makes a solid case for farm-to-fork, nose-to-tail eating, from bacon-braised collard greens to the lamb meatballs Sappington stuffs with chard and goat cheese. His signature entrée presents Sweet Briar Farms pork three ways atop a bed of creamy grits; it's cleverly named the Whole Hog.

The restaurant's spirited pastry chef (and Adam's wife), Jackie Sappington, provides a sweet finish to every meal — and plenty of baked goods for the daily brunch menu as well. Baskets of her cinnamon rolls have become a brunch staple, and her tender sweet-cream biscuits are legendary among neighborhood regulars.

Outside their restaurant work, the two extend their passion for local agriculture into the

Jackie and Adam Sappington

surrounding community: Adam presents chef demos at neighborhood farmers' markets, and together they host an annual farmers' market benefit dinner at The Country Cat to further support the farmers and artisans who make their jobs possible day after day.

Spring Lamb Ragù

In this shoulder-season recipe, Chef JC Mersmann partners a hearty lamb ragù with a homemade pasta made with spring nettles (page 61) foraged from the property at Gathering Together Farm. Serve this comforting ragù over the nettle pasta or a noodle of your choice.

4–6 SERVINGS

All-purpose flour

Salt and freshly ground black pepper

1½ pounds boneless lamb shoulder, cut into ½-inch chunks

2 tablespoons extra-virgin olive oil

2 large carrots, peeled and finely diced (about 1½ cups)

1 large yellow onion, finely diced (about 1½ cups)

1 small fennel bulb, finely diced (about 1 cup)

2 strips thick-cut bacon, diced into ¼-inch pieces

5 garlic cloves, minced

3 tablespoons tomato paste

1¼ cups dry red wine

3 cups low-sodium chicken broth

⅓ cup crushed tomatoes

2 bay leaves

2 fresh thyme sprigs

Fresh flat-leaf parsley, for garnish (optional)

Grated Parmesan cheese, for garnish (optional)

1. Fill a shallow dish with flour and lightly season it with salt and pepper. Dredge the lamb through the flour and set aside. Warm the olive oil in a large lidded pot over medium heat. Add the lamb and cook, turning occasionally, until browned all over, about 10 minutes.

2. Remove the lamb from the pot and add the carrots, onion, fennel, and bacon. Cook over medium heat, stirring occasionally, until the vegetables are slightly softened, about 5 minutes. Stir in the garlic and tomato paste with a wooden spoon and cook until the tomato paste begins to brown, about 3 minutes. Stir in the wine and scrape up the flavorful browned bits from the bottom of the pan. Add the chicken broth, crushed tomatoes, bay leaves, thyme, and lamb to the pot. Bring the mixture to a boil.

3. Reduce the heat to low and simmer the ragù, covered, until the lamb is fork-tender and the sauce has thickened slightly, about 2 hours 30 minutes. Continue to cook the ragù, uncovered, until it reaches the desired thickness, about 15 minutes longer.

4. Discard the bay leaves and thyme sprigs. Garnish the ragù with the parsley and Parmesan, if desired, and serve immediately.

Beef and Lamb Burgers with Herb Aioli

Cutting ground beef with a bit of ground lamb, then adding herbs and warming spices, gives these patties a depth of flavor that plain beef burgers lack. Wooldridge Creek's wine club members gave this burger rave reviews — particularly after they tried it with the southern Oregon winery's full-bodied syrah.

¾ cup fresh flat-leaf parsley

¼ cup fresh cilantro

1 medium shallot, roughly chopped (about 3 tablespoons)

2 teaspoons garlic salt

½ teaspoon ground cinnamon

½ teaspoon ground cumin

¾ pound ground chuck or sirloin

¼ pound ground lamb

Salt and freshly ground black pepper

½ cup mayonnaise

4 hamburger buns

4 ¼-inch-thick tomato slices (optional)

4 lettuce leaves (optional)

4 SERVINGS

1. Preheat the grill for direct grilling over medium-hot charcoal or medium-high heat. Oil the grill grates.

2. Blend the parsley, cilantro, shallot, garlic salt, cinnamon, and cumin in the bowl of a food processor fitted with a steel blade attachment until well combined.

3. Mix three-quarters of the herb mixture, the beef, and the lamb together with a rubber spatula in a medium bowl until well combined. Form the burgers into four equal-size patties, each slightly wider than the hamburger buns. Make a small depression in the center of each patty with your thumb to reduce shrinkage. Sprinkle both sides of the patties with salt and pepper and set aside.

4. Combine the remaining herb mixture and the mayonnaise with a rubber spatula in a small bowl. Cover and refrigerate until ready to use.

5. Grill the patties, turning once, until medium-rare, about 4 minutes per side. Lightly toast the buns on the grill. Place the burgers on the bun bottoms and top with the herb mayonnaise and a slice of tomato and lettuce, if desired. Cover the patties with the top buns and serve immediately.

Lamb Tagine with Sweet Tomato Jam

Lamb shoulder from Cattail Creek's grass-fed flock grooves with jammy tomatoes and warming spices in this Moroccan-themed supper. Cattail Creek's founder John Neumeister and his wife, Gwen Meyer, serve this fragrant tagine over a scoop of steamed couscous or rice.

½ teaspoon crumbled saffron threads

½ cup hot water

2 tablespoons extra-virgin olive oil

2½ pounds boneless lamb shoulder, cut into 1-inch cubes

Salt and freshly ground black pepper

1½ cups low-sodium chicken broth

1 yellow onion, coarsely grated

2 garlic cloves, minced

2 teaspoons ground cinnamon

1 teaspoon ground ginger

1 (28-ounce) can whole tomatoes

2 tablespoons tomato paste

¼ cup honey

3 tablespoons toasted sesame seeds

4 SERVINGS

1. Steep the saffron threads in the hot water. Set aside.

2. Warm the olive oil in a large lidded pot over medium-high heat. Season the lamb with salt and pepper and add to the pot. Cook, stirring occasionally, until browned on all sides, about 5 minutes.

3. Add the saffron and hot water, chicken broth, onion, garlic, 1 teaspoon of the cinnamon, and ginger to the pot. Bring to a boil. Reduce the heat to low, cover, and simmer until the lamb is tender, about 1 hour.

4. Purée the tomatoes in the bowl of a food processor fitted with a steel blade attachment. Stir the puréed tomatoes, tomato paste, and a pinch of salt into the pot. Simmer uncovered over low heat, stirring occasionally, until the sauce thickens, about 35 minutes.

5. Add the honey and remaining 1 teaspoon cinnamon and cook for a few minutes longer to let the flavors meld. Salt and pepper to taste. Serve the tagine warm with the sesame seeds sprinkled on top.

CATTAIL CREEK LAMB

JOHN NEUMEISTER strides across the pasture on his 17-acre plot, then suddenly stoops down and ruffles the lush greens growing beneath his feet. This open pasture, he explains, is the foundation of his sheep farm. "Rapidly growing young lambs on lush green feed is the key to our success — that's why we have a great product," he says.

Though Neumeister didn't plan on becoming a second-generation sheep farmer, he has spent nearly 30 years raising grass-fed lamb near Corvallis. After bolting from his family's Ohio farm for college, he dabbled in various jobs before returning to his roots by re-creating his family's sheep farm in Oregon in 1983.

The business plan for his Oregon farm shifted slightly when a fortuitous meeting put Neumeister in touch with the buyer for Chez Panisse. Soon, he was shipping his sustainably raised lambs directly to the famous farm-to-table restaurant. It was then that he realized he didn't have to sell his lamb to a local broker. He could skip the middleman and sell it to chefs who wanted to buy their lamb directly from his farm.

"Chefs realized that they knew what they wanted in terms of quality and portion size and that if they worked with farmers and communicated those things, they had a much better chance of getting what they wanted," he says. "The lamb they get is much fresher and meets the political and environmental goals of reducing food miles as well."

The driving force behind Cattail Creek's success, however, is the fact that the farm's high-quality lamb has the mild taste and tenderness chefs and

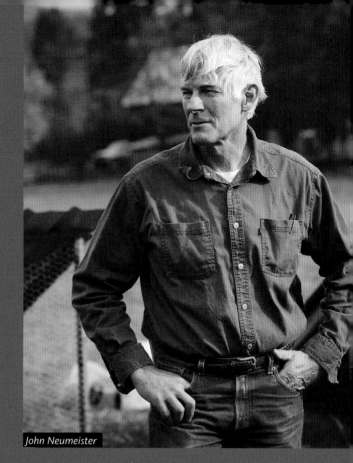

John Neumeister

consumers desire. Neumeister attributes the flavor and tenderness of his lamb to the farming practices he and his business partner use. All the lamb they produce is grass fed, sustainably raised, and rapidly grown. The meat is processed in small batches at a USDA-certified facility, after which the carcasses are dry aged for six days to concentrate the flavor and maximize the tenderness of the meat.

Neumeister is pleased with Cattail Creek's outstanding reputation but, more importantly, proud of his efforts to expand and enhance the local food community. "It feels like we are building something by working together, and that enriches everyone's experience," he says. "It makes the customers and restaurant owners and meat shop owners and farmers feel like we're all working together to do a good thing."

T. R. and Jen McCrystal

JEN'S GARDEN

SISTERS HAS ALWAYS been a sleepy mountain town, more known for its famous quilt show and eponymous bakery than its dining scene. But when T. R. McCrystal and his wife, Jen, relocated to Sisters to escape the fray of bigger cities, they opened a restaurant that's given gourmands a reason to pull into town and stay awhile.

In 2006, the couple transformed a cozy downtown cottage into a 28-seat dining room. There, McCrystal serves an elegant prix fixe menu that rotates with the seasons and his whims. Despite its upscale reputation and white tablecloth ambiance, however, the little bistro is devoid of pretense. Ever the consummate host, McCrystal often joins in the dining room chatter, catching up with guests old and new as they tuck into his southern French–inspired cuisine.

Main courses of gnocchi Bolognese, hazelnut-crusted rack of lamb, and quail stuffed with ratatouille and rice and desserts like Jen's lavender-honey crème brûlée have put this Sisters spot on the map. But the hosts' warm welcome is the piece that makes diners want to return to the small town again and again.

Hazelnut-crusted Rack of Lamb

Chef T. R. McCrystal has served this versatile entrée with mushroom risotto, roasted potatoes, and wild rice throughout the years at Jen's Garden in Sisters. Serve this special occasion dish atop a bed of creamy polenta or mashed potatoes for a presentation that's elegant but easy to pull off. For a first course, serve an eye-catching salad like Shaved Radish "Carpaccio" (page 23) and for dessert something classically Oregonian like Apple-Huckleberry Crisp (page 265).

2 tablespoons mayonnaise

2 tablespoons whole-grain mustard

½ cup fresh bread crumbs

½ cup roasted hazelnuts, skinned and roughly chopped

⅓ cup fresh flat-leaf parsley

¼ cup grated Parmesan cheese or similarly hard cheese, like Juniper Grove's Redmondo

Salt and freshly ground black pepper

1 (2-pound) frenched rack of lamb

1 tablespoon extra-virgin olive oil

¾ cup white wine

¾ cup water

4 SERVINGS

1. Whisk the mayonnaise and mustard together in a small bowl and set aside. Blend the bread crumbs, hazelnuts, parsley, and Parmesan in the bowl of a food processor fitted with a steel blade attachment until well combined. Salt and pepper to taste. Put the breading in a shallow baking dish and set aside.

2. Position a rack in the center of the oven and preheat the oven to 500°F. Season the lamb generously with salt and pepper. Warm the olive oil over medium-high heat in a large skillet. Add the lamb to the skillet and cook until browned, turning once, about 4 minutes per side.

3. Spread the mayonnaise-mustard sauce on top of the lamb (the ribs should be curving down), then press into the breading to coat. If necessary, pat additional breading over the meat to patch up the crust. Discard any remaining breading.

4. Arrange the lamb in a large baking dish with the crust side up and the ribs curving down. Pour the wine and water around the lamb and roast until the crust is brown and the lamb reaches an internal temperature of 130°F for medium-rare, about 25 minutes.

5. Remove the pan from the oven and cover with foil. Let the lamb rest for 10 minutes, then carve into individual ribs and serve, two ribs to a serving.

Fennel-roasted Rabbit Salad
with Fennel-Pollen Aioli

The famous English Chef Fergus Henderson introduced Chef Vitaly Paley to fennel twigs while visiting Portland a few years ago; now Paley obtains fennel twigs from Dancing Roots Farm to add flavor to soups and stews and the rabbit salad he serves at his respected bistro. Serve this main-course salad with a thick slab of artisan bread and a glass of viognier from Penner-Ash Wine Cellars, Paley's favorite wine pairing with this dish.

4–6 SERVINGS

- 1 large bundle dried fennel twigs or dried tops from 3 fennel bulbs
- 1 rabbit (about 3 pounds), cut into 8 pieces
- 2 teaspoons fennel pollen or ground fennel seed
- 1 teaspoon cayenne pepper
- Salt and freshly ground black pepper
- 3 tablespoons extra-virgin olive oil
- 1 cup dry white wine
- 4 medium shallots, unpeeled
- 2 garlic heads
- 2 large carrots, peeled and cut into ½-inch pieces
- 4 strips thick-cut bacon
- 5 ounces hearty greens, such as arugula or frisée, stemmed
- 1 medium fennel bulb, thinly sliced
- 1½ cups loosely packed fresh flat-leaf parsley
- ½ cup loosely packed fresh tarragon leaves
- ½ cup loosely packed fresh chervil
- ¼ cup dried cranberries
- ⅓ cup Fennel-Pollen Aioli (page 196)

1. Position a rack in the center of the oven and preheat the oven to 350°F.

2. Arrange the fennel twigs or dried fennel tops in the bottom of a large roasting pan. Rub the rabbit pieces with the fennel pollen and cayenne. Sprinkle with salt and pepper.

3. Warm the olive oil in a large skillet over medium heat. Working with a few pieces at a time, cook the rabbit until golden brown on all sides, about 1 minute per side. Arrange the rabbit pieces on top of the fennel twigs as they come out of the skillet. Discard any remaining oil.

4. Add the wine to the skillet and bring to a boil over high heat, scraping the bottom of the skillet with a wooden spoon to loosen the flavorful browned bits. Pour the wine over the rabbit in the roasting pan. Nestle the shallots, garlic heads, and carrots around the meat. Lay the bacon slices over the rabbit pieces.

5. Cover the roasting pan with foil. Roast for 45 minutes. Remove the foil and roast until the rabbit is tender and flavorful, about 35 minutes longer. Remove the pan from the oven and let the rabbit rest for 30 minutes.

6. Peel the shallots and squeeze them into a large bowl to break them apart. Transfer the cooked carrots to the bowl. Add the greens, fennel, parsley, tarragon, chervil, and dried cranberries.

7. Transfer the bacon and the rabbit to a cutting board. Pick large chunks of the rabbit off the bones and place them into the bowl. Roughly chop the bacon and add it to the bowl.

8. Whisk 2 tablespoons of the pan juices and the aioli together in a small bowl. Discard the remaining pan juices, fennel twigs, and garlic (or reserve roasted garlic for another use). Toss the salad with the aioli. Salt and pepper to taste and serve immediately.

NOTE: Since fennel twigs are a rare market find, Paley has found an easy substitute for home cooks. Buy three fennel bulbs with their tops still attached. Cut off the tops and dry them in a 175°F oven for 1 hour 30 minutes. Then use the tops in place of the twigs in this recipe. Look for fennel pollen in specialty food stores.

Recipe from CHEF VITALY PALEY OF PALEY'S PLACE BISTRO AND BAR

Fennel-Pollen Aioli

Making aioli by hand takes a bit of muscle, but it makes for a silky, unparalleled sauce. Chef Vitaly Paley recommends using a mortar and pestle to make his fennel aioli; if you do not have a large mortar and pestle, finely chop the garlic cloves and use a whisk and a mixing bowl to blend the aioli instead. The process will seem impossibly slow, but you need to incorporate the oil a little at a time so the aioli doesn't break. Look for fennel pollen in specialty food stores.

3 large garlic cloves, crushed

1 teaspoon kosher salt, plus more if needed

1 teaspoon fennel pollen or ground fennel seed

3 egg yolks

1 teaspoon Dijon mustard

1 teaspoon lemon juice

¾ cup grapeseed oil

2 tablespoons extra-virgin olive oil

NOTE: This dish contains raw eggs. Consuming raw eggs may increase your risk of foodborne illness.

MAKES ABOUT 1 CUP

1. Place the garlic, salt, and fennel pollen in a mortar. Work the garlic with the pestle until it forms a paste. Blend in the egg yolks, mustard, and lemon juice with the pestle until smooth.

2. Drizzle 1 teaspoon of the grapeseed oil into the mortar with one hand while stirring with the pestle with the other hand to fully incorporate the oil. Continue to drizzle the oil into the bowl slowly while stirring to maintain the emulsion. Make sure the oil is completely absorbed before adding more.

3. When all of the grapeseed oil is incorporated, drizzle and blend in the olive oil, 1 tablespoon at a time. Taste the aioli and adjust the salt if needed. Use the aioli immediately, or transfer to an airtight container and store in the refrigerator for up to 1 week.

PALEY'S PLACE BISTRO AND BAR

THE HOUR IS APPROACHING 3 PM at Paley's Place and though the dining room is dark and silent, the kitchen is bustling as the cooks collaborate on the evening's menu. Wielding their knives and cutting boards, they prep the ingredients for classic dishes and on-the-fly specials while Hall & Oates streams in overhead. Occasionally, a few cooks pop out to the counter bar to paw through deliveries from local farmers. Then they return to the kitchen to transform those farm-fresh ingredients into an inviting menu before the restaurant comes alive that night.

Vitaly Paley

Chef Vitaly Paley stands calm and collected in the center of this bustling scene, just as he has on many previous afternoons. Paley and his wife, Kimberly, opened their renowned restaurant in a charming old Victorian home during an extraordinary time for Portland's restaurant scene. The first farm-to-table restaurants were popping up in town, and Paley eagerly joined the ranks of a few passionate chefs serving local, seasonal cuisine. His appreciation and deep understanding of the local food scene won the sophisticated restaurant accolade after accolade in the following years.

But while trendy restaurants come and go, Paley's Place has remained a constant — and innovative — force in Portland's dining scene for more than 15 years. Paley still displays a childlike excitement when a delivery of pristine lettuce or the season's first tomatoes arrive at his door; the constant feeling of discovery fuels his creative process day after day. "We are more creative now than we have ever been. We went to a new menu format and print the menu every day now because we needed an outlet for creativity and to be able to react on the fly to everything that comes in the door," he says.

Deliveries of seasonal produce and artisan products from respected vendors like farmer George Weppler and John Neumeister of Cattail Creek Lamb lay the groundwork for the restaurant's regional Northwest menu. Those products appear in dishes like rabbit ravioli with local mushrooms and spring garlic or a braised lamb and eggplant terrine to delight customers when the curtain comes up every evening.

But what pleases devoted diners even more is the fact that Paley values his ingredients in the same way that the diners appreciate his food. "I really feel privileged to be able to work with this kind of product," he says. "Not many places in this world can say they deal with product this good."

Elk Tartare

Gilt Club made a name for itself in part with house-made spirit infusions that extend the season of local produce. To complement the bar program's local bent, Chef Chris Carriker serves dishes like this twist on traditional steak tartare in the adjacent dining room. Elk is available through farmers' market vendors such as Pine Mountain Ranch. You can also special order elk from an artisan butcher. Serve this appetizer with crostini and a mixed green salad on the side.

4 SERVINGS

2 medium shallots, finely diced (about ¼ cup)

4 cornichons, finely diced

2 tablespoons fresh flat-leaf parsley, finely chopped

1 teaspoon fresh thyme

½ teaspoon capers, minced

½ teaspoon lemon juice

½ teaspoon extra-virgin olive oil

½ pound elk top sirloin

2 egg yolks

½ teaspoon Dijon mustard, plus more as needed

Salt and freshly ground black pepper

Fleur de sel, for garnish (optional)

NOTE: This dish contains raw egg and raw meat. Consuming raw eggs or meat may increase your risk of foodborne illness.

1. Mix the shallots, cornichons, parsley, thyme, capers, lemon juice, and olive oil together in a medium bowl. Cover and refrigerate the mixture until ready to use.

2. Trim the elk of any visible fat. Chop it into approximately ¼-inch pieces, with a few slightly larger pieces and a few slightly smaller pieces to create a varied texture.

3. Mix the meat, egg yolks, mustard, and shallot-herb mixture together in a large bowl with a rubber spatula until well combined. Salt and pepper to taste. Mix in additional mustard, if desired.

4. Divide the tartare among four plates. Garnish with a pinch of fleur de sel, if desired, and serve immediately.

Duck Confit and Butternut Squash Risotto

Roasted butternut squash lends its sweet character to a hearty risotto made even more indulgent with the addition of duck confit. Innkeeper Bruce Bandstra makes his own duck confit, but I find it more convenient to pick up prepared duck confit from butchers like Chop or Laurelhurst Market. Bandstra serves this hearty entrée with slices of duck breast and roasted Brussels sprouts.

1 (1½-pound) butternut squash, peeled, seeded, and cut into ½-inch cubes

¼ cup plus 1 tablespoon extra-virgin olive oil

Salt and freshly ground black pepper

5 cups low-sodium chicken broth

¼ cup finely diced shallots

2 cups Arborio rice

1 cup dry white wine

2 confit duck legs

¾ cup finely grated Parmesan cheese, plus more for garnish (optional)

4–6 SERVINGS

1. Position a rack in the center of the oven and preheat the oven to 400°F. Toss the squash with ¼ cup of the olive oil and a pinch of salt and pepper. Place the squash in a shallow baking pan and roast, stirring once, until just tender, about 25 minutes.

2. Meanwhile, bring the broth to a simmer in a large saucepan over medium heat. Reduce the heat to low and cover to keep warm.

3. Heat the remaining 1 tablespoon olive oil in a large skillet over medium-low heat. Add the shallots and cook, stirring occasionally, until the shallots are soft but not brown, about 2 minutes. Stir in the rice and continue cooking until the grains of rice are opaque, about 2 minutes longer.

4. Add the wine and cook over medium-low heat until the rice absorbs the wine. Ladle 1 cup of the hot broth over the rice and simmer, stirring frequently, over medium-low heat until absorbed. Continue to add the broth ½ cup at a time and reduce it, stirring frequently, until the rice is creamy and tender but still slightly chewy in the center, about 20 minutes. Turn off the heat and salt to taste. Reserve any remaining broth for another use.

5. While the risotto finishes cooking, heat the duck confit in a medium skillet over medium heat until warmed through, turning once, about 5 minutes. Transfer the duck to a cutting board and tear it into bite-size pieces. Discard the bones.

6. Stir the duck and Parmesan into the risotto. Gently fold in the butternut squash. Divide the risotto among four to six plates. Garnish with additional Parmesan, if desired. Serve immediately.

Pan-seared Duck Breasts on Wild Rice Pancakes
with Mushrooms and Cilantro Sauce

For more than a decade, the historic Joel Palmer House has delighted wine country visitors with menus that revolve around wild mushrooms. When Chef Chris Czarnecki took over the kitchen from his dad, Jack, one of the dishes he added to the menu was this Asian-inspired pan-seared duck. The fat from the duck, the salt from the hoisin sauce, and the umami of the mushrooms combine to create what Czarnecki calls "an awesome dance in the mouth."

CILANTRO SAUCE

- 1½ cups fresh cilantro leaves (from about ½ bunch)
- 1 bunch scallions, light green and white parts only, chopped (about ½ cup)
- ½ cup extra-virgin olive oil
- Juice of 1 lime

WILD RICE PANCAKES

- ½ cup all-purpose flour
- ¼ cup wild rice, cooked
- 2 tablespoons basmati rice, cooked
- 4 tablespoons reduced-fat milk
- 1 egg
- 2 tablespoons finely chopped red onion
- ½ teaspoon salt

DUCK WITH MUSHROOMS

- 4 (5- to 6- ounce) Muscovy duck breasts
- 1 medium red onion, thinly sliced
- 1 large portobello mushroom, thinly sliced
- 1 tablespoon hoisin sauce
- Corn oil, if needed

4 SERVINGS

1. **Make the cilantro sauce:** Blend the cilantro, scallions, olive oil, and lime juice in the bowl of a food processor fitted with a steel blade attachment until well combined but not completely smooth. Cover and refrigerate until ready to use.

2. **Make the pancakes:** Whisk the flour, wild rice, basmati rice, milk, egg, onion, and salt together in a small bowl. Set aside.

3. **Make the duck:** Score the skin side of the duck breasts by making four slices across each piece, cutting through the skin and down almost to the meat so fat can escape. Cook the duck, skin side down, in a large skillet over medium heat until the skin is brown and crisp, about 6 minutes. Turn the duck over and cook until medium-rare, about 4 minutes longer. Test a piece for doneness.* If it is too rare, continue cooking for 1 to 2 minutes longer. Remove the duck from the skillet and cover with foil to keep warm.

4. Add the onion to the skillet and cook over medium heat until transparent, about 4 minutes. Add the mushroom and cook over medium heat until softened, about 5 minutes longer. Transfer the onion and mushroom to a small bowl and mix with the hoisin sauce. Cover and set aside.

5. Check the skillet to make sure there is enough duck fat to cook the pancakes. If there is not enough left, coat the bottom of the skillet with a thin layer of corn oil. Pour ¼-cup portions of the pancake batter into the skillet to make four small pancakes. Cook the pancakes over medium heat until light brown on both sides and cooked through, about 4 minutes per side.

6. Divide the pancakes among four plates and top each pancake with a serving of the mushroom sauce. Slice each duck breast along the score lines. Fan the slices out over the sauce-topped pancakes. Drizzle with the cilantro sauce and serve immediately.

*NOTE: Duck can turn tough quickly, so time the searing carefully and trust your eye. You can test the duck for doneness by poking the center of the breast with the point of a knife; if the meat is pleasantly pink, it is done.

THE JOEL PALMER HOUSE

IN 1996, Jack and Heidi Czarnecki shuttered their well-regarded restaurant Joe's, packed up their family, and moved from Reading, Pennsylvania, to Dayton, Oregon, to pursue their passion for wild mushrooms and fine wines.

The couple transformed a historic home into a fine dining restaurant that put Oregon wines, wild mushrooms, and truffles on a pedestal. "We wanted to have a restaurant that was reflective of everything you saw when you came into the valley," says Jack of The Joel Palmer House. "We also wanted to make people aware of the quality of the local wines, mushrooms, and truffles. People were peripherally aware that we have these things here, but we gave them a place to try them together."

Today, Jack and Heidi are settling into retirement while their son Chris works to transform foraged finds into the restaurant's mushroom-centric menu. "The main focus of our menu has always been the seasonality of the mushrooms," says Chris. "Most people think of the seasons in terms

of spring, summer, fall, and winter, but we think of them in terms of morels, chanterelles, matsutake, and truffles. We adjust the menu based on those changing seasons, which can vary significantly from year to year based on the weather and what the spores are doing."

Sometimes mushroom seasons overlap and the kitchen has a glut of local mushrooms. Other times, Chris has to dip into the stash of mushrooms he dries and freezes throughout the year. In either case, wine country guests can always count on a few menu standards, among them a full-bodied wild mushroom soup and Heidi's wild mushroom tart.

However, Chris has found room to inject his personality into the menu as well. His self-described freestyle approach draws inspiration from various cuisines, with mushrooms serving as the common thread. "I do not limit myself to French or Italian or even a Northwest style of cuisine," he says. "I can do all of those things because we've got the local mushrooms serving as the core of what we do."

6 COOKING WITH OREGON'S BOTTLED BOUNTY

Black Butte Porter Mustard

Instead of serving ubiquitous bottled condiments at Deschutes Brewery in Bend, Chef Matt Neltner makes his own spicy mustard for brewpub diners. The condiment is a great accompaniment to soft pretzels and a standout spread for roast beef sandwiches as well. Black Butte Porter is widely available, but you can substitute your favorite porter instead.

½ cup dry mustard

2 tablespoons packed dark brown sugar

2 tablespoons honey

2 tablespoons lemon juice

2 tablespoons malt vinegar

¾ cup mayonnaise

¼ cup Black Butte Porter

MAKES ABOUT 1½ CUPS

1. Whisk the dry mustard and sugar together in a medium bowl. Whisk in the honey, lemon juice, and vinegar until a thick paste forms.

2. Fold in the mayonnaise with a rubber spatula until well combined. Gently stir in the porter until well combined. The mustard will be slightly runny.

3. Cover the bowl with plastic wrap and refrigerate until the mustard sets, about 1 hour. Transfer to a lidded container and refrigerate until ready to use. Stored in the refrigerator, the mustard will keep for about 1 month.

Sweet Cider-Onion Marmalade

I first tried a jammy red wine–onion marmalade at a restaurant called Trellis in Washington. I later adapted the recipe to use one of my favorite market finds: hard apple cider from Wandering Aengus Ciderworks. The marmalade can serve as a cheese plate condiment and as a spread for grilled cheese sandwiches, though I've been known to use it as a pizza or flatbread topping as well. This recipe yields ample marmalade, so plan on packing some into jars to share with family and friends.

2 cups fresh orange juice

2 tablespoons unsalted butter

2 tablespoons extra-virgin olive oil

3 red onions, thinly sliced

2 yellow onions, thinly sliced

2 tablespoons sugar

1 teaspoon salt, plus more for seasoning

¾ cup hard apple cider

⅓ cup honey

Zest from 1 orange

Leaves from 5 fresh thyme sprigs

MAKES ABOUT 5 CUPS

1. Bring the orange juice to a simmer in a small saucepan over medium heat. Continue to simmer until the orange juice has reduced to ½ cup, about 30 minutes. Cover and set aside.

2. Warm the butter and olive oil in a large saucepan over medium heat. Once the butter has melted, add the red onions, yellow onions, sugar, and salt. Cook, stirring occasionally, until the onions are translucent and soft, about 20 minutes.

3. Stir in the cider and reduced orange juice. Continue to cook, stirring occasionally, until the liquid has reduced by half, about 15 minutes. Stir in the honey, orange zest, and thyme and cook for 5 minutes longer. Taste and adjust salt as needed.

4. Use the marmalade immediately or cool and transfer to an airtight container. Stored in the refrigerator, the marmalade will keep for about 1 week.

Recipe from HANK SAWTELLE

Lambic Vinaigrette

In classic vinaigrettes, the sourness comes from vinegar or citrus juice. Here, my beer-loving friend Hank Sawtelle substitutes a sour fruit beer called lambic for vinegar to create a dressing with a subtly fruity flavor. Use this vinaigrette to dress a green salad or grilled vegetables. Sour fruit beers are available from Cascade Brewing in seven states and through the brewery's website.

¼ cup sour fruit beer

2 tablespoons apple cider vinegar

1 tablespoon minced shallot

1 teaspoon Dijon mustard

¼ teaspoon salt

½ cup neutral-flavored oil, such as grapeseed oil or canola oil

1 tablespoon sugar (optional)

MAKES 1 CUP

1. Whisk the beer, vinegar, shallot, mustard, and salt together in a small bowl until well combined.

2. Continue to whisk the dressing while drizzling the oil into the bowl in a thin stream. Whisk until emulsified. Taste the dressing and, if desired, whisk in the sugar. Stored in an airtight container in the refrigerator, the vinaigrette will keep for about 1 week. Re-whisk before using.

Arugula Salad with Glazed Walnuts
and Pinot Noir–Tarragon Vinaigrette

Chef Dolan Lane served this zippy arugula salad at a Plate & Pitchfork farm dinner years ago. The inspiration: plump blueberries from Smith BerryBarn's 30-acre family farm. Lane boils the blueberries with Oregon pinot noir to create this deep garnet vinaigrette. A bit of crumbled blue cheese would be a nice garnish here.

GLAZED WALNUTS

- 1 cup walnuts
- 1½ tablespoons light corn syrup
- 2 teaspoons sugar
- Salt and freshly ground black pepper

ARUGULA SALAD WITH PINOT NOIR–TARRAGON VINAIGRETTE

- ¼ cup pinot noir
- 3 tablespoons blueberries, plus more for garnish (optional)
- 3 tablespoons balsamic vinegar
- 2 tablespoons red wine vinegar
- 1 small shallot, minced (about 3 tablespoons)
- 2 fresh tarragon sprigs, leaves removed and finely chopped
- ½ cup extra-virgin olive oil
- Salt and freshly ground black pepper
- 14 ounces arugula

8 SERVINGS

1. **Make the glazed walnuts:** Position a rack in the center of the oven. Preheat the oven to 350°F and line a small baking sheet with parchment paper. Arrange the walnuts on the baking sheet and bake until lightly toasted, about 4 minutes.

2. Stir the warm walnuts, corn syrup, sugar, and a pinch of salt and pepper together in a small bowl with a rubber spatula until well combined. Spread the walnuts out on the baking sheet and bake, stirring occasionally, until the walnuts are golden and shiny but not sticky, about 5 minutes. Remove from the oven and set aside to cool.

3. **Make the salad and vinaigrette:** Combine the pinot noir and blueberries in a small saucepan. Bring the mixture to a simmer over medium heat and continue simmering until the blueberries release their juices, about 3 minutes. Add the balsamic vinegar and reduce the mixture by half over medium heat.

4. Strain the berry mixture into a medium bowl. Discard the berry pulp. Whisk the red wine vinegar, shallot, and tarragon into the bowl. Whisk in the olive oil. Salt and pepper to taste.

5. Toss the arugula with the vinaigrette in a large bowl until well combined. Divide the salad among eight salad plates. Garnish with the walnuts and additional blueberries, if desired. Serve immediately.

Recipe from LINDA KISTNER OF ABACELA VINEYARD & WINERY

Shrimp and White Bean Salad
with Lime-Cilantro Vinaigrette

Earl and Hilda Jones moved from Pensacola, Florida, to southern Oregon's Umpqua Valley to find the perfect climate to produce Spanish wines. Many of their grape varietals were firsts for Oregon, including their albariño. Tasting room manager Linda Kistner developed the recipe for this citrusy summer salad that uses the crisp white wine to poach shrimp. It's always a hit when she serves it with tortilla chips for dipping at the winery's annual fiesta.

SHRIMP AND WHITE BEAN SALAD

- 1½ cups Abacela albariño, or similarly crisp white wine
- ½ pound medium shrimp, peeled and deveined
- 1 (15-ounce) can cannellini beans, rinsed and drained
- ½ medium cucumber, peeled, seeded, and finely diced
- ½ red bell pepper, seeded and finely diced
- ¼ cup fresh cilantro leaves, roughly chopped

LIME-CILANTRO VINAIGRETTE

- ½ cup fresh cilantro leaves
- 1 tablespoon honey
- ¼ teaspoon ground cumin
- 1 small jalapeño chile, seeded and finely diced
- Zest and juice of 1 lime
- Juice of ½ lemon
- 1 garlic clove, minced (optional)
- ⅓ cup extra-virgin olive oil
- Salt and freshly ground black pepper

4 SERVINGS

1. **Make the salad:** Bring the wine to a simmer in a small saucepan over medium heat. Poach the shrimp in the wine until pink, about 3 minutes. Drain the shrimp and transfer to a medium bowl. Discard the wine.

2. Add the beans, cucumber, bell pepper, and cilantro to the bowl and toss with the shrimp until well combined. Set aside.

3. **Make the vinaigrette:** Blend the cilantro, honey, cumin, jalapeño, lime zest, lime juice, lemon juice, and garlic, if desired, in the bowl of a food processor fitted with a steel blade attachment until smooth. Slowly pour in the olive oil with the motor running and blend until well combined. Salt and pepper to taste.

4. Pour the vinaigrette over the salad and toss until well combined. Salt and pepper to taste. Let the salad sit for a few minutes to let the flavors meld, then serve.

ABACELA VINEYARD & WINERY

EARL AND HILDA JONES brought a slice of Spanish culture to an unassuming southern Oregon hillside when they planted it with the grape they'd long loved: Spain's noble tempranillo.

In the mid-1990s, the Joneses made a cross-country move to Roseburg after they discovered that the city's climate was well suited to growing tempranillo grapes. In just a few years, their gamble — one backed by exhaustive research and many hours of hard work — paid off. The Joneses realized their dream of making the first commercial tempranillo in the Pacific Northwest.

Earl is now lauded as the forerunner in the tempranillo movement in the United States. "I started the tempranillo trend in the States, and now there are something like 100 wineries making it," he says. "I am the granddaddy of tempranillo in America — of fine, quality, premium tempranillo."

But it was Hilda who encouraged her husband to diversify their portfolio beyond the noble grape. "She said we shouldn't put all of our eggs in one basket, and I listened to her," Earl admits. Abacela's deep portfolio now encompasses multiple tempranillos and other Spanish varietals like albariño and garnacha. Each Abacela wine offers a taste of Spanish culture, just as the Joneses envisioned it would when they moved west to make wine.

Watermelon Panzanella
with Aged Balsamic Vinegar

The Italian bread salad known as panzanella traditionally consists of basil, onions, tomatoes, and hunks of bread tossed with vinegar and olive oil. In my version, chunks of juicy watermelon replace the tomato while peppery arugula and aromatic mint stand in for the basil. A finishing drizzle of aged balsamic vinegar gives the salad greater complexity. You can purchase locally produced aged balsamic vinegar from Cooper Mountain Vineyards.

4 SERVINGS

- ½ loaf rustic country bread, crust removed and torn into ½-inch pieces (about 2 cups)
- 3 tablespoons extra-virgin olive oil
- 2 tablespoons champagne vinegar
- ¼ teaspoon honey
  Salt and freshly ground black pepper
- 1 (3½-pound) watermelon, rind removed and cut into ½-inch cubes (about 5 cups)
- 4 ounces fresh mozzarella cheese, roughly chopped
- 2 ounces baby arugula
- 12 fresh mint leaves, torn
  Aged balsamic vinegar

1. Position a rack in the center of the oven and preheat the oven to 375°F. Arrange the bread pieces on a large baking sheet and bake until lightly toasted, about 5 minutes. Remove from the oven and set aside to cool.

2. Whisk the olive oil, vinegar, and honey together in a small bowl. Salt and pepper to taste.

3. Toss the bread, watermelon, mozzarella, arugula, and mint with the vinaigrette in a large salad bowl until well combined. Salt and pepper to taste. Drizzle the aged balsamic vinegar over the salad and serve immediately.

Dr. Robert Gross

COOPER MOUNTAIN VINEYARDS

THE FLAVOR OF Cooper Mountain Vineyards' Apicio balsamic vinegar can come as a surprise to anyone used to the thin, watery balsamic vinegar most Americans stock in their pantries. The distinct vinegar is sweet, slightly syrupy, and pungent — an Oregon-made version of the famed Italian balsamic vinegar from Modena.

During trips to Italy in the late 1990s, Cooper Mountain's founder, Dr. Robert Gross, became fascinated with aged balsamic vinegar and began wondering why no one was making it from grape juice in Oregon. The hurdle, he quickly learned, was acquiring the famous barrels that give aged balsamic vinegar its unique flavor profile.

Gross eventually charmed a battery of barrels out of master barrel maker F. Renzi; in 2000, he put the barrels to use and set about making balsamic vinegar from a blend of Cooper Mountain's chardonnay and pinot noir juice. The winery staff put the first vinegar into barrels following the fall crush and aged it for six years before a drop hit the local market. Now, they bottle a small batch of vinegar each fall and boil down another 150 gallons of grape juice postcrush to keep the balsamic making tradition alive.

Cooper Mountain's Apicio balsamic vinegar is subtly sweet, with a viscosity that makes it an ideal finishing vinegar for everything from a cheese plate to salmon (page 166) and watermelon panzanella (page 212). In the years to come, Gross believes the winery's aged balsamic vinegar will become even more intruging and valuable to home chefs. "The longer it ages, the more complex the vinegar will become," says Gross. "We still have some years to go, but we are looking forward to releasing our 12-, 15-, and ultimately 25-year-old balsamic vinegar."

Grilled Quail with Tempranillo Syrup

The Steamboat Inn's general manager (and resident chef) Patricia Lee turns local tempranillo from Abacela Vineyard & Winery or Reustle Prayer Rock Vineyards into a vivid crimson syrup to accompany tender grilled quail. Since quail are quite small, Lee recommends serving this dish as a first course for a dinner party. It is also a nice light summer supper when served over a bed of greens.

GRILLED QUAIL

- 6 quail, breastbone and backbone removed
- ⅓ cup extra-virgin olive oil
- 3 garlic cloves, roughly chopped
- 3 tablespoons finely chopped fresh rosemary

TEMPRANILLO SYRUP

- 1 (750-milliliter) bottle tempranillo
- 3 tablespoons packed dark brown sugar

  Salt and freshly ground black pepper

6 SERVINGS

1. **Make the quail:** Place the quail in a dish large enough to fit the quail in a single layer. Whisk the olive oil, garlic, and rosemary together in a small bowl and pour the mixture over the quail. Cover the dish with plastic wrap and refrigerate for at least 2 hours or up to 6 hours.

2. **Make the tempranillo syrup:** Bring the wine and sugar to a boil, stirring occasionally, in a medium saucepan. Reduce the heat to medium and cook until the wine is syrupy and has reduced to about ½ cup, about 40 minutes. (The syrup will thicken slightly as it cools.) Remove the saucepan from the heat, cover, and set aside.

3. Preheat the grill for direct grilling over medium-hot charcoal or medium heat. Oil the grill grates. Remove the quail from the marinade and brush off any excess rosemary. Sprinkle the quail with salt and pepper.

4. Grill the quail until the skin is golden brown and the meat is cooked through, about 4 minutes per side. The meat will still be slightly pink. Transfer the quail to a plate and cover with foil. Let rest for 5 minutes.

5. Transfer the quail to a serving platter or individual plates and drizzle with the tempranillo syrup before serving.

Espresso Stout–braised Pork Shoulder

My husband improvised a version of this recipe after we toured Laurelhurst Brewery in Portland and came home with a giant bottle of their Espresso Stout. The flavors of the beer and coffee combine to create an earthy sauce, perfect for coating shredded pork shoulder. Serve the meat in sandwiches or piled atop mashed potatoes with a pint of stout on the side to wash it down. Laurelhurst Brewery's Espresso Stout or Hopworks Urban Brewery's Organic Survival Seven-Grain Stout works well for this dish.

1 (3-pound) bone-in pork shoulder blade roast

Salt and freshly ground black pepper

2 tablespoons vegetable oil

1 medium yellow onion, thinly sliced

5 cups (40 ounces) espresso stout

⅓ cup packed dark brown sugar

3 tablespoons balsamic vinegar

6 SERVINGS

1. Rub the pork with the salt and pepper. Heat the oil in a large lidded pot over medium-high heat and brown the meat on all sides. Remove the pork from the pot.

2. Add the onion to the pot and cook, stirring occasionally, until translucent, about 5 minutes. Stir in the stout, sugar, and balsamic vinegar and bring to a simmer over high heat.

3. Reduce the heat to low and return the pork to the pot. Cover the pot with a tight-fitting lid and simmer until the meat is fork-tender and easily pulls away from the bone, about 3 hours.

4. Position a rack in the center of the oven and preheat the oven to 350°F. Remove the pork from the pot and place it in a large baking dish. Bake until lightly browned, about 20 minutes.

5. While the pork browns, place a large strainer over a large bowl and pour the contents of the pot through the strainer, discarding the solids. Bring the liquid to a boil in a medium saucepan over high heat until it has reduced by about half and has a consistency similar to barbecue sauce.

6. Remove the pork from the oven and shred it into large pieces using two forks. Discard any large pieces of fat. Ladle the sauce over the shredded pork (you may not need all of it) and toss gently to coat the meat. Serve immediately.

CLEAR CREEK DISTILLERY

THE NEIGHBORHOOD RESIDENTS are just waking when Clear Creek Distillery's small staff arrives at their northwest Portland facility and begins turning nearly 30,000 pounds of cherries into the clear, powerful spirit called kirschwasser. The taut-skinned cherries are one of the first fruits to arrive at the distillery each year. As the seasons progress, the talented team will distill an abundance of blackberries, raspberries, loganberries, plums, pears, and apples into Clear Creek's renowned pure fruit spirits.

However, the distillery didn't always work with such a broad range of fruits. When Steve McCarthy founded the company in 1985, he focused on making the bone-dry digestif known as eau-de-vie from Oregon pears — and with good reason. During his European travels, he'd learned that Oregon's Bartlett pears were the same pear variety the French used to make the eau-de-vie *au poire* he loved to drink abroad.

McCarthy decided he would learn to make the spirit using traditional techniques, European pot stills, and pears from his family orchard. Once he perfected his pear eau-de-vie, he imagined, he'd start experimenting with spirits made from other Oregon fruits.

"My instant conceptual leap was to go from making eau-de-vie of pear on one still to making all of the kinds of eau-de-vie that you'll find in Alsace or parts of Switzerland," he says. "There's eau-de-vie of blue plum, eau-de-vie of cherries, apple brandy, eau-de-vie of holly berries, spruce buds, pine cones — you name it — all over Europe. My instant vision was that we'd do all of that."

Over the next 25 years, McCarthy slowly expanded his product line to include seven different eaux-de-vie; he also created a handful of fruit liqueurs that appease customers who find eau-de-vie to be too bracing. From a raspberry eau-de-vie to the kirschwasser, the distillery's products now rival the best in Europe. But most importantly, the spirits capture the essence of Oregon's finest fruits in every bottle.

Steve McCarthy

Flat-Iron Steaks with Apple Brandy Pan Sauce

Lucinda Parker uses the apple brandy her husband, Steve McCarthy, makes at Portland's renowned Clear Creek Distillery to create a pan sauce for steak. I added shallots, beef broth, and butter to her recipe to give the pan sauce a silky texture and flavor boost.

4 **(6-ounce) flat-iron steaks**

Kosher salt and freshly ground black pepper

4 **garlic cloves, peeled**

2 **teaspoons fresh thyme**

1 **teaspoon red pepper flakes**

3 **tablespoons vegetable oil**

¼ **cup minced shallots**

½ **cup beef broth**

¼ **cup apple brandy**

3 **tablespoons unsalted butter, cut into ¼-inch cubes**

1 **tablespoon finely chopped fresh flat-leaf parsley**

1 **teaspoon lemon juice**

4 SERVINGS

1. Pat the steaks dry with a paper towel. Sprinkle the steaks with salt and pepper. Smash the garlic cloves with the side of a knife and smear one on each steak. Discard the cloves. Rub the thyme and red pepper flakes onto the steaks and set aside.

2. Heat the oil in a large skillet over medium-high heat until almost smoking. Add the steaks to the skillet and cook over medium-high heat until the edges begin to brown, about 4 minutes. Turn the steaks over and reduce the heat to medium. Continue cooking until the steaks reach the desired level of doneness, about 4 minutes for medium-rare. Transfer the steaks to a cutting board and cover with foil to keep warm.

3. Discard all but 1 tablespoon of the oil from the skillet. Add the shallots to the skillet and cook over medium-low heat, stirring occasionally, until golden brown, about 3 minutes. Add the beef broth and brandy to the skillet and scrape the flavorful browned bits from the bottom of the pan with a wooden spoon.

4. Reduce the heat to low and stir in the butter, one piece at a time, until melted. Continue to cook over low heat until the sauce thickens slightly, about 2 minutes. Stir in the parsley and lemon juice and remove the skillet from the heat.

5. Thinly slice the steaks and divide among four plates. Spoon the pan sauce over the steaks and serve immediately.

Red Wine–braised Beef Short Ribs
with Gremolata and Gorgonzola Cheese

Beef short ribs get a flavor boost from full-bodied cabernet sauvignon, Gorgonzola cheese, and the sprightly Italian garnish known as gremolata in this hearty winter dish. Chef Dustin Clark serves these fork-tender short ribs with his Balsamic-braised Radicchio Risotto (page 60), but the dish would be excellent with boiled potatoes or pasta as well.

NOTE: The short ribs must marinate for at least 8 hours.

RED WINE–BRAISED BEEF SHORT RIBS

- 3 pounds bone-in beef short ribs, about 2½ inches thick

  Salt

- 3 cups cabernet sauvignon
- 1 tablespoon canola oil
- 2 medium yellow onions, diced into ½-inch pieces
- 1 medium fennel bulb, diced into ½-inch pieces
- 1 large carrot, peeled and diced into ½-inch pieces
- 2 cups beef broth
- 2 bay leaves

GREMOLATA

- ¼ cup walnuts, toasted and roughly chopped
- 3 tablespoons fresh flat-leaf parsley, finely chopped

  Zest of 1 orange

- ¼ cup Gorgonzola cheese, at room temperature

4 SERVINGS

1. **Make the short ribs:** Rub the short ribs generously with salt and place in a large, shallow baking dish. Set aside.

2. Bring the wine to a boil over medium-high heat in a medium saucepan. Continue simmering the wine over medium-high heat until reduced by one-third. Let cool to room temperature. Pour the wine over the ribs, cover, and refrigerate for at least 8 hours or overnight.

3. Heat the oil over medium heat in a large, lidded ovenproof pot. Add the onions, fennel, and carrot and cook, stirring occasionally, until they start to soften and caramelize, about 5 minutes. Remove the short ribs from the marinade and add the marinade to the pot. Reduce by half over medium-high heat, about 5 minutes. Add the beef broth and bring to a simmer.

4. Add the short ribs and bay leaves to the pot, cover, and cook over low heat until the short ribs are fork-tender, about 2 hours 30 minutes. Remove the pot from the heat and discard the bay leaves. Let the short ribs rest in the pot for 45 minutes.

5. **Make the gremolata:** Mix the walnuts, parsley, and orange zest together in a small bowl. Crumble the cheese into a separate small bowl and set aside.

6. Position a rack in the top of the oven and preheat the oven to broil. Slide the pot into the oven and brown the short ribs for 5 minutes.

7. Divide the short ribs among four plates. Discard the broth. Garnish with the gremolata and cheese and serve immediately.

Coffee Caramel Sauce

This coffee-scented sauce celebrates Oregon's ever-evolving coffee culture. It is lovely spooned over vanilla ice cream, but you can also use it to dress up such baked goods as a fudgy brownie.

1¼ cups heavy cream
1 tablespoon finely ground coffee
1½ cups sugar
⅓ cup water
¾ teaspoon vanilla extract

MAKES ABOUT 1½ CUPS

1. Warm the cream and coffee over low heat in a small saucepan until the cream turns light brown. Strain the cream through a fine-mesh strainer into a small bowl to remove the coffee particles. Strain again if necessary. Cover the cream to keep warm.

2. Combine the sugar and water in a medium saucepan and cook over low heat until the sugar dissolves, about 5 minutes. Do not stir the mixture.

3. Increase the heat to medium and boil uncovered until the sugar turns butterscotch brown or until it reaches 350°F on a candy thermometer, about 8 minutes. Occasionally, gently swirl the pan, but do not stir it, as it will ruin the sauce. Watch the mixture very carefully at the end, as it will burn quickly.

4. When the sugar has caramelized, remove the saucepan from the heat. Stand back to avoid splattering and slowly add the coffee-infused cream and vanilla to the saucepan. The cream will bubble and the caramel will solidify slightly.

5. Return the saucepan to the stove and simmer the sauce over low heat, stirring constantly with a wooden spoon, until the caramel dissolves and the sauce is smooth, about 2 minutes. Pour the caramel into a jar. Let the caramel cool to room temperature on the counter for at least 2 hours before using. The sauce will thicken slightly as it sits. Stored in an airtight container in the refrigerator, the sauce will keep for about 2 weeks.

Recipe from LOUISA NEUMANN

Grilled Honey-Balsamic–glazed Stone Fruits
with Honeyed Mascarpone Whipped Cream

Local honey from the farmers' market or a company like Eugene-based GloryBee Foods glazes grilled fruit in this summer dessert. I make the dessert with a mix of peaches and nectarines so that each individual gets a taste of both fruits. The honey-mascarpone whipped cream is a fitting topping, but you can serve this dish with plain whipped cream or scoops of vanilla ice cream if you prefer.

HONEY-BALSAMIC–GLAZED STONE FRUITS

- ½ cup honey
- ¼ cup balsamic vinegar
- ½ teaspoon vanilla extract
- ⅛ teaspoon ground cinnamon
- 6 peaches or nectarines, or combination thereof, halved and pitted

HONEYED MASCARPONE WHIPPED CREAM

- 1 cup heavy cream
- ¼ cup plus 2 tablespoons mascarpone cheese
- 1 tablespoon honey
- ¼ teaspoon vanilla extract

6 SERVINGS

1. **Make the glazed fruit:** Whisk the honey, vinegar, vanilla, and cinnamon together in a small bowl. Place the fruit in a shallow baking dish and pour the honey glaze over the top. Gently toss the fruit to combine. Cover the dish with plastic wrap and let the fruit marinate for 30 minutes at room temperature.

2. **Make the whipped cream:** Beat the cream, cheese, honey, and vanilla in a medium bowl with an electric mixer on medium speed until soft peaks form, about 3 minutes. Cover and refrigerate until ready to use.

3. Preheat the grill for direct grilling over medium-hot charcoal or medium-high heat. Oil the grill grates. Grill the fruit, cut side down, until lightly colored but not black, about 3 minutes. Flip the fruit over and grill for 2 minutes longer, skin side down. Baste the fruit with the marinade several times during grilling. Remove the fruit from the grill.

4. Pour the remaining marinade into a small saucepan and reduce over medium-high heat until warm and slightly syrupy, about 5 minutes.

5. Divide the fruit among six bowls. Garnish the fruit with a drizzle of the warm sauce and a dollop of the whipped cream. Serve immediately.

Recipe from **COURTNEY SPROULE OF DIN DIN**

Brandied Cherries

Courtney Sproule macerates sweet summer cherries in pinot noir and the cherry brandy called kirschwasser to give brandied cherries a local twist. Clear Creek Distillery's kirschwasser and a pinot noir with strong cherry notes play up the flavor of the fruit. After the cherries soak for four days, Sproule uses them to top savory dishes like chicken liver mousse and to gild desserts like a hazelnut panna cotta at dinners for her roving supper club, din din.

1 large orange

1 cup sugar

1 cup water

2 cups pinot noir

3 tablespoons kirschwasser (cherry brandy)

1 tablespoon vanilla extract

2 pounds sweet dark cherries, such as Bing cherries, stemmed, pitted, and halved

MAKES ABOUT 4½ CUPS

1. Remove the orange peel, but not the pith, in long strips using a vegetable peeler. Reserve the orange for another use. Bring the orange peel, sugar, and water to a simmer over medium heat in a medium saucepan. Continue simmering, stirring occasionally, until the sugar dissolves, about 2 minutes. Stir in the wine and simmer gently over medium-low heat for 5 minutes.

2. Strain the wine mixture into a medium bowl. Discard the orange peel. Stir the kirschwasser and vanilla into the mixture.

3. Divide the cherries between two 1-pint mason jars. Pour the wine mixture over the cherries, dividing it equally between the jars. Let cool, then cover and refrigerate for 4 days before using. Stored in the refrigerator, the cherries will keep for about 1 month.

Athena Pappas and Stewart Boedecker

BOEDECKER CELLARS

IN THEIR CAVERNOUS URBAN WINERY, Stewart Boedecker and Athena Pappas handcraft small lots of high-quality, food-oriented wines from a fruit-forward chardonnay to limited releases like the syrah they bottled in 2008. But what sets this Portland-based winery apart are bottlings of structured pinot noir — particularly two cuvées that reflect the individual palate and winemaking style of each winemaker.

After learning the winemaking ropes through classes and apprenticeships at various Willamette Valley wineries, the couple transitioned to making wine under the Boedecker Cellars label in 2003. They quickly learned, however, that they had different opinions about which style of pinot noir they should produce. Rather than cause a marital row, the couple decided to make two cuvée blends and bottle them under the name of the individual winemaker, Stewart or Athena.

Every year, Boedecker and Pappas obtain fruit from a handful of Willamette Valley vineyards, ferment the grapes in vineyard blocks, and age the wine in barrels for 18 months. When the time comes to determine which wines will go into their blends, they spend a series of weekends blind-tasting through the barrels and discussing the body, character, and expressions of each wine. They reserve wine from any particularly interesting barrels for single-vineyard pinots, then mark the rest as his and hers to blend into their individual cuvées.

The couple's distinct winemaking styles show through in their individual labels. Boedecker appreciates classic Oregon pinot noir with light red fruit, soft tannins, and bright, zingy acidity, while Pappas prefers dark black fruit flavors, heartier tannins, and a little spice. "When you put those two styles together, they become average wine, but when you separate them into two blends, they each become something unique," says Pappas. "Stewart's blend is gorgeous and refined and elegant, and my blend tends to be bigger and a little heartier."

What the winemakers have in common is a desire to create food-friendly wines and a passion for the challenging pinot noir grape. "Pinot noir is so finicky, delicate, and high maintenance," says Pappas. "You can't predict what it is going to do or where it is going to go. The flavors change so much when the wine ages in the barrel. It's so much work but it keeps it interesting. I think that's why we like it."

Molasses-Ginger Stout Cake with Ginger Glaze

Kir Jensen is a sugar pusher. From the window of her bubble gum pink and chocolate brown food cart, she encourages consumption of all things sweet, from her chocolaty Triple Threat cookies to daily specials that highlight Oregon's bounty. Here, she's adapted a recipe from lauded pastry chef Claudia Fleming to use Oregon stout and create a complex, deeply spiced molasses-ginger cake. You can make it at least one day ahead of serving it as it gets better with age.

NOTE: The batter needs to chill for a few hours before baking.

MOLASSES-GINGER STOUT CAKE

- 1 cup stout
- 1 cup blackstrap molasses
- ½ teaspoon baking soda
- ½ cup packed dark brown sugar
- ½ cup granulated sugar
- 3 eggs, at room temperature
- ¾ cup vegetable oil
- 1 tablespoon finely grated fresh ginger
- 1½ teaspoons vanilla extract
- 2 cups all-purpose flour
- 2 tablespoons ground ginger
- 1½ teaspoons baking powder
- 1 teaspoon ground cinnamon
- ¼ teaspoon ground cardamom
- ¼ teaspoon ground cloves
- ¼ teaspoon freshly grated nutmeg
  Salt
  Cooking spray

GINGER GLAZE

- ½ cup granulated sugar
- ½ cup water
- 2 tablespoons peeled and sliced fresh ginger

MAKES 1 (9-INCH) CAKE

1. **Make the cake:** Bring the stout and molasses to a boil in a large saucepan. Remove the saucepan from the heat and whisk in the baking soda. The beer will bubble and foam a bit. Let cool.

2. Whisk the brown sugar, granulated sugar, and eggs together in a medium bowl until well combined. Whisk in the vegetable oil, fresh ginger, and vanilla. Whisk in the cool beer mixture.

3. Whisk the flour, ground ginger, baking powder, cinnamon, cardamom, cloves, nutmeg, and a pinch of salt together in a large bowl. Add the beer-sugar mixture to the bowl and whisk until smooth and well combined. The batter will be thin. Cover the bowl with plastic wrap and refrigerate for a few hours or overnight to thicken.

4. Position a rack in the center of the oven and preheat the oven to 350°F. Coat a 9-inch round baking pan with cooking spray. Pour the batter into the pan and bake until a tester stick inserted into the center of the cake comes out clean, about 55 minutes.

5. **Make the glaze:** Heat the granulated sugar, water, and ginger in a small saucepan over medium heat, stirring occasionally, until slightly syrupy, about 20 minutes. Strain the syrup into a small bowl. Discard the ginger. Let cool slightly before brushing the warm cake liberally with the syrup. Let the syrup cool on the cake for 10 minutes before serving.

FULL SAIL BREWING COMPANY

FULL SAIL BREWING COMPANY opened for business in the bones of an old Hood River fruit cannery with a recipe for Oregon's original amber ale and four employees. Though the veteran craft brewery has seen a great deal of growth since it began brewing in 1987 — production has increased from 287 barrels of beer that first year to more than 100,000 barrels a year today — the values CEO Irene Firmat instilled in her business have not changed.

Central to Full Sail's culture is a commitment to maintain a high-quality standard for their lineup of craft beers. In the brewery's early years, Executive Brewmaster Jamie Emmerson designed a manual brewing system to ensure consistent quality for decades to come. "It's really easy to make beer, but hard to make good beer and really hard to make good beer exactly the same way every time," says the brewery's marketing manager, Sandra Evans. "We need our amber ale, for example, to taste the same way every time, and we really strive for that high quality through the hands-on brewing process."

Full Sail's brewers recognized early on that ingredients matter too: The brewers only use four ingredients in their beers, and they find 95 percent of those ingredients locally. They purchase the majority of their hops and barley from Northwest farms and use water and yeast from their own backyard. The high-quality brews that result from their careful ingredient selection have won more than 100 medals and awards to date.

The amber ale that put Full Sail on the craft beer map is still the brewery's flagship beer. But the brewery has also garnered attention for its pale ales and lagers — and a culture that goes beyond the beer.

Environmental stewardship is at the core of Full Sail's culture and has been since the start. "Sustainability was part of our DNA from day one. Instead of building a brand-new building on a piece of property, we took this shell of an old dilapidated building and made it into a working business that provides family-wage jobs," says Evans.

The company further committed itself to environmentally friendly practices in the following years; the staff has implemented energy- and water-saving strategies and created a recycling program that allows them to reuse everything from wooden pallets to spent grain.

Full Sail is also recognized for being an employee-owned brewery. In 1999, the move to become employee owned fulfilled a long-held vision for Firmat and created an open work environment that allows every employee to participate in the dialogue concerning company decisions. "We're all pulling the rope in the same direction," says Evans. "We all have a personal interest in the company and take pride in it because we own a piece of this business."

Stout Ice Cream

Portland-based cooking instructor and writer Hank Sawtelle uses cornstarch as a thickener instead of egg yolks (which would interfere with the stout's flavor) in this inventive frozen treat. His recipe works well with any good stout, such as Ninkasi Brewing's Oatis Oatmeal Stout, Pelican Brewery's Tsunami Stout, or Full Sail Brewing Company's seasonal Imperial Stout.

1 (12-ounce) bottle stout
1½ cups heavy cream
⅓ cup sugar
⅛ teaspoon salt
2 tablespoons cornstarch
2 tablespoons water
½ teaspoon vanilla extract

MAKES ABOUT 1 QUART

1. Whisk the stout, cream, sugar, and salt together in a large saucepan over medium heat until the sugar and salt dissolve.

2. Whisk the cornstarch and water together in a small bowl to create a slurry. Whisk the slurry into the stout mixture until dissolved.

3. Bring the mixture to a simmer over medium heat. Continue simmering over medium heat, stirring frequently, until the liquid coats the back of a wooden spoon, about 5 minutes. Do not allow the mixture to boil.

4. Remove the saucepan from the heat and stir in the vanilla. Let cool until warm to the touch, then cover and refrigerate until well chilled, preferably 24 hours.

5. Transfer the chilled mixture to an ice cream maker and process according to the manufacturer's instructions. Serve immediately for soft-serve ice cream or transfer to an airtight container and place in the freezer for 2 hours to firm before serving. The ice cream will keep for about 2 weeks.

Vin Glacé Cake

Pastry chef Tobi Sovak's moist, golden vin glacé cake makes use of one of my favorite King Estate wines. The vin glacé dessert wine lends the cake a sweet backbone, while the olive oil imparts delicate fruity notes. In King Estate's hilltop restaurant outside Eugene, Sovak serves slices of the cake with estate-grown berries and a dollop of lightly sweetened whipped crème fraîche.

Cooking spray

- 3 cups all-purpose flour
- 2 teaspoons baking powder
- 2 teaspoons salt
- ½ teaspoon baking soda
- 2 cups plus 2 tablespoons sugar
- ½ cup plus 2 tablespoons (1¼ sticks) unsalted butter, at room temperature
- ½ cup extra-virgin olive oil
- 4 eggs
- 2 teaspoons lemon zest
- 1 (375-milliliter) bottle King Estate Vin Glacé or similar sweet white dessert wine

MAKES 1 (9-INCH) CAKE

1. Position a rack in the center of the oven and preheat the oven to 375°F. Coat a 9-inch round baking pan with cooking spray.

2. Sift the flour, baking powder, salt, and baking soda together in a medium bowl.

3. Mix 2 cups of the sugar and ½ cup of the butter together in the bowl of an electric mixer fitted with a paddle attachment on medium speed until light and fluffy. With the motor running, pour the olive oil into the bowl and mix until fully incorporated into the batter. Mix in the eggs and lemon zest on medium speed until well combined.

4. Mix the flour mixture into the bowl on medium speed, one-third at a time, alternating with the vin glacé, until both the flour and vin glacé are fully incorporated into the batter.

5. Pour the batter into the prepared cake pan. Bake until the top of the cake is set and starting to turn golden brown, about 20 minutes. Remove the cake from the oven.

6. Cut the remaining 2 tablespoons butter into ¼-inch pieces and dot the top of the cake with the pieces. Sprinkle the remaining 2 tablespoons sugar over the top of the cake. Return the cake to the oven and bake until the top is golden brown and a tester stick inserted into the middle of the cake comes out clean, about 25 minutes longer.

7. Let the cake cool slightly before removing it from the pan. Slice the cake into wedges and serve warm.

Blueberry, Lemon Cream, and Olive Oil Trifle

Chef Earl Hook became an early supporter of the Oregon Olive Mill when he started buying the mill's olive oil to serve at his northwest Portland restaurant. Here, he uses it in a light and lemony summer trifle. Hook quickly dips the ladyfingers in a mixture of sweet dessert wine and fruity olive oil before layering them with lemon cream and berries in a trifle dish.

NOTE: The trifle needs to chill at least three hours before serving.

LEMON CREAM

- 4 eggs
- 1 cup granulated sugar
- Zest of 1 lemon
- ⅔ cup lemon juice (from about 3 lemons)
- 4 tablespoons (½ stick) unsalted butter, cut into ½-inch cubes
- 1 cup heavy cream

OLIVE OIL TRIFLE

- 3 cups fresh blueberries
- ¼ cup confectioners' sugar, plus more for garnish (optional)
- 2 cups sweet white dessert wine
- ¼ cup extra-virgin olive oil
- 24 crisp ladyfingers

NOTE: Hook makes his trifle with huckleberries, but I found that it works equally well with more readily available blueberries. If you can find local huckleberries during their short, late-summer season, you can substitute them for the blueberries.

8 SERVINGS

1. **Make the lemon cream:** Bring 3 inches of water to a simmer in a large saucepan. Prepare an ice-water bath.

2. Mix the eggs and sugar together in the bowl of an electric mixer fitted with a whisk attachment on medium speed until light and fluffy. Mix in the lemon zest and lemon juice. Transfer the mixture to a medium stainless steel bowl and place the bowl above, but not in, the simmering water. Heat, whisking constantly, until the mixture is warm and thick like pudding, about 10 minutes.

3. Remove the bowl from the heat and whisk in the butter until melted. Place the bowl in the ice-water bath to cool.

4. Beat the cream in the bowl of an electric mixer fitted with a whisk attachment until stiff peaks form. Gently fold the whipped cream into the lemon mixture. Cover the bowl with plastic wrap and refrigerate until ready to use.

5. **Make the trifle:** Toss the blueberries with the confectioners' sugar in a medium bowl. Whisk the wine and olive oil together in a small bowl. Dip the ladyfingers in the wine-oil mixture, one at a time. Cover the bottom of a trifle dish or a large glass bowl with a layer of the soaked ladyfingers.

6. Spread a layer of the lemon cream over the ladyfingers. Scatter a handful of the blueberries over the top of the lemon cream. Dip another layer of ladyfingers in the wine-oil mixture and repeat the layering process until all of the ladyfingers, lemon cream, and blueberries are used up, ending with a layer of blueberries on top.

7. Cover the trifle with plastic wrap and refrigerate for at least 3 hours or overnight. Garnish with a dusting of confectioners' sugar, if desired, before serving.

OREGON OLIVE MILL

KEN AND PENNY DURANT are comfortable being front-runners in a new industry. In the early 1970s, they were among the first farmers to plant wine grapes in the Willamette Valley. And though neighboring farmers raised their eyebrows at the risk-taking couple, the vineyard venture paid off: The Durant's vineyard continues to thrive in an area now known for producing fine wine.

So when Ken decided to plant olive trees on the family's hillside property in 2005, he was prepared to deal with skeptics. The new venture was a gamble, but the family believed that olives could flourish in Oregon in the same way the grapes they once planted had. "We think it has great potential, and it fits really well with the wine grapes. A lot of the same techniques, from equipment to trellising and to a certain extent pruning, well, we can adapt those skills," says Ken's son Paul. "And honestly, it's just been a hell of a lot of fun and people have responded to it really well."

The olive oil project began with tree trials to determine which olive varieties could withstand Oregon's cool winters. Varieties like the cold hardy Arbequina olive survived cold snaps and produced enough fruit that the family decided to build Oregon's first olive mill in 2008. The mill stays busy each November, when the Durants harvest and press their olives. Currently, olives from their property account for about 15 percent of the oil they produce. Until the rest of their olive trees mature, they'll augment their harvest with California-grown olives to produce their oil.

But even a small percentage of Oregon-grown olives makes a difference in the final product. "It shows an impact when you blend it with other oils," says Paul. "It adds some flavor because it is generally a stronger-tasting oil. It has that grassy, green-banana taste and the fruitier parts of it are stronger."

Eventually, the family hopes other farmers will follow their lead and gamble with growing olives. "We hope at some point in the next few years that there will be the Oregon Olive Oil Council or something along those lines," says Paul. "We're not at that point where the grape industry was in the '70s where there are enough people to collaborate with, but I'm sure the olive oil industry will eventually get to that point too."

Paul Durant

HOUSE SPIRITS DISTILLERY

TAKE A GLANCE at the rustic wood shelves at the House Spirits Distillery tasting room and you'll spot the standbys: bottles of botanical gin and a bold aquavit that's developed a cult following over the years. Look beyond those buzzed-about bottles, however, and you'll discover a lesser-known lineup of niche, small-batch spirits called the Apothecary Line. This line showcases the diverse passions of a team of talented craft distillers and is just one of the many ways House Spirits keeps things interesting after nearly a decade in the business.

Back in 2002, former brewers and winemakers Lee Medoff and Christian Krogstad founded House Spirits with hopes of one day making fine Oregon whiskey. After a short stint in Corvallis, they moved production to Portland's Eastside neighborhood and continued to chase their whiskey dreams while perfecting a variety of other spirits. As the years passed, accolades for their flagship vodka, a genever-inspired style of gin, and that distinct aquavit racked up; in 2009, they released their first whiskey and started peddling it alongside other passion projects like ouzo, rum, and aged aquavit under their Apothecary Line.

Medoff branched off from the distillery in 2010, but the focus and intent of House Spirits remains the same. No matter the spirit, every House Spirits product captures the character of Oregon. The distillers don't reinvent the wheel, but rather give age-old spirits their own impression, stamp, or vision. In the case of their gin, for example, they don't make a Dutch gin or English gin. They make Oregon's Aviation Gin, which is their brainchild and indicative of Oregon's DIY spirit.

The same goes for the whiskey that motivated them all along. The House Spirits whiskey is unlike bourbon or Irish or Canadian whiskey. Tasting room guests can't pigeonhole it because the distillers are making a whiskey that's all Oregon — which is precisely why they love it.

Recipe from ALI JEPSON AND EVAN DOHRMANN

PDX Coffee Cocktail
with Chocolate Whipped Cream

The flavors of chocolate and orange combine in this warming, whiskey-laced coffee from one of Portland's favorite, but sadly shuttered, brunch spots, Little Red Bike Café. After many tests, former owners Ali Jepson and Evan Dohrmann discovered that whiskey from House Spirits Distillery gives this wintery cocktail the boozy boost they crave.

4 SERVINGS

CHOCOLATE WHIPPED CREAM

- 1 cup heavy cream
- 2 tablespoons confectioners' sugar
- 1½ tablespoons unsweetened Dutch-processed cocoa powder

COFFEE COCKTAIL

- 2½ cups freshly brewed strong coffee
- 2 tablespoons packed dark brown sugar
- 4 (1½-ounce) shots whiskey
- 4 ¼-inch orange slices

1. **Make the whipped cream:** Whip the cream in a small bowl with a hand mixer on medium speed until soft peaks form. Add the confectioners' sugar and cocoa powder and continue beating until thoroughly combined. Cover and refrigerate until ready to use.

2. **Make the cocktail:** Fill four small coffee mugs with hot water. Let the mugs warm up for a few minutes before discarding the water.

3. Fill each mug about three-quarters full with the coffee. Stir 1½ teaspoons of the brown sugar into each mug until dissolved. Stir 1 shot of the whiskey into each mug.

4. Rub and garnish the rim of each mug with an orange slice. Top with the whipped cream and serve immediately.

Berry Rosé Sangria

Spanish-born sangria gets an Oregon update care of local rosé wine and juicy berries. I adapted this blushing pink sangria from a recipe from Suzanne Bozarth that ran in Portland's *MIX* magazine; my twist substitutes raspberries and strawberries for peaches and blueberries and triple sec for the brandy she used. Play around with this flexible recipe to see which fruit and booze combinations suit your tastes.

1 cup fresh raspberries

1 cup fresh strawberries, hulled and halved

3 tablespoons sugar

¼ cup triple sec

1 (750-milliliter) bottle dry rosé wine

¾ cup sweet white dessert wine

6 SERVINGS

1. Combine the raspberries and strawberries in the bottom of a large pitcher. Sprinkle the berries with the sugar. Pour the triple sec into the pitcher and stir gently with a wooden spoon to combine. Refrigerate the berry mixture for 30 minutes.

2. Pour the rosé and dessert wine over the berries. Stir gently with a wooden spoon to combine. Chill for 1 hour longer before serving, as is or over ice.

7 SWEET TREATS FROM FRUIT TO NUTS

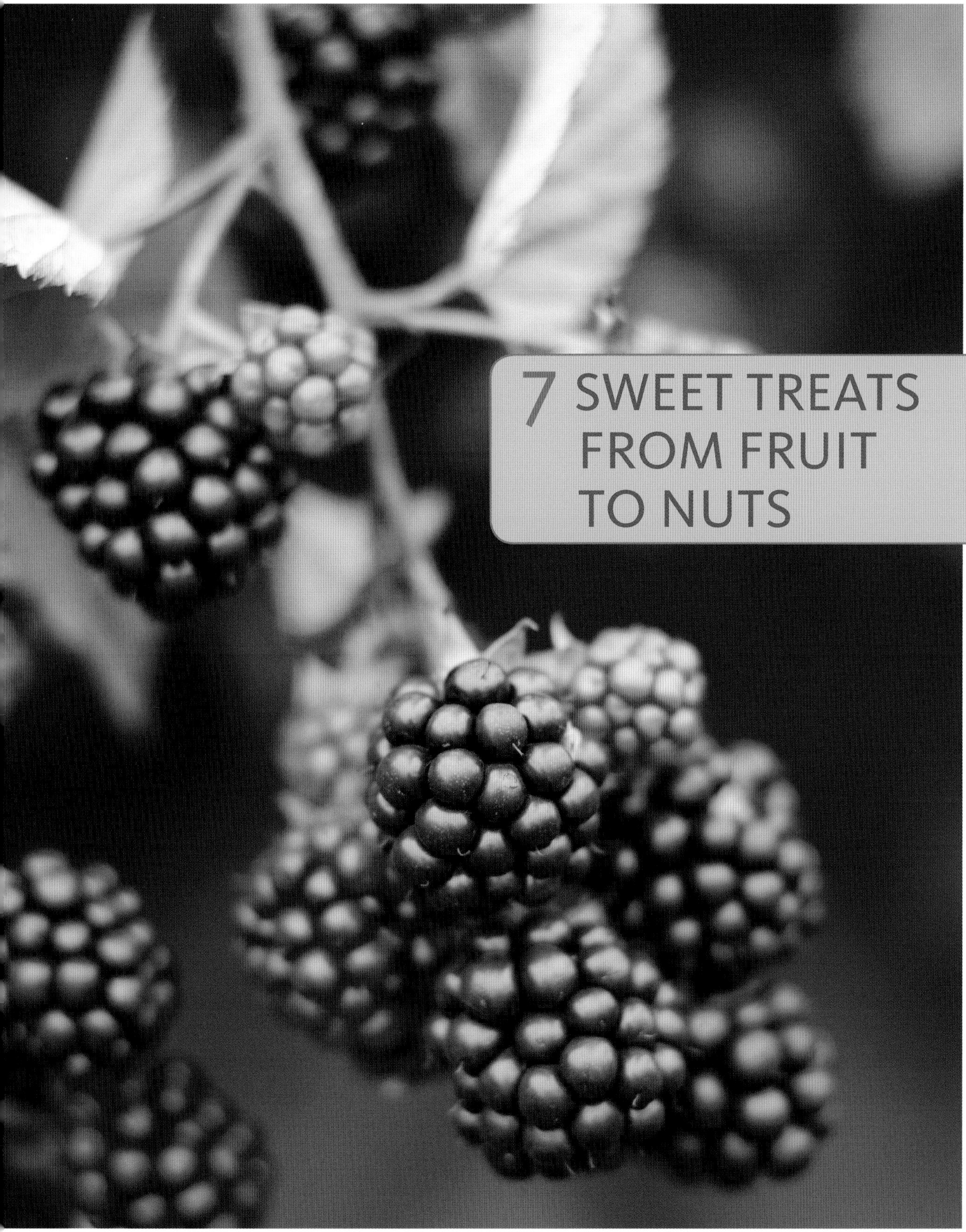

Sally Lunn Bread

Award-winning baker Tim Healea based the recipe for his light, buttery Sally Lunn Bread on James Beard's original recipe. Use slabs of the bread to make French toast or a BLT sandwich. Or enjoy lightly-toasted slices for breakfast with a generous spoonful of strawberry jam. Unlike the other baked-good recipes in this chapter, this recipe requires use of a kitchen scale. Healea asked that I call for ingredients by weight rather than volume to ensure that home cooks could successfully make this popular loaf at home.

370	grams all-purpose flour
44	grams sugar
12	grams instant yeast
8	grams salt
2	eggs
1	egg yolk
80	grams warm water
80	grams whole milk
90	grams unsalted butter, at room temperature and cut into ½-inch cubes
	Canola oil
	Cooking spray

MAKES 2 (4- BY 8-INCH) LOAFS

1. Mix the flour, sugar, yeast, and salt together on low speed in the bowl of an electric mixer fitted with a paddle attachment. Whisk the eggs, egg yolk, water, and milk together in a large measuring cup. Pour the egg mixture into the bowl with the mixer running, reserving about ¼ cup. Mix the dough on low speed until it starts to come together, about 1 minute.

2. Keeping the mixer running, add the remaining ¼ cup egg mixture to the dough. Once the liquid is incorporated, increase the speed to medium and add the butter, a few cubes at a time. Continue mixing the dough until well combined, about 4 minutes. The dough will look like a slightly rough cake batter and be quite wet.

3. Coat a large bowl with the canola oil. Transfer the dough to the bowl using a rubber spatula. Cover the bowl with plastic wrap, and let the dough rise in a warm place for 2 hours.

4. Coat two 4- by 8-inch loaf pans with cooking spray. Divide the dough between the pans. With lightly floured fingertips, gently press the dough to the edges of each pan to distribute it evenly. Allow the dough to rise, uncovered, in a warm place until it approaches the top of the pan, about 1 hour 30 minutes.

5. Position a rack in the center of the oven and preheat the oven to 375°F. Bake the bread until deep brown on top, about 35 minutes. Remove the bread from the pans immediately and transfer to a cooling rack to let cool completely before slicing.

Recipe from **DEANNA JOYER OF SAKURA RIDGE FARM AND LODGE**

Cherry Granola

Every summer, the owners of Sakura Ridge Farm and Lodge dry a portion of their cherry harvest to use in this subtly sweet from-scratch granola. If you have trouble finding brown rice syrup or barley malt syrup at your local grocer, look for them at a natural foods market.

8	cups old-fashioned oats
½	cup brown rice syrup
½	cup canola oil
¼	cup barley malt syrup
1	cup roasted hazelnuts, skinned
1	cup pumpkin seeds
1	cup walnuts, coarsely chopped
3	cups dried cherries
1	cup unsweetened flaked coconut

MAKES ABOUT 14 CUPS

1. Position two racks in the center of the oven and preheat the oven to 350°F. Line two large rimmed baking sheets with parchment paper.

2. Stir the oats, brown rice syrup, canola oil, and barley malt syrup together in a large bowl with a wooden spoon until the oats are moist and slightly clumpy. Divide the oats between the prepared baking sheets, spreading them out evenly. Bake for 10 minutes.

3. Remove the baking sheets from the oven and stir in the hazelnuts, pumpkin seeds, and walnuts, dividing them equally between the two baking sheets. Bake the granola for 10 minutes longer.

4. Remove the baking sheets from the oven and stir in the dried cherries and coconut flakes, dividing them equally between the two baking sheets. Bake until the oats are crisp and golden brown, about 15 minutes longer, removing the baking sheets from the oven every 5 minutes to give the granola a quick stir.

5. Let the granola cool on the baking sheets and then transfer it to an airtight container. The granola will keep for 1 week at room temperature or in the freezer for about 1 month.

Sakura Ridge Farm and Lodge

AT FIRST GLANCE, Sakura Ridge Farm and Lodge appears to be the sort of charmingly rustic retreat you'd expect to find in a small town like Hood River. But guests who look closely among the 3,000 fruit trees bordering the lodge will see that this peaceful getaway is also a working farm. At Sakura Ridge, the orchards are vast, the pear trees hang heavy with fruit, and the farm tools and tractors rest roadside waiting for the next morning's tasks.

Lodge guests who want to experience life on the farm can rise with the sun and meet resident farmer and co-owner John Joyer to help harvest fruit and complete the daily farm chores. They might sling half-moon-shaped pails over their shoulders and start plucking ripe red cherries from the trees.

Or they can try their hands at herding sheep and laying gopher traps as the sun creeps higher overhead. The reward comes when the inn's accomplished chef (and John's wife) Deanna serves breakfast hours later. Unlike guests who stayed in bed, the newly minted farmers know exactly where their food came from.

Blackberry-Cardamom Muffins

Pockets of blackberries give these sweet, subtly spiced muffins a tart bite, while grapeseed oil creates a light crumb. If you don't have grapeseed oil on hand, substitute another neutral oil, like canola oil, for similar results. As the market seasons shift, replace the blackberries with other fruits like peaches, blueberries, or rhubarb.

3 cups whole-wheat pastry flour

2 teaspoons baking powder

2 teaspoons ground cinnamon

½ teaspoon baking soda

½ teaspoon ground cardamom

½ teaspoon salt

2 eggs

1 cup packed dark brown sugar, plus more for topping (optional)

¾ cup unsweetened applesauce

¾ cup grapeseed oil

1½ cups fresh or frozen blackberries

MAKES 12 MUFFINS

1. Position a rack in the center of the oven and preheat the oven to 375°F. Line a standard-size 12-cup muffin tin with paper liners.

2. Whisk the flour, baking powder, cinnamon, baking soda, cardamom, and salt together in a large bowl. Whisk the eggs, sugar, applesauce, and grapeseed oil together in a separate bowl.

3. Make a well in the center of the flour mixture. Pour the oil mixture into the well and stir gently with a rubber spatula until the batter is just combined. Gently fold in the blackberries until evenly distributed throughout the batter.

4. Divide the batter among the cups, filling each one nearly full. If desired, sprinkle with additional sugar.

5. Bake the muffins until a tester stick inserted into the center comes out clean, about 20 minutes. Let the muffins cool in the tins for 10 minutes before transferring them to a rack. Serve warm or at room temperature. Stored in an airtight container at room temperature, the muffins will keep for about 3 days.

Lemon-Blueberry Scones

I firmly believe that the best foods are of the simple sort. Such is the case with these seemingly ordinary scones that bake up beautifully into golden wedges laced with juicy blueberries and lemon zest. If you've squirreled away plenty of summer blueberries in your freezer, you can make these scones with local berries all year long.

2 cups all-purpose flour

¼ cup sugar

1 tablespoon plus ½ teaspoon baking powder

1½ teaspoons lemon zest

½ teaspoon salt

7 tablespoons unsalted butter, chilled and cut into ¼-inch cubes

½ cup low-fat buttermilk

¼ cup lemon juice

½ cup fresh or frozen blueberries

MAKES 8 SCONES

1. Position a rack in the center of the oven and preheat the oven to 375°F. Line a large baking sheet with parchment paper.

2. Whisk the flour, sugar, baking powder, lemon zest, and salt together in a medium bowl. Add the butter cubes to the bowl and place the bowl in the freezer for 5 minutes to allow the ingredients to chill. Remove the bowl from the freezer and, using your fingers or a pastry blender, work the butter into the flour mixture until the butter is reduced to the size of peas.

3. Pour the buttermilk and lemon juice into the bowl and bring the dough together with a rubber spatula. Once the dough starts to come together, knead it with your hands until the dough forms a ball in the bowl.

4. Turn the dough out onto a lightly floured surface and gently knead in the blueberries. Shape the dough into a circle 7 inches in diameter and cut it into eight wedges. Arrange the wedges on the prepared baking sheet, spacing them a few inches apart.

5. Loosely cover the scones with plastic wrap and chill in the freezer for 10 minutes. Remove the scones from the freezer and bake until the tops are golden brown, about 20 minutes. Serve warm.

Recipe from JACKIE SAPPINGTON OF THE COUNTRY CAT DINNER HOUSE & BAR

Basil-infused Strawberry Shortcakes

At the Portland restaurant Jackie Sappington owns with her husband, Adam, she updates summer shortcakes by adding a whisper of basil to the strawberry topping. Her impossibly tender biscuits melt in your mouth and soak up the sweet, delicate strawberry juices perfectly. If you prefer a classic flavor profile, simply omit the basil. The dessert will be more traditional but no less enjoyable.

SHORTCAKES

- 3 cups all-purpose flour
- ¼ cup light brown sugar
- 1½ tablespoons baking powder
- ¾ teaspoon salt
- 2 sticks (1 cup) unsalted butter, chilled and cut into ½-inch cubes
- 2 eggs
- 2 tablespoons buttermilk
- ¾ teaspoon vanilla extract
- 1 tablespoon heavy cream
- 1 tablespoon turbinado sugar

BASIL-INFUSED STRAWBERRIES

- 3 pints fresh strawberries (about 6 cups), hulled and quartered
- ⅓ cup granulated sugar
- 1 tablespoon lemon juice
- 6 medium fresh basil leaves, torn into small pieces

WHIPPED CREAM

- 2 cups heavy cream
- 2 tablespoons granulated sugar
- 1 teaspoon vanilla extract

8 SERVINGS

1. **Make the shortcakes:** Mix the flour, brown sugar, baking powder, and salt together on low speed in the bowl of an electric mixer fitted with a paddle attachment. Mix in the butter on medium speed until it is reduced to the size of peas. Mix in the eggs, buttermilk, and vanilla on medium speed until well combined.

2. Turn the dough out onto a lightly floured work surface and press it together to form a disc. Fold the disk in half and press it together with your hands. Turn counterclockwise and fold in half again; repeat the turn and fold process three more times. Shape the dough into a round disk and wrap it in plastic wrap. Refrigerate for 20 minutes.

3. **Make the infused strawberries:** Mix the strawberries, granulated sugar, lemon juice, and basil together with a rubber spatula in a medium bowl. Cover the bowl with plastic wrap and let sit at room temperature until the berries are juicy, about 30 minutes.

4. Position a rack in the center of the oven and preheat the oven to 350°F. Line a large baking sheet with parchment paper. Roll the dough out with a rolling pin into a ½-inch-thick circle on a clean lightly floured surface. Cut the circle into eight wedges. Arrange the wedges on the prepared baking sheet. Brush the wedges with the cream and sprinkle with the turbinado sugar. Bake until golden brown on top, about 20 minutes. Remove the biscuits from the oven and let cool on the baking sheet for 10 minutes.

5. **Make the whipped cream:** Whip the cream, granulated sugar, and vanilla together with a hand mixer on medium speed or in the bowl of an electric mixer fitted with a whisk attachment until soft peaks form.

6. Cut the shortcakes in half along their equator and place the bottom halves on eight plates. Spoon the strawberries over the biscuits, dividing them equally among the plates. Top each serving with a generous spoonful of whipped cream. Set the top halves of the biscuits over the whipped cream and strawberries. Garnish with another dollop of whipped cream, if desired, and serve immediately.

Blackberry Bread Pudding

When guests at the Tuscan-style Black Walnut Inn bring freshly picked blackberries back from a summer hike, innkeeper Karen Utz uses them to make Blackberry Bread Pudding for breakfast. Though Utz uses brioche for this popular inn breakfast, I've substituted more widely available challah for home cooks. Serve the bread pudding for breakfast or dessert accompanied by a dollop of whipped cream.

NOTE: The pudding needs to be prepped at least 8 hours in advance.

6–8 SERVINGS

4 eggs
1 cup packed light brown sugar
1 teaspoon vanilla extract
¼ teaspoon ground cinnamon
⅛ teaspoon freshly grated nutmeg
2¼ cups half-and-half
½ loaf challah, crust removed and cut into 1-inch cubes (about 4 cups)
   Unsalted butter
1 pint (2 cups) fresh blackberries

1. Whisk the eggs, sugar, vanilla, cinnamon, and nutmeg together in a large bowl until well combined. Whisk in the half-and-half until well combined. Fold the bread into the egg mixture with a rubber spatula until all of the bread cubes are well coated. Cover the bowl with plastic wrap and refrigerate for at least 8 hours or overnight.

2. Position a rack in the center of the oven and preheat the oven to 325°F. Butter a 9-inch square baking pan.

3. Gently fold the blackberries into the bread mixture. Transfer the mixture to the prepared baking pan and bake until the top is golden brown and the center is set, about 1 hour. To check for doneness, gently press a spoon into the center of the pan. The bread pudding is done when the center feels firm and the custard doesn't pool over the spoon.

4. Remove the baking pan from the oven. Set it on a cooling rack to cool for 15 minutes before serving.

Spiced Walnut Brownies

Though less common than hazelnuts, locally grown walnuts are reappearing at Oregon farmers' markets. Familiarize yourself with the local nut in these subtly spiced, walnut-studded brownies. At little t, Posey bakes the brownies in individual tart tins until the edges are firm but the brownies are still gooey in the middle. For home cooks, the recipe works best in an 8-inch square baking pan, as described below.

Cooking spray

¾ cup all-purpose flour, sifted

½ teaspoon ground cinnamon

½ teaspoon kosher salt

¼ teaspoon ground nutmeg

⅛ teaspoon ground cloves

Scant ⅛ teaspoon cayenne pepper

7 tablespoons unsalted butter, cut into ¼-inch cubes

3½ ounces unsweetened chocolate, roughly chopped

1¼ cups sugar

2 eggs

1 teaspoon vanilla extract

1 cup walnuts, toasted and roughly chopped

MAKES 12–16 BROWNIES

1. Position a rack in the center of the oven and preheat the oven to 350°F. Coat an 8-inch square baking pan with cooking spray and set aside.

2. Whisk the flour, cinnamon, salt, nutmeg, cloves, and cayenne together in a small bowl. Set aside.

3. Melt the butter and chocolate in a small metal bowl set over a small saucepan of barely simmering water, stirring frequently, until smooth. Remove the bowl from the heat and allow the chocolate to cool slightly.

4. Whisk the sugar, eggs, and vanilla together in a medium bowl. Whisk in the chocolate mixture. Whisk in the flour mixture until well combined. Fold in the walnuts with a rubber spatula.

5. Pour the batter into the prepared baking pan. Bake the brownies until the batter is set around the edges but still soft in the middle, about 20 minutes. Let the brownies cool before slicing. Stored in an airtight container at room temperature, the brownies will keep for about 5 days.

Recipe from CATHERINE AND CHERYL REINHART OF SWEET LIFE PÂTISSERIE

Vanilla Custard and Berry Tart

Creamy, vanilla-infused custard meets bright, juicy berries in this seasonal tart from Eugene's Sweet Life Pâtisserie. Owners (and sisters) Catherine and Cheryl Reinhart put the tart back on the menu when local berries arrive each spring. Though I've called for a mix of blueberries, raspberries, and blackberries in this version, you can top the custard with fresh strawberries as well if you like.

VANILLA CUSTARD FILLING

- 2 cups whole milk
- ½ cup sugar
- ¼ cup all-purpose flour
- 1 tablespoon plus 1 teaspoon cornstarch
- ½ cup egg yolks (from about 7 eggs)
- 4 tablespoons (½ stick) salted butter, at room temperature
- 1 tablespoon vanilla extract

SHORTBREAD CRUST

- 1 cup all-purpose flour
- ¼ cup sugar
- ¼ teaspoon salt
- ½ cup (1 stick) unsalted butter, chilled and cut into ½-inch cubes

- 1 pint (2 cups) fresh blueberries, raspberries, or blackberries, or any combination thereof

MAKES 1 (9-INCH) TART

1. **Make the custard filling:** Prepare an ice-water bath. Heat the milk in a medium saucepan over medium-low heat until warm but not boiling. Remove the saucepan from the heat.

2. Whisk the sugar, flour, and cornstarch together in a small bowl. Place the egg yolks in a medium bowl. Slowly whisk 1 cup of the milk into the yolks. Whisk the egg mixture into the sugar mixture until well combined.

3. Combine the egg-sugar mixture with the milk remaining in the saucepan. Cook over medium-low heat, stirring constantly with a wooden spoon, until the mixture is thick like pudding, about 4 minutes. Remove the saucepan from the heat and stir in the butter and vanilla. Transfer the custard to a clean bowl and cool in the ice-water bath. Cover the surface of the custard with a layer of plastic wrap to prevent a skin from forming. Refrigerate it until chilled and thickened, about 3 hours.

4. **Make the shortbread crust:** Position a rack in the center of the oven and preheat the oven to 350°F. Mix the flour, sugar, salt, and butter together in the bowl of a food processor fitted with a steel blade attachment until the dough forms a ball.

5. Press the dough into a 9-inch tart pan with a removable bottom, covering the bottom and sides of the pan evenly. Bake the crust until golden brown, about 25 minutes. Remove from the oven and let cool completely.

6. Transfer the tart shell to a serving plate. Fill with the chilled custard and arrange the berries on top. Serve the tart immediately or cover loosely with plastic wrap and refrigerate. Stored covered in the refrigerator, the tart will keep for 1 day.

Fig Bars

When figs come into season in midsummer, Portland-based pastry chef Kristen Murray reaches for her great-aunt's recipe for homemade fig bars. Murray learned to make the fig-filled snack as a kid using figs from a backyard fruit tree, and she makes them today using local Black Mission figs.

FIG JAM

- 1 pound fresh Black Mission figs, stemmed and roughly chopped
- ½ cup granulated sugar
- 2 teaspoons lemon juice
- 1 small vanilla bean, seeds scraped and pod reserved

PASTRY DOUGH

- 2 cups all-purpose flour
- ¼ cup granulated sugar
- ½ teaspoon baking powder
- ¼ teaspoon salt
- ½ cup (1 stick) unsalted butter, chilled and cut into ½-inch cubes
- 3 eggs
- ½ teaspoon water
  Confectioners' sugar (optional)

MAKES 12 BARS

1. **Make the jam:** Combine the figs, sugar, lemon juice, and vanilla seeds and pod together in a medium saucepan. Cook the fig mixture, stirring frequently, over medium-low heat until the figs break down and become jammy, about 1 hour. Discard the vanilla bean and let cool slightly before using.

2. **Make the dough:** Whisk the flour, granulated sugar, baking powder, and salt together in a medium bowl. Rub the butter into the flour mixture using your hands until the mixture is the consistency of cornmeal. Transfer the flour mixture to the bowl of an electric mixer fitted with a paddle attachment. Mix in 2 of the eggs on medium speed until well combined. The dough will be slightly wet.

3. Turn the dough out onto a lightly floured work surface and knead briefly to bring together. Flatten the dough into a 1-inch-thick rectangle and wrap it in plastic wrap. Refrigerate until well chilled, about 1 hour.

4. Position a rack in the center of the oven and preheat the oven to 325°F. Line a baking sheet with parchment paper.

5. Slice the dough in half and rewrap and return one piece to the refrigerator. Roll the dough out on a lightly floured work surface into a ¼-inch-thick, approximately 4- by 12-inch rectangle. Transfer to the prepared baking sheet.

6. Spread the jam down the center of the rectangle with a rubber spatula, leaving about a 1½-inch border on the sides and a ½-inch border on the top and bottom. Fold the long sides of the dough over to meet in the middle. Press the edges together gently to join them and erase the seam. Repeat the process with the remaining piece of dough.

7. Beat the remaining egg and the water together in a small bowl. Brush the egg wash on top of the dough. Bake until the dough is firm to the touch and light brown, about 15 minutes.

8. Let the bars cool on the baking sheet before slicing each rectangle into six small bars with a serrated knife. Dust the bars with confectioners' sugar, if desired, before serving. Stored in an airtight container at room temperature, the bars will keep for 1 week.

Lavender-Honey Crème Brûlée

Lavender and honey give crème brûlée added depth at Jen's Garden, where this updated recipe has become a favorite dessert with Sisters diners. Splurge on a kitchen blowtorch to melt the sugar topping — a broiler doesn't deliver a crust that shatters the right way.

NOTE: The custards require at least an 8-hour chill.

8 SERVINGS

Unsalted butter
1¾ cups heavy cream
1½ cups whole milk
½ cup honey
2 teaspoons dried culinary lavender
8 egg yolks
2 eggs
¼ cup granulated sugar
¼ cup packed dark brown sugar

1. Position a rack in the center of the oven and preheat the oven to 325°F. Lightly butter eight 6-ounce ramekins.

2. Heat the cream, milk, honey, and lavender in a heavy saucepan over medium heat until the mixture comes to a simmer. Remove the saucepan from the heat.

3. Whisk the egg yolks, eggs, and granulated sugar together in a medium bowl until well combined. Slowly whisk the hot cream mixture into the egg mixture. Pour the custard through a fine-mesh strainer into another medium bowl. Discard the lavender.

4. Bring a medium saucepan of water to a boil. Place the ramekins in a large roasting pan and fill the pan with enough hot water to come halfway up the sides of the ramekins. Divide the custard among the ramekins and bake until the custards are set but still tremble slightly in the center, about 35 minutes.

5. Remove the ramekins from the pan and refrigerate uncovered until cool. Once cool, cover the custards with plastic wrap and refrigerate at least 8 hours or overnight.

6. Divide the brown sugar among the ramekins, sprinkling it lightly over the top of the custards. Using a kitchen torch, heat the brown sugar until melted and deep amber, about 2 minutes. Refrigerate the custards until the sugar hardens, about 15 minutes, before serving.

Hazelnut-Cherry Nibby Cookies

Alma Chocolate's resident baker Ruth E. Fox adds local hazelnuts and dried cherries to sandy shortbread cookies at the Portland chocolate shop. Tied up in a pretty cellophane bag, these cookies make a beautiful gift.

1 cup (2 sticks) unsalted butter, at room temperature

¾ cup sugar

1½ teaspoons vanilla extract

¼ heaping teaspoon fleur de sel

2 cups unbleached all-purpose flour

¼ cup dried cherries, roughly chopped

¼ cup hazelnuts, roasted, skinned, and roughly chopped

1 heaping tablespoon cacao nibs

1 teaspoon water (if needed)

MAKES ABOUT 18 COOKIES

1. Combine the butter, sugar, vanilla, and fleur de sel in the bowl of an electric mixer fitted with a paddle attachment and beat on medium speed until smooth and creamy, about 1 minute.

2. Mix in the flour on low speed until just blended. Add the cherries, hazelnuts, and cacao nibs, and the water if the dough appears dry, and mix on low speed until just combined.

3. Turn the dough out onto a lightly floured work surface. Shape the dough into a log about 12 inches long and 2 inches wide. Wrap the log in plastic wrap and refrigerate until firm, at least 2 hours or overnight.

4. Position two racks in the center of the oven and preheat the oven to 350°F. Line two large baking sheets with parchment paper. Remove the dough from the refrigerator and cut the log into ½-inch slices. Space the cookies 1 inch apart on the baking sheets and bake for 8 minutes. Rotate the baking sheets and bake until the edges of the cookies are golden brown, about 8 minutes longer.

5. Remove the baking sheets from the oven and let the cookies rest on the sheets until cool enough to handle, about 3 minutes. Transfer the cookies to a cooling rack to cool completely before serving. Stored in an airtight container at room temperature, the cookies will keep for about 1 week.

Hazelnut Butter Cookies

I'd long heard that using natural peanut butter in cookie recipes led to crumbly, dry treats. Imagine my surprise when I substituted natural hazelnut butter in cookbook author David Lebovitz's peanut butter cookie recipe and (with a few tweaks) created a cookie that is delightfully crunchy around the edges and moist and chewy in the center. I use hazelnut butter from Freddy Guys Hazelnuts for this recipe, but nut butter from the mainstream Kettle Foods brand will also work.

1¼ cups all-purpose flour

1 tablespoon baking powder

¼ teaspoon salt

½ cup (1 stick) unsalted butter, at room temperature

½ cup plus 1 tablespoon granulated sugar, plus more for coating the cookies

½ cup plus 1 tablespoon dark brown sugar

1 cup natural unsalted hazelnut butter

1 egg, at room temperature

1 teaspoon vanilla extract

MAKES ABOUT 30 COOKIES

1. Whisk the flour, baking powder, and salt together in a small bowl. Set aside.

2. Cream the butter, granulated sugar, brown sugar, and hazelnut butter together on medium speed in the bowl of an electric mixer fitted with a paddle attachment until smooth. Beat in the egg and vanilla until well combined. Mix in the flour mixture until the dough just comes together.

3. Shape the dough into a ball and cover with plastic wrap. Refrigerate for at least 2 hours or overnight.

4. Remove the dough from the refrigerator and let it come to room temperature. Position a rack in the center of the oven and preheat the oven to 350°F. Line two baking sheets with parchment paper. Fill a small bowl with granulated sugar.

5. Pinch off small pieces of the dough and shape into 1-inch balls. Roll the dough balls in the granulated sugar to coat. Place the balls 3 inches apart on the prepared baking sheets. Use a fork to flatten the cookies, making a crosshatch pattern on each. Rewrap the remaining dough and refrigerate between batches.

6. Bake the cookies, rotating the baking sheets halfway through, until the cookies begin to brown around the edges but the centers are still slightly soft, about 9 minutes. Let the cookies cool on the baking sheets until firm enough to handle. Transfer the cookies to a cooling rack to cool completely. Stored in an airtight container at room temperature, the cookies will keep for about 3 days.

Hazelnut Tassies

Buttery, bite-size, hazelnut-filled cookies from Two Tarts Bakery are the Oregon version of classic pecan tassies. Though I prefer the cookies unadorned, for added indulgence, owner and artisan baker Elizabeth Beekley suggests topping each cookie with a dollop of chocolate ganache after the cookies have cooled.

1 cup unbleached all-purpose flour

½ cup (1 stick) plus 1 tablespoon unsalted butter, chilled

3 ounces cream cheese, chilled

Cooking spray

1 cup hazelnuts, roasted and skinned

¾ cup packed dark brown sugar

1 egg

1 teaspoon vanilla extract

¼ teaspoon fine sea salt

MAKES 24 COOKIES

1. Pulse the flour, ½ cup of the butter, and cream cheese together in the bowl of a food processor fitted with a steel blade attachment until the dough comes together in a ball. Remove the dough from the processor, wrap it in plastic wrap, and refrigerate until chilled, about 30 minutes.

2. Position a rack in the center of the oven and preheat the oven to 350°F. Grease 24 miniature muffin cups with cooking spray.

3. Remove the dough from the refrigerator and divide it into two equal portions. Rewrap and return one portion to the refrigerator. Divide the remaining dough into 12 equal portions. Roll each piece into a ball and, using your thumbs, press a dough ball into each of the muffin cups to cover the bottom and sides of the cups evenly. Repeat the process with the remaining half of the dough.

4. Melt the remaining 1 tablespoon butter in the microwave. Blend the melted butter, hazelnuts, sugar, egg, vanilla, and salt in a clean food processor bowl fitted with a steel blade attachment until just combined. The filling should still have small pieces of hazelnuts visible. Using a small spoon, distribute the filling among the muffin cups.

5. Bake the cookies until the dough starts to brown around the edges and the filling has set, about 15 minutes. Remove the cookies from the oven and let cool in the muffin cups for 10 minutes. Invert the muffin tins and tap gently to release the cookies. Let the cookies cool completely on a cooling rack. Stored in an airtight container at room temperature, the cookies will keep for about 4 days.

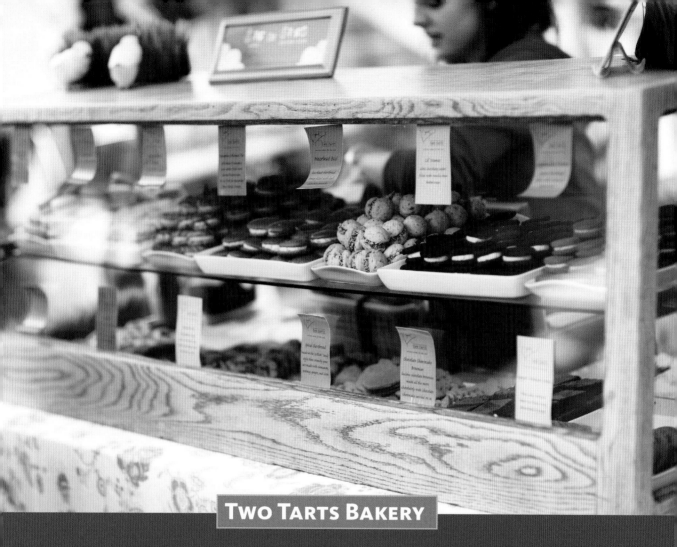

TWO TARTS BAKERY

BACK IN 2006, Portlander Elizabeth Beekley grew tired of eating mammoth bakery shop sweets. Massive pastries and manhole-size cookies made her feel alternately guilty for indulging or wasteful for throwing most of the oversize treats away. So she called on her culinary school training and her sister Cecelia to create a menu of miniature, seasonally inspired cookies to peddle at the Portland Farmers Market's 2007 season.

Armed with golden tassies and sublime sandwich cookies slathered with peanut butter cream, the sisters sold out of their bite-size treats by 10:30 AM. Throughout the season, locals continued to line up for artisan cookies that satisfied on multiple levels because of their small size.

After Cecelia moved to Australia, Beekley grew her business by making connections with local, sustainably minded purveyors. Readied with her Rolodex of new contacts, Beekley opened a brick-and-mortar storefront in northwest Portland and extended the buzz born from her market stand. Inside the cozy shop, she proves that bigger cookies aren't necessarily better cookies with a pastry case filled with cappuccino creams, marionberry linzers, and rhubarb rugelach that fit in the palms of her customers' hands.

FREDDY GUYS HAZELNUTS

NEARLY A DECADE AGO, Barb and Fritz Foulke moved their family from rural Washington to the Willamette Valley and bought a 60-acre hazelnut farm. With help from Barb's dad and uncle — themselves lifelong farmers — they learned the filbert farming trade and entered a niche Oregon industry.

But when their daughter Jocie decided to attend a fancy university, the enterprising couple knew they needed to hone their business model to support her schooling. With help from their savvy daughter, they perfected their product and transitioned to a direct-sales model that would pay for Jocie's tuition and for her siblings' schooling down the road.

Business really began booming when Barb started peddling their hazelnuts and hazelnut products at regional farmers' markets. Now the nuts are in high demand among local chefs, artisan bakers, and filbert-loving market shoppers. Barb often sells bags of her fresh-roasted nuts to out-of-towners at the market, then fields an order from the same customers the next week. They simply can't find direct-to-consumer, roasted-to-order hazelnuts in their hometowns.

Nor can shoppers easily find specialty products like hazelnut meal and hazelnut granola through other vendors. "When my customers realize they can order what suits them, they become dedicated, because no one else does that," says Barb. "And even if you don't order something special, you're getting a hazelnut that was shelled less than a week ago and roasted less than three days ago when you get it from us."

Spiced Cranberry-Hazelnut Bundt Cake

I have always admired the sloping shoulders and elegant simplicity of Bundt cake — particularly when the cake in question is this tender-crumbed, cranberry-studded version. Inspired by a recipe from baking maven Dorie Greenspan, this cake works equally well for breakfast and dessert. For dessert, serve it with a scoop of vanilla bean ice cream or a spoonful of whipped cream. This cake gets better with age, so do make it a day ahead.

Cooking spray

- 1 cup all-purpose flour
- 1 cup white whole-wheat flour
- ¾ cup hazelnut flour (also called hazelnut meal; see Note)
- 1½ teaspoons ground cinnamon
- 1½ teaspoons ground cloves
- 1 teaspoon baking powder
- ¾ teaspoon ground ginger
- ½ teaspoon baking soda
- ½ teaspoon salt
- ½ cup (1 stick) unsalted butter, at room temperature
- 1 cup packed dark brown sugar
- ¾ cup granulated sugar
- ½ cup unsweetened applesauce
- 3 eggs
- 1½ teaspoons vanilla extract
- 1 cup (8 ounces) Greek-style 2 percent plain yogurt
- 1½ cups frozen cranberries

Confectioners' sugar, for dusting

NOTE: Purveyors like Freddy Guys Hazelnuts sell hazelnut meal at local farmers' markets. You can also make your own meal by grinding toasted, skinned hazelnuts into a fine powder in the bowl of a food processor fitted with a steel blade attachment.

8–10 SERVINGS

1. Position a rack in the center of the oven and preheat the oven to 350°F. Generously coat a 12-cup Bundt pan with cooking spray.

2. Whisk the all-purpose flour, white whole-wheat flour, hazelnut flour, cinnamon, cloves, baking powder, ginger, baking soda, and salt together in a small bowl.

3. Beat the butter on medium speed in the bowl of an electric mixer fitted with a paddle attachment until smooth. Add the brown sugar and granulated sugar and beat until fluffy, about 2 minutes. Add the applesauce and beat for 1 minute longer. Add the eggs, one at a time, beating for 30 seconds after each addition and scraping down the sides of the bowl as needed. Beat in the vanilla, then the yogurt. Mix in the flour mixture until just combined.

4. Gently fold the cranberries into the batter with a rubber spatula. Transfer the batter to the prepared pan. Bake the cake until the crust is deep brown and a tester stick inserted near the center comes out clean, about 1 hour.

5. Let the cake cool in the pan until the pan is cool enough to handle before inverting the cake onto a cooling rack to cool completely. Transfer the cake to a serving plate and sift the confectioners' sugar over the top. Cut the cake into thick slices and serve.

SWEET LIFE PÂTISSERIE

ASK ANYONE WHO LIVES IN EUGENE where to head for dessert and you'll likely hear the words "Sweet Life Pâtisserie." The colorful, European-style sweet shop serves a tempting assortment of petits fours, cookies, tartlets, tortes, and cakes and has satisfied local sweet tooths for more than a decade.

The bakery looks quite different than it did when co-owners Catherine and Cheryl Reinhart began baking out of a certified kitchen in their garage in 1993, but the pâtisserie's focus remains the same. From day one, the sisters made high-quality pastries and cakes from scratch; their baking methods were new in an era when most American bakeries relied on shortening and box mixes to fill the pastry case. Locals recognized the difference in taste and quality when they sampled Sweet Life's pastries and quickly got behind the sisters' efforts to introduce better baked goods to the town.

Many customers also grew to appreciate the bakery's lineup of vegan-friendly sweets. Pastries like cinnamon rolls, cheesecakes, and peanut butter cups cater to alternative diets — and have been known to sway nonvegan skeptics with one bite. Eugene might be a tofu-loving hippie town, but even the health-conscious locals love their dessert.

Raspberry-Rhubarb Fool

Rhubarb — whose puckery flavor is often masked with an abundance of sugar and sweet strawberries — makes an excellent partner for raspberries as well. I adapted this fool recipe from a charming cookbook called *Rustic Fruit Desserts*. A fool is an old-fashioned English dessert that blends whipped cream with tart fruit. Serve this light, simple dessert at the end of a dinner party with a shortbread cookie slipped into the glass.

4 SERVINGS

1 pound rhubarb, trimmed and cut into ½-inch slices (about 2⅔ cups)

½ cup honey

Zest and juice of 1 lemon

½ vanilla bean, split

Salt

1½ cups fresh raspberries

1 cup heavy cream

1 tablespoon confectioners' sugar

¼ teaspoon vanilla extract

1. Combine the rhubarb, honey, lemon zest, lemon juice, vanilla bean, and a pinch of salt in a medium saucepan. Cover and simmer over medium heat, stirring occasionally, until the rhubarb has softened, about 10 minutes. Remove the rhubarb sauce from the heat and discard the vanilla bean. Transfer the sauce to a medium bowl and let cool to room temperature.

2. When the rhubarb sauce is cool, purée ¾ cup of the raspberries in a food processor fitted with a steel blade attachment until smooth. Pass the purée through a fine-mesh strainer into a medium bowl, pressing on the berry pulp with a rubber spatula to extract as much juice as possible. Discard the pulp.

3. Gently fold the raspberry purée and the remaining ¾ cup raspberries into the rhubarb sauce. Refrigerate, uncovered, until well chilled, about 30 minutes.

4. Whip the cream, sugar, and vanilla together on medium speed in the bowl of an electric mixer fitted with a whisk attachment until soft peaks form. Fold all but ½ cup of the rhubarb-raspberry sauce into the whipped cream. Divide the mixture among four stemmed glasses and chill for 1 hour. Refrigerate the reserved rhubarb-raspberry sauce.

5. Top each serving with about 2 tablespoons of the remaining rhubarb-raspberry sauce. Serve immediately.

Rhubarb Buckle with Candied Ginger Crumb

Pastry chef Steve Bouton partners complementary rhubarb and ginger in this moist, delicate cake. At Belly, Bouton serves individual cakes with scoops of strawberry ice cream. I've adapted his recipe to fit a 9-inch round baking pan and serve a crowd. "Buckle" is an old name for a simple, single-layer cake made with fruit, and it is as good for breakfast as it is for dessert.

CANDIED GINGER CRUMB

- ¼ cup all-purpose flour
- ¼ cup sugar
- ¼ cup finely chopped candied ginger
- 2 tablespoons unsalted butter, melted

RHUBARB BUCKLE

- Cooking spray
- 1¾ cups all-purpose flour
- 2 teaspoons ground ginger
- 1 teaspoon baking powder
- ½ teaspoon baking soda
- ¼ teaspoon salt
- ½ cup (1 stick) unsalted butter, at room temperature
- 1 cup sugar
- 2 eggs
- ¾ cup plus 2 tablespoons buttermilk
- ¾ pound rhubarb, trimmed and cut into ½-inch slices (about 2 cups)

MAKES 1 (9-INCH) CAKE

1. **Make the candied ginger crumb:** Mix the flour, sugar, and candied ginger together in a small bowl. Mix in the melted butter with a fork until crumbly. Cover and refrigerate until ready to use.

2. Position a rack in the center of the oven and preheat the oven to 350°F. Coat a 9-inch round baking pan with cooking spray.

3. **Make the buckle:** Whisk the flour, ginger, baking powder, baking soda, and salt together in a medium bowl.

4. Cream the butter and sugar together on medium speed in the bowl of an electric mixer fitted with a paddle attachment until light and fluffy, about 3 minutes. Mix in the eggs on medium speed, scraping down the sides of the bowl with a spatula as needed.

5. Add the flour mixture in two parts, alternating with the buttermilk, on medium speed until just combined. Gently fold in the rhubarb with a rubber spatula.

6. Pour the batter into the prepared cake pan. Sprinkle the candied ginger crumb evenly over the top. Bake the cake until the top is golden and firm, about 45 minutes. Cool on a rack for 30 minutes before serving.

Apple-Huckleberry Crisp

Portland-based pastry chef Lauren Fortgang makes a variety of fruit crisps each fall and rarely has any left of the day's selection by evening's end. In her twist on apple crisp, huckleberries prove an apt partner for local apples. You can, however, substitute other berries — such as fresh or frozen blackberries, blueberries, or cranberries — when huckleberries aren't available.

1⅓ cups old-fashioned oats

1 cup granulated sugar

¾ cup packed dark brown sugar

½ cup all-purpose flour

1 tablespoon ground cinnamon

¼ teaspoon salt

½ cup (1 stick) plus 1 tablespoon unsalted butter, chilled and cut into ¼-inch cubes

4 medium tart baking apples, peeled, cored, and diced into ½-inch pieces

¼ cup fresh or frozen huckleberries

6–8 SERVINGS

1. Position a rack in the center of the oven and preheat the oven to 375°F.

2. Mix the oats, ½ cup of the granulated sugar, brown sugar, flour, cinnamon, and salt on low speed in the bowl of an electric mixer fitted with a paddle attachment until well combined. Mix in the butter on low speed until the mixture is crumbly and no butter chunks are visible.

3. Toss the apples in a medium bowl with the remaining ½ cup granulated sugar until well combined. Add the huckleberries and toss lightly. Spoon the fruit evenly into a 9-inch square baking pan.

4. Pinch the topping between your fingers to form a clumpy texture. Scatter the topping over the apples and huckleberries.

5. Bake the crisp until the topping is golden brown and the apple juices are bubbling around the edges of the baking pan, about 45 minutes. Serve the crisp warm in individual bowls with a scoop of vanilla or ginger ice cream, if desired.

Recipe from **BLAKE VAN ROEKEL OF KEUKEN**

Tomatillo–Green Apple Sorbet

Blake Van Roekel creates art-inspired culinary events, like her popular Art + Palate Supper Club, through her Portland-based company Keuken. In this refreshing savory sorbet, she proves there is indeed life beyond salsa for the summer tomatillo crop. Tomatillos are available locally at farmers' markets from late summer through early fall.

2 medium green apples

1½ cups water

1 cup sugar

1 jalapeño chile, halved, seeded, and stemmed (optional)

3 medium tomatillos, husked and rinsed

2 teaspoons lemon juice

MAKES ABOUT 2½ CUPS

1. Peel and core the apples, reserving the peels and cores. Simmer the water and sugar in a medium saucepan over medium heat, stirring occasionally, until the sugar dissolves. Add the apple peels and cores and jalapeño, if desired. Simmer the mixture over medium-high heat until syrupy and reduced by one-third, about 35 minutes. Remove the saucepan from the heat.

2. Meanwhile, chop the apples and tomatillos into 1-inch pieces. Cook the apples and tomatillos in a medium saucepan over low heat, covered and stirring occasionally, until soft, about 25 minutes. Remove the saucepan from the heat and let cool slightly. Purée the mixture with the lemon juice in the bowl of a food processor fitted with a steel blade attachment.

3. Strain the apple-jalapeño syrup into the tomatillo-apple purée and discard the solids. Blend the syrup and the purée together until well combined. Refrigerate the mixture until cool, about 1 hour.

4. Transfer the mixture to an ice cream maker and process according to the manufacturer's instructions. Transfer the sorbet to an airtight container and freeze until firm before serving, at least 4 hours. Stored in an airtight container, the sorbet will keep for about 1 month.

Heritage Apple Pie

When the holidays arrive, the bakers at this Portland coffeehouse and bakery go into overdrive turning out pie after pie to fill holiday orders. A filling made from heritage apple varieties makes this homespun pie a well-loved local favorite.

PIECRUST

- 2⅓ cups pastry flour (see Note)
- 1 tablespoon granulated sugar
- 1⅛ teaspoons salt
- 1 teaspoon baking powder
- ½ cup plus 6 tablespoons (1¾ sticks) unsalted butter, chilled and cut into ½-inch cubes
- 5–8 tablespoons ice water
- 1 tablespoon apple cider vinegar

APPLE FILLING

- ¼ cup packed dark brown sugar
- ¼ cup granulated sugar
- 2 tablespoons cornstarch
- 1 tablespoon lemon juice
- 1 teaspoon ground cinnamon
- ¼ teaspoon ground nutmeg
- ¼ teaspoon salt
- 2½ pounds heritage apples, such as Cox's Orange Pippin
- 1 tablespoon unsalted butter

  Heavy cream
  Turbinado sugar

NOTE: If you can't find pastry flour, make your own. To make 4 cups of pastry flour, combine 2⅔ cups of all-purpose flour with 1⅓ cups of cake flour. Reserve any extra flour for another use.

MAKES 1 (9-INCH) PIE

1. **Make the piecrust:** Mix the flour, granulated sugar, salt, and baking powder together in the bowl of a food processor fitted with a steel blade attachment. Add the butter to the bowl and pulse until the dough resembles a coarse meal.

2. Transfer the dough to a medium bowl. Work 5 tablespoons of the ice water and the apple cider vinegar into the dough with your hands. Incorporate up to 3 tablespoons more water as needed if the dough is dry and needs additional water to come together.

3. Divide the dough into two equal balls. Shape each ball into a 5-inch disk on a lightly floured work surface. Wrap the disks in plastic wrap and refrigerate until chilled, about 30 minutes.

4. **Make the filling:** Mix the brown sugar, granulated sugar, cornstarch, lemon juice, cinnamon, nutmeg, and salt together in a large bowl. Peel and core the apples. Cut the apples into ½-inch cubes and toss them in the sugar mixture to prevent them from browning.

5. Position a rack in the center of the oven and preheat the oven to 400°F. Remove the chilled pastry dough from the refrigerator and let the dough rest at room temperature for 5 minutes.

6. Roll out one of the disks of dough on a lightly floured work surface into a circle large enough to line a shallow 9-inch pie pan. Transfer the dough to the pie pan and trim the edges of the dough with a knife or kitchen scissors so it is even with the rim of the pan. Fill the pie pan with the apples and dot the filling with the butter.

7. Roll out the second disk of dough and set it over the apple filling. Crimp the edges of the dough together and cut a few

small, decorative steam vents in the top of the crust with a paring knife. Brush the top of the crust, but not the crimped edges, lightly with the heavy cream, and sprinkle the turbinado sugar over the top.

8. Bake the pie until the crust begins to turn golden brown, about 20 minutes. Reduce the heat to 375°F. Tent the rims with foil or a pie protector if the edges are browning too quickly, and bake the pie until the crust is golden brown and the apple juices are bubbling, about 50 minutes longer. Transfer the pie to a cooling rack to cool for 1 hour before serving.

Rustic Pear Galette

The Steamboat Inn's pies earn high praise from guests, but during peak pear season it's this rustic galette that draws accolades in the dining room. If you can't find almond paste for the filling, you can omit it entirely or substitute ½ cup toasted and chopped walnuts, almonds, or pecans in its place. The inn's general manager, Patricia Lee, recommends serving her galette with a scoop of vanilla ice cream or caramel sauce drizzled over the top.

GALETTE DOUGH

- 2 cups all-purpose flour
- 1 tablespoon granulated sugar, plus more for sprinkling the dough (optional)
- ½ teaspoon salt
- ¾ cup (1½ sticks) unsalted butter, chilled and cut into ½-inch cubes
- ⅓ cup ice water, plus more as needed

PEAR FILLING

- 4 firm-ripe Bartlett pears
- ½ cup packed dark brown sugar
- 2 teaspoons vanilla extract
- ¼ teaspoon ground cinnamon
- ¼ teaspoon ground nutmeg
  Salt
- ½ cup (about 5 ounces) crumbled almond paste
- 1 teaspoon unsalted butter, cut into tiny pieces

- 1 egg, lightly beaten

MAKES 1 (12-INCH) GALETTE

1. **Make the dough:** Whisk the flour, granulated sugar, and salt together. Cut in the butter using a pastry blender or your hands until the butter is reduced to pea-size pieces. Sprinkle the ice water over the flour mixture, about 1 tablespoon at a time, using a fork to distribute the liquid. The dough will be shaggy but will come together when squeezed. If the dough doesn't come together, add additional water by the tablespoonful as needed.

2. Turn the dough onto a lightly floured work surface and gently knead it until it comes together. Flatten the dough into a 1-inch-thick disk. Wrap in plastic wrap and refrigerate for 30 minutes.

3. **Make the filling:** Peel and core the pears and cut them into ½-inch slices. Mix the pears, brown sugar, vanilla, cinnamon, nutmeg, and a pinch of salt together with a rubber spatula in a large bowl until well combined.

4. Line a large baking sheet with parchment paper. Remove the dough from the refrigerator and roll it out into a 13-inch circle. Transfer the dough to the prepared baking sheet; it may hang over the edge of the sheet. Sprinkle the crumbled almond paste over the dough, leaving about a 1½-inch border. Layer the pear slices over the almond paste. Discard any juices that have accumulated in the bowl.

5. Fold the outer edge of the dough over the outside layer of pears, pleating the dough as needed and leaving the center of the galette open. Dot the butter evenly over the pears. Brush the edge of the dough with the beaten egg and lightly sprinkle the edges with sugar. Refrigerate the galette for 20 minutes.

6. Position a rack in the lower third of the oven and preheat the oven to 350°F. Bake the galette until the crust is golden brown and the pears are tender, about 40 minutes. Let cool slightly on the baking sheet before slicing into wedges to serve.

STEAMBOAT INN

ON THE WINDING HIGHWAY that runs from Roseburg along the scenic North Umpqua River, you'll find the requisite fly-fishing lodges and roadside pit stops. But if you drive far enough — 38 miles — you'll also discover an inn that's admired equally by fly fisherman and gourmands.

Since it opened in the mid-1970s, the Steamboat Inn's seasonally driven restaurant has given Oregonians a reason to visit the region beyond fishing expeditions and scenic drives. By day, the staff at the mom-and-pop café serves guests and passersby honest home cooking and their famed fruit pies. But in the evening, the cozy space transforms into a fine-dining restaurant where guests gather for multicourse dinners that begin with a trio of appetizers and end with an elegant dessert. The menu changes nightly, so guests might sample pinot noir–glazed short ribs one night and peppered duck breast with marionberry ketchup or fresh roasted halibut the next.

Every year from March through mid-June, general manager Patricia Lee also orchestrates a series of guest chef and winemaker dinners. The dinners delight locals and out-of-town guests and give chefs from popular Oregon restaurants like Wildwood and Nick's Italian Cafe the chance to take over the inn's kitchen. Each meal provides guests with a rare opportunity to sample local culinary talents and Oregon wines in a riverside setting that's as intimate as they come.

Parsnip-Carrot Cupcakes with Cream Cheese Icing

Though I adore carrot cake, I also like turning a classic recipe on its head by incorporating the humble parsnip into the batter. Grated parsnips lend a natural sweetness and delicate flavor to these wintery cupcakes. Rum raisins strewn through the batter give them added adult appeal.

PARSNIP-CARROT CUPCAKES

- 1 cup golden raisins
- 3 tablespoon dark rum
- 2 cups whole-wheat pastry flour
- 2 teaspoons baking powder
- 2 teaspoons baking soda
- 1 teaspoon salt
- 1 teaspoon ground cinnamon
- ¾ teaspoon freshly grated nutmeg
- 1¼ cups packed dark brown sugar
- ¾ cup grapeseed oil
- 4 eggs
- ½ cup unsweetened applesauce
- 1 teaspoon vanilla extract
- 1½ cups finely grated peeled carrots (from about 2 medium carrots)
- 1½ cups finely grated peeled parsnips (from about 2 medium parsnips)
- ½ cup pecans, toasted and roughly chopped

CREAM CHEESE ICING

- 4 ounces cream cheese
- 3 tablespoons unsalted butter, at room temperature
- 1½ cups confectioners' sugar
- ½ teaspoon vanilla extract
- ½ teaspoon grated orange zest
- 1–2 tablespoons orange juice

MAKES 18 CUPCAKES

1. **Make the cupcakes:** Position a rack in the center of the oven and preheat the oven to 325°F. Line one standard-size 12-cup muffin tin and one standard-size 6-cup muffin tin with paper liners.

2. Combine the raisins and rum in a microwave-safe bowl. Cover the bowl with plastic wrap and microwave the raisins on high for 30 seconds. Uncover the raisins and set aside to cool.

3. Whisk the flour, baking powder, baking soda, salt, cinnamon, and nutmeg together in a medium bowl.

4. Beat the brown sugar and grapeseed oil together on medium speed in the bowl of an electric mixer fitted with a paddle attachment until well combined. Add the eggs, one at a time, scraping down the sides of the bowl with a rubber spatula as needed. Mix in the applesauce and vanilla. Mix in the flour mixture, scraping down the sides of the bowl with a rubber spatula as needed.

5. Fold in the carrots, parsnips, pecans, and ¾ cup of the raisins with a rubber spatula until just combined. Fill the prepared muffin tins about two-thirds full with batter. Bake the cupcakes until they are golden brown and a tester stick inserted into the middle comes out clean, about 20 minutes.

6. Remove the cupcakes from the oven and let cool for 10 minutes in the muffin tins. Transfer the cupcakes to a cooling rack to cool completely.

7. **Make the icing:** Blend the cream cheese and butter in a medium bowl on medium speed with a hand mixer. Sift the confectioners' sugar into the bowl and mix on medium speed until well combined. Mix in the vanilla, orange zest, and 1 tablespoon of the orange juice on medium speed. Add the remaining 1 tablespoon of orange juice if needed to thin out the frosting.

8. Spread the icing on top of the cooled cupcakes. Top each cupcake with a few of the remaining ¼ cup rum-soaked raisins before serving. Stored in an airtight container at room temperature, the cupcakes will keep for about 1 day.

Recipe Contributors and Suppliers

The following information listed here for the contributors was accurate as of the first printing of this book (2011).

PORTLAND METRO AREA

Alma Chocolate
140 Northeast 28th Avenue
Portland, OR 97232
503-517-0262
www.almachocolate.com
  Hazelnut-Cherry Nibby Cookies

Beaker & Flask
727 Southeast Washington Street
Portland, OR 97214
503-235-8180
www.beakerandflask.com
  Grilled Corn on the Cob with
    Roasted Poblano Aioli and
    Parmigiano-Reggiano

Boedecker Cellars
2621 Northwest 30th Avenue
Portland, OR 97210
503-288-7752
www.boedeckercellars.com

Clarklewis Restaurant
1001 Southeast Water Avenue
Portland, OR 97214
503-235-2294
www.clarklewispdx.com
  Arugula Salad with Glazed Walnuts and
    Pinot Noir–Tarragon Vinaigrette

Clear Creek Distillery
2389 Northwest Wilson Street
Portland, OR 97210
503-248-9470
www.clearcreekdistillery.com
  Flat-Iron Steaks with Apple Brandy Pan
    Sauce

Clyde Common
1014 Southwest Stark Street
Portland, Oregon 97205
503-228-3333
www.clydecommon.com
  Broccoli Rabe Salad with Lemon
    Vinaigrette and Prosciutto

Cooper Mountain Vineyards
20121 SW Leonardo Lane
Beaverton, OR 97007
503-649-0027
www.coopermountainwine.com

The Country Cat Dinner House & Bar
7937 Southeast Stark Street
Portland, OR 97215
503-408-1414
www.thecountrycat.net
  Basil-infused Strawberry Shortcakes
  Honey-Paprika Potatoes
  Lamb Meatballs Stuffed with Swiss
    Chard and Goat Cheese

din din
971-544-1350
www.dindinportland.com
  Brandied Cherries
  Dill-Hazelnut Pesto
  Sorrel Salsa Verde
  Steamed Clams in Tomato-Fennel Broth
    with Dill-Hazelnut Pesto

Firehouse Restaurant
711 Northeast Dekum Street
Portland, OR 97211
503-954-1702
www.firehousepdx.com
  English Pea Pesto
  Thyme-roasted Chicken with Warm
    Potato, Kale, and Pancetta Salad

Foster & Dobbs Authentic Foods
2518 Northeast 15th Avenue
Portland, OR 97212
503-284-1157
www.fosteranddobbs.com
  Oregon Albacore Tuna Melts

Genoa
2832 Southeast Belmont Street
Portland, OR 97214
503-238-1464
www.genoarestaurant.com
  Bagna Cauda
  Sunchoke and Fennel Gratin

Gilt Club
306 Northwest Broadway
Portland, OR 97209
503-222-4458
www.giltclub.com
  Elk Tartare

Grand Central Bakery
(multiple locations)
www.grandcentralbakery.com
  Cranberry-Apple Chutney

Grüner
527 Southwest 12th Avenue
Portland, OR 97205
503-241-7163
www.grunerpdx.com
  Shaved Radish "Carpaccio"

House Spirits Distillery
65 SE Washington Street
Portland, Oregon 97214
503-235-3174
www.housespirits.com

In Good Taste Cooking School
231 Northwest 11th Avenue
Portland, OR 97209
503-248-2015
www.ingoodtastestore.com

Keuken
503-753-1655
www.goodkeuken.com
  Tomatillo–Green Apple Sorbet

Laurelhurst Market
3155 East Burnside Street
Portland, OR 97214
503-206-3099 (butcher shop)
503-206-3097 (restaurant)
www.laurelhurstmarket.com
  Grilled Pork Chops with Grilled
    Nectarine Salsa

Lauro Kitchen
3377 Southeast Division Street, #106
Portland, OR 97202
503-239-7000
www.laurokitchen.com
  Pear and Prosciutto Pizza

Le Pigeon
738 East Burnside Street
Portland, OR 97214
503-546-8796
www.lepigeon.com
  Apple-Huckleberry Crisp

Lincoln Restaurant
3808 North Williams Avenue,
  No. 127
Portland, OR 97227
503-288-6200
www.lincolnpdx.com
  Malfatti with Pumpkin and Sage Brown-
    Butter Sauce
  Roasted Pears with Sage

Little Bird
219 Southwest 6th Avenue
Portland, OR 97204
503-688-5952
www.littlebirdbistro.com
  Apple-Huckleberry Crisp

little t american baker
2600 Southeast Division Street
Portland, OR 97202
503-238-3458
www.littletbaker.com
  Sally Lunn Bread
  Spiced Walnut Brownies

Meat Cheese Bread
1406 Southeast Stark Street
Portland, OR 97214
503-234-1700
www.meatcheesebread.com
  Razor Clam Po' Boys

Meriwether's Restaurant
2601 Northwest Vaughn Street
Portland, OR 97210
503-228-1250
www.meriwethersnw.com
  Blueberry, Lemon Cream, and Olive Oil
    Trifle
  Farmhouse Salad with Lemon-Shallot
    Vinaigrette

Metrovino
1139 Northwest 11th Avenue
Portland, OR 97209
503-517-7778
www.metrovinopdx.com
  Heirloom Carrot Bisque with Manila
    Clams and Chorizo
  Homemade Ricotta
  Whole Roasted Fava Beans with
    Maitakes and Ricotta

Kristen D. Murray
www.sweetsavantkdm.com
  Fig Bars
  Nectarine-Basil Lemonade

Ned Ludd
3925 Northeast MLK Jr. Boulevard
Portland, OR 97212
503-288-6900
www.nedluddpdx.com
  Radicchio Salad with Parsley-Hazelnut
    Pesto

Louisa Neumann
www.louisaneumann.com
  Eggs Lyonnaise
  Grilled Honey-Balsamic-glazed Stone
    Fruits with Honey Marscapone
    Whipped Cream

Newman's Fish Company
(multiple locations)
www.newmansfish.com

Nostrana
1401 Southeast Morrison Street
Portland, OR 97214
503-234-2427
www.nostrana.com
  Chanterelle Rillettes
  Yogurt Panna Cotta with Strawberry-
    Rhubarb Sauce

Olympic Provisions
107 Southeast Washington Street
Portland, OR 97214
503-954-3663
www.olympicprovisions.com
  Spring Strata

Paley's Place Bistro and Bar
1204 Northwest 21st Avenue
Portland, OR 97209
503-243-2403
www.paleysplace.net

Fennel-roasted Rabbit Salad and
  Fennel-Pollen Aioli

Park Kitchen
422 Northwest 8th Avenue
Portland, OR 97209
503-223-7275
www.parkkitchen.com
  Morel Mojo
  Parsnip-Almond Soup with Kumquat-
    Caperberry Garnish

Pazzo Ristorante
627 Southwest Washington Street
Portland, OR 97205
503-228-1515
www.pazzo.com
  Grilled Quail with Apple, Sunchoke,
    and Fennel Salad

Plate & Pitchfork
P.O. Box 82744
Portland, OR 97282
503-477-7565
www.plateandpitchfork.com

Portland Farmers Market
240 North Broadway, Suite 129
Portland, OR 97227
503-241-0032
www.portlandfarmersmarket.org

**Random Order Coffeehouse &
  Bakery**
1800 Northeast Alberta Street
Portland, OR 97211
971-340-6995
www.randomordercoffee.com
  Heritage Apple Pie

The Robert Reynolds Chefs Studio
2818 Southeast Pine Street
Portland, OR 97214
503-233-1934
www.thechefstudio.com
  Strawberry Risotto

Salt, Fire & Time
1902 Northwest 24th Avenue
Portland, OR 97210
503-208-2758
www.saltfireandtime.com
  Potted Cheese

Hank Sawtelle
www.cuisinology.com
  Lambic Vinaigrette
  Stout Ice Cream

Screen Door
2337 East Burnside Street
Portland, OR 97214
503-542-0880
www.screendoorrestaurant.com
  Peach-Herb Salad with Pickled Red
    Onions and Balsamic Vinaigrette

Simpatica Dining Hall
828 Southeast Ash Street
Portland, OR 97214
503-235-1600
www.simpaticacatering.com
  Baby Romaine Salad with Pickled
    Blueberries and Creamy Tarragon
    Dressing

The Sugar Cube
4262 Southeast Belmont Street
Portland, OR 97215
503-890-2825
www.thesugarcubepdx.com
  Molasses-Ginger Stout Cake with
    Ginger Glaze

Tabla Mediterranean Bistro
200 Northeast 28th Avenue
Portland, OR 97232
503-238-3777
www.tabla-restaurant.com
  Crispy-Skinned Black Cod with Salsa
    Mojo Verde
  Gin and Citrus Salt–cured Salmon
    Gravlax

Tails & Trotters
6829 North Curtis Avenue
Portland, OR 97217
503-680-7697
www.tailsandtrotters.com
  Spring Pork Braise

Trébol
4835 North Albina Avenue
Portland, OR 97217
503-517-9347
www.trebolpdx.com
  Halibut Ceviche

Two Tarts Bakery
2309 Northwest Kearney Street
Portland, OR 97210
503-312-9522
www.twotartsbakery.com
  Hazelnut Tassies

Wildwood Restaurant
1221 Northwest 21st Avenue
Portland, OR 97209
503-248-9663
www.wildwoodrestaurant.com
  Balsamic-braised Radicchio Risotto
  Red Wine–braised Beef Short Ribs with
    Gremolata and Gorgonzola Cheese
  Yogurt-Peach Coffee Cake

Recipe Contributors and Suppliers (continued)

PORTLAND AREA (CONTINUED)

Xocolatl de David (inside Meat Cheese Bread)
1406 Southeast Stark Street
Portland, OR 97214
503-459-1044
www.xocolatldedavid.com
  Chocolate Crab Bisque

WILLAMETTE VALLEY

Ayers Creek Farm
P.O. Box 1150
Gaston, OR 97119
503-985-3556
  Moroccan Tomato Soup

Belly
291 East 5th Avenue
Eugene, OR 97401
541-683-5896
www.eatbelly.com
  Rhubarb Buckle with Candied Ginger
    Crumb
  Shaved Zucchini and Basil Salad with
    Guajillo Chile Vinaigrette
  Smoked Salmon and Sea Bean Salad
    with White Wine–Chive Vinaigrette

Black Walnut Inn
9600 Northeast Worden Hill Road
Dundee, OR 97115
503-538-8663
www.blackwalnut-inn.com
  Blackberry Bread Pudding

The Brookside Inn on Abbey Road
8243 Northeast Abbey Road
Carlton, OR 97111
503-852-4433
www.brooksideinn-oregon.com
  Duck Confit and Butternut Squash
    Risotto
  Polenta Cakes with Goat Cheese, Cured
    Salmon, and Poached Eggs

Cattail Creek Lamb
95363 Grimes Road
Junction City, OR 97448
541-998-8505
www.cattailcreeklamb.com
  Lamb Tagine with Sweet Tomato Jam

Champoeg Farm
21579 Champoeg Creek Lane Northeast
St. Paul, OR 97137
503-678-3333
www.champoegfarm.com

Cuvée Restaurant
214 West Main Street
Carlton, OR 97111
503-852-6555
www.cuveedining.com
  Cuvée's Coveted Crab Juniper

Freddy Guys Hazelnuts
12145 Elkins Road
Monmouth, OR 97361
503-606-0458
www.freddyguys.com

Gathering Together Farm
25159 Grange Hall Road
Philomath, OR 97370
541-929-4270
www.gatheringtogetherfarm.com
  Fresh Nettle Pappardelle
  Spring Lamb Ragù

The Joel Palmer House
600 Ferry Street
Dayton, OR 97114
503-864-2995
www.joelpalmerhouse.com
  Pan-seared Duck Breasts on Wild
    Rice Pancakes with Mushrooms and
    Cilantro Sauce

King Estate Winery
80854 Territorial Road
Eugene, OR 97405
541-942-9874
www.kingestate.com
  Vin Glacé Cake

Marché
296 East 5th Avenue
Eugene, OR 97401
541-342-3612
www.marcherestaurant.com
  Curried Bay-Shrimp Salad
  French Onion Soup
  Pear-Pepper Chutney

Newman's Fish Company
(multiple locations)
www.newmansfish.com

Oregon Black Truffles
503-997-8881
www.oregonblacktruffles.com

Oregon Olive Mill at Red Ridge Farms
5510 Northeast Breyman Orchards Road
Dayton, OR 97114
503-864-8502
www.oregonolivemill.com

Oregon Raspberry & Blackberry Commission
4845 B Southwest Dresden Avenue
Corvallis, OR 97333
541-758-4043
www.oregon-berries.com

The Painted Lady Restaurant
201 South College Street
Newberg, OR 97132
503-538-3850
www.thepaintedladyrestaurant.com
  Heirloom Tomato Tart
  Oregon Shrimp Napoleons

Queener Fruit Farm
40385 Queener Drive
Scio, OR 97374
503-769-8965
  Blackcurrant Barbecue Sauce

Springfield Creamery
29440 Airport Road
Eugene, OR 97402
541-689-2911
www.nancysyogurt.com

Sweet Briar Farms
28475 Spencer Creek Road
Eugene, OR 97405
541-683-7447
www.sweet-briar-farms.com

Sweet Life Pâtisserie
755 Monroe Street
Eugene, OR 97402
541-683-5676
www.sweetlifedesserts.com
  Vanilla Custard and Berry Tart

Sybaris Bistro
442 1st Avenue West
Albany, OR 97321
541-928-8157
www.sybarisbistro.com
  Grilled Oregonzola Figs

Thistle
228 North Evans Street
McMinnville, OR 97128
503-472-9623
www.thistlerestaurant.com
  Northwest Black Truffle Butter

Viridian Farms
18525 Southeast Lower Island Road
Dayton, OR 97114
503-830-7086
www.viridianfarms.com
  Basque-style Chicken with Espelette
    Piperade
  Fried Pimientos de Padrón

Recipes by Category

INDEX

Page numbers in *italics* indicate photos.

DISHING UP®
More Delicious State Flavors from Storey

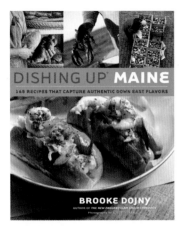

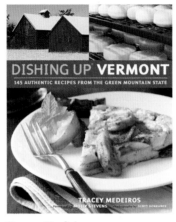

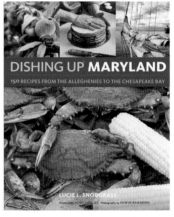

Brooke Dojny
Journey through the foodways of the Pine Tree State — from fresh seafood to blueberries and maple syrup.

Tracey Medeiros
Get an insider's view of Vermont dishes made with natural meats, fresh produce, and rich dairy products.

Lucie L. Snodgrass
This culinary tour of the Old Line State includes 150 recipes highlighting Maryland's best from local chefs, farmers, and fishermen.

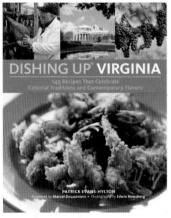

Patrick Evans-Hylton
Colonial traditions mingle with contemporary flavors in this gastro celebration of the Old Dominion state.

Jess Thomson
Celebrate the Evergreen State's bounty, both wild and cultivated, with recipes from many of Washington's world-class chefs.

Dave DeWitt
Taste what fuels the Land of Enchantment, from Chipotle-Pumpkin Seed Pesto to Blue Corn Chicken Taquitos.

Join the conversation. Share your experience with this book, learn more about Storey Publishing's authors, and read original essays and book excerpts at storey.com. Look for our books wherever quality books are sold or by calling 800-441-5700.